The Rise and Fall of Ireland's Celtic Tiger

In 2008 Ireland experienced one of the most dramatic economic crises of any economy in the world. It remains at the heart of the international crisis, sitting uneasily between the US and European economies. Not long ago, however, Ireland was celebrated as an example of successful market-led globalisation and economic growth. How can we explain the Irish crisis? What does it tell us about the causes of the international crisis? How should we rethink our understanding of contemporary economies and the workings of economic liberalism based on the Irish experience? This book combines economic sociology and comparative political economy to analyse the causes, dynamics and implications of Ireland's economic 'boom to bust'. It examines the interplay between the financial system, European integration and Irish national politics to show how financial speculation overwhelmed the economic and social development of the 1990s 'Celtic Tiger'.

SEÁN Ó RIAIN is Professor of Sociology in the Department of Sociology and National Institute for Regional and Spatial Analysis (NIRSA) at the National University of Ireland Maynooth. He is the author of *The Politics of High-Tech Growth* (Cambridge University Press, 2004), which was awarded the James S. Donnelly Book Prize of the American Conference of Irish Studies in 2004. In 2011 he was awarded the prestigious European Research Council Starting Investigator Grant for a project entitled 'New Deals in the New Economy: European Workplaces in an Era of Transformation'.

The Rise and Fall of Ireland's Celtic Tiger

Liberalism, Boom and Bust

SEÁN Ó RIAIN

CAMBRIDGE UNIVERSITY PRESS

CAMBRIDGE
UNIVERSITY PRESS

University Printing House, Cambridge CB2 8BS, United Kingdom

Published in the United States of America by Cambridge University Press, New York

Cambridge University Press is part of the University of Cambridge.

It furthers the University's mission by disseminating knowledge in the pursuit of education, learning and research at the highest international levels of excellence.

www.cambridge.org
Information on this title: www.cambridge.org/9780521279055

First published 2014

Printed in the United Kingdom by T. J. International Ltd, Padstow

A catalogue record for this publication is available from the British Library

Library of Congress Cataloguing in Publication data
Ó Riain, Seán, 1968–
The rise and fall of Ireland's Celtic tiger : liberalism, boom and bust / Seán Ó Riain.
    pages cm
Includes bibliographical references.
ISBN 978-1-107-00982-0 (Hardback) – ISBN 978-0-521-27905-5 (Paperback)
1. Ireland–Economic policy. 2. Ireland–Economic conditions–1949– 3. Finance–
Ireland. 4. Financial crises–Ireland. 5. Debts, Public–Ireland. I. Title.
HC260.5.O75 2014
330.9417–dc23 2013041806

ISBN 978-1-107-00982-0 Hardback
ISBN 978-0-521-27905-5 Paperback

Contents

Figures

Tables

Acknowledgements

This book is built on a number of different stages of research and academic work. First, it is a dialogue in parts with my earlier writing on Ireland's 'developmental state' in *The Politics of High-Tech Growth* (2004). I owe a debt of gratitude here to all those acknowledged in that book. Second, it draws on various projects and articles between 2003 and 2008 about the shifting character of the Celtic Tiger. This was also a period when I was Head of the Department of Sociology at the National University of Ireland, Maynooth, a position that brought me into contact with many aspects of education and innovation policy. Third, it has been written during the more traumatic years since 2008 as Ireland's crisis has unfolded as part of a global 'Great Recession'. Unlike the earlier book, which was largely written as an occasionally returning academic emigrant, this book was shaped by ten years as a citizen and as a member of the outer edges of the policy world. I appreciate the engagement of all those I met in that world, particularly in the sociological community, at NUI Maynooth and in the Secretariat of the National Economic and Social Council.

I have benefited greatly from the intellectual community of my colleagues at NUI Maynooth, including in the Department of Sociology, the National Institute for Regional and Spatial Analysis, the Political Economy and Work research cluster and the 'New Deals in the New Economy' project. Particular thanks for comments, support and encouragement related to this project go to Michael Ash, David Begg, Felix Behling, Chris Benner, Fred Block, Mark Boyle, Michael Burawoy, Bruce Carruthers, Peter Cassells, Rossella Ciccia, Vincent Comerford, Mary Corcoran, Pauline Cullen, Mary Daly, Peter Evans, Justin Gleason, Jane Gray, Niamh Hardiman, Colin Hay, Bora Isyar, Matt Keller, Sinéad Kelly, Tom Kelly, Rob Kitchin, Basak Kus, Joe Larragy, Erik Larson, Steve Lopez, Muiris MacCárthaigh, Andrew MacLaran, Jim Mahoney, Lars Mjøset, Mary Murphy, John O'Brennan, Anne O'Brien, Ronan O'Brien, Aileen O'Carroll, Larry O'Connell,

Rory O'Donnell, Seán Ó Foghlú, Mike O'Sullivan, Monica Prasad, Joe Ruane, Andrew Schrank, Gay Seidman, Damian Thomas and James Wickham.

Invited talks on material in this book were given at the Departments of Sociology, Trinity College, Dublin, University College Dublin (UCD), the University of Wisconsin–Madison, University of California, Davis and Northwestern University; the Centre for the Study of Wider Europe, NUI Maynooth; the Department of Economics, NUI Galway; the Department of Politics, UCD; the International Workshop on Finance, Credit and the Welfare State, Geary Institute, UCD; the Sociological Association of Ireland Conference; the Hungarian Sociological Association/Central European University; the School of Information, University of California, Berkeley; the Buffett Centre for International and Comparative Studies, Northwestern University; the University of Aarhus, Denmark; and the German Political Science Association. I would like to offer my thanks for the opportunities to discuss the ideas and evidence with these audiences.

I am very grateful to Brian Hansen, Hendrik Spruyt and all their colleagues at the Buffett Centre for International and Comparative Studies at Northwestern University for most generously hosting me during a sabbatical in 2008–9 and every summer since as a visiting scholar. I benefited enormously from discussions with my colleagues at Northwestern and owe a special thanks to Art Stinchcombe for his always insightful and stimulating comments on any number of sociological issues, as well as a great deal of encouragement with this and other projects.

The research for this book has been funded through a European Research Council Starting Investigator Grant ('New Deals in the New Economy', 2012–16), funding from the Irish Research Council (2005–8, 2012–13) and NUI Maynooth ERC Incentive Funding (2010). Particular thanks for encouragement and support on research funding go to Caroline Ang, Ray O'Neill and Andrea Valova.

I have been very fortunate to have exceptional research assistance with this project. Patricia Connerty's support with transcribing drafts of the chapters and encouraging me to get finished was exceptional and invaluable. Both Fergal Rhatigan and Eoin Flaherty provided support and stimulating comments as well as expert research assistance. Many thanks are also due to Rhona Bradshaw, Orla Dunne and Áine Edmonds.

Many thanks to Carrie Parkinson and John Haslam, my editors at Cambridge University Press, for their expertise and, particularly, patience. The cover photograph was taken by an outstanding architectural photographer, Donal Murphy, and was generously made possible by Aaron O'Donohue. I am very grateful to two anonymous reviewers for helpful comments on the general framework and approach of the book. As ever, neither they nor anyone else mentioned here can be blamed for any remaining flaws.

Having written about Ireland for eleven years from the vantage point of life in California, this book was written across ten years in suburban Kildare. My friends and neighbours in Celbridge and the world of the Gaelic Athletic Association have been a great help in keeping me sane. Hon the Bridge! My love and thanks as always to my 'older' family – Seán, Brighdín, Ciarán, Clíona, Gearóid, Claire, Eimer and Tony, and all their children. In my 'new' family, my debts to Aoife, Aisling and Aidan go beyond words – all my love always.

My wife, Rebecca King-O'Riain, encouraged me to keep going to get finished and to stop working every now and then and take a break. As two sociologists, our lives have been linked not only by our passion for our subjects but also by a much more important set of bonds. All my love and thanks go to Becky for her support, encouragement and for sharing our life in the Celtic Tiger and its aftermath. I dedicate this book, for all its faults, to her.

1 | *Liberalism in crisis*

Ireland and the Great Recession: liberalism's crisis or liberalism betrayed?

In early 2013, as I completed this manuscript, the Great Recession was in its fifth year. The shock of the acute crisis of 2008 had given way to the recognition of the chronic, long-term character of the recession. The outrage of the early months of the crisis had turned into a deeper erosion of trust and legitimacy of private and public institutions, often accompanied by despair that either public or private institutions could deliver economic recovery, let alone reconstruction.

Europe was at the heart of the crisis, even if its economy as a whole was performing at least as well as others that were struggling to respond to the recession around the world. However, Europe's problems went deeper than specifically economic woes to the foundations of its socio-economic system, as the euro currency hung in the balance and the European project fractured in the face of economic crisis and political division. In the midst of this broader regional crisis, Ireland was one of the countries at the very centre of the economic storm. Not long before celebrated as the 'Celtic Tiger', Ireland was now experiencing one of the deepest and most sustained crises in Europe and beyond. After almost five years of recession and austerity, the Irish economy remained mired in an economic slump, with only fleeting glimpses of economic growth, burdened by banking and government debt and facing serious questions of solvency and sovereignty. Behind the public face of its status as the 'poster child' of austerity in Europe, Ireland was poised on a knife-edge between potentially unsustainable debt and the growing social and political costs of recession and fiscal consolidation.

In the five years of the Great Recession, Ireland had staggered from one historically memorable event to another, with each tumultuous occasion quickly passed over as new events took centre stage. The Irish state guaranteed the liabilities of its most significant domestic financial institutions in September 2008, in the face of a collapse in those institutions' liquidity and solvency and to the tune of over double the value of gross domestic product (GDP). In the following year, Irish citizens took on these private debts as their responsibility, with the costs of the banking bailout reaching at least €64 billion over the course of the recession. GDP collapsed with the bursting of the property bubble and as measures to cut the public deficit began to bite. Nonetheless, the Irish electorate approved the Lisbon Treaty promoting further European integration in October 2009, despite a sharp loss of trust in the previously popular EU and having rejected it just over a year before.

Almost uniquely among EU states, Ireland pursued a policy response that was focused almost exclusively on fiscal consolidation, particularly through expenditure cuts. This resolute commitment to 'austerity' was not enough to reassure financial markets, however, as uncertainty around the future of the euro and Irish banking debt saw interest rates on state borrowing rise sharply in 2010. Ireland entered a bailout programme in November 2010, involving detailed oversight of fiscal measures by the 'troika' of the European Union (EU), the International Monetary Fund (IMF) and European Central Bank (ECB) funders.

Ireland's electorate took their revenge on the parties that had presided over the bubble and the recession in March 2011, decimating the historically dominant Fianna Fáil party and returning a new coalition government of Fine Gael and Labour (the Christian Democratic and Social Democratic Parties, respectively). Once more in May 2012, Ireland faced a referendum on signing the fiscal treaty that brought together all these dilemmas of crisis, austerity and Europeanisation into a single vote on legally binding measures to control the public finances. Once more, despite the erosion of faith in the European and domestic elites, the electorate comfortably passed the Fiscal Treaty – with both Yes and No voters driven primarily by fear of the future rather than by positive agendas for recovery.

The Irish public deficit came down in 2011 and 2012 even as the economy stagnated and the social costs and political tensions grew. Despite some indicators of stabilisation and perhaps even growth in the economy, it was clear that many years of high unemployment lay ahead. With at least two years of significant cuts in public spending still to come, political difficulties remained. The growth in the number of home-owners with significant mortgage arrears prompted policies to allow for debt restructuring, but also offered the prospect of politically explosive home repossessions. A negotiated agreement with public sector unions to cut wages and change a variety of other payments and conditions faced great difficulty in getting union member approval. All the while, the EU was still capable of shooting itself in the foot as a proposal in March 2013 to impose part of Cyprus' bailout costs on ordinary depositors threatened for a time to fatally damage the prospects of a European banking union.

Much of the popular narrative of the Great Recession has focused on the frailties of national systems of economic management, or mismanagement. In particular, countries like Ireland suffered from major failures of regulation in the financial and property sectors, in developing the real economy and in the public finances. However, the Irish experience was only one of a number of similar stories that had unfolded across the European periphery over the previous five years. The various national economic stories combined into a European crisis. While the economies of Europe foundered in different ways, the politics of adjustment after the crisis – including the 'fiscal compact' of late 2011 and the European Stability Mechanism Treaty of February 2012 – fundamentally re-ordered European political relations. The question of the unequal development of the EU's regions and of relations between core and periphery had long been a sideshow in European politics – it now took centre stage.

Even more fundamentally, the European and international crises raised profound questions regarding the international financial system, the European and international economic orders, and the place of national governments and new forms of governance in shaping the political economy. Coming at the end of at least three decades of financialisation, Europeanisation and worldwide experiments in economic governance, the crisis cast a dim light on all these developments, placing economic liberalism profoundly in question. However, an economic crisis that seemed to signal the exhaustion of a period of aggressive international economic liberalisation has paradoxically reinforced liberal policy prescriptions.

This book explores these broader questions of liberalism, development and crisis through an analysis of the changing fortunes of the Irish economy, a poster child since the 1990s but one of the first to hit the rocks in 2008. Having spent many decades in the years after independence in 1922 as one of the laggards of the European economy, to everyone's surprise, Ireland became a model for economic growth and regional development in the 1990s. An economic crisis in the 1980s saw massive government debt accompanied by severe unemployment, immigration and weak labour force participation among women. Nonetheless, in the 1990s Ireland experienced rapid economic growth and, even more significantly, exceptionally high employment growth in the second half of the decade. The numbers employed in Ireland almost doubled between 1988 and 2008, increasing by one million jobs. The sources of this growth are of course controversial, with some seeing it as the outcome of Ireland finally 'converging' on European living standards through free market reforms, while others dismiss the gains of the period as unsustainable and rooted in a bubble inflated by liberal policies. Ireland's crisis since 2008 was sudden and severe, and appeared to bear out the argument of these critics. However, in the eyes of those who had seen the 'Celtic Tiger' years of the 1990s as a process of economic convergence, it was not continuity with those liberal policies that produced the crash but the departure from those policies in the 2000s through lack of discipline in public finances and weak prudential regulation in the financial sector.

This book shares the view that the Irish economy significantly shifted in its underlying dynamic between the 1990s and the 2000s. However, I argue that the growth of the 1990s was not due to a convergence on market-led orthodoxy, but to a partial move toward a European-style combination of industrial policy, social investment and social partnership. In the 2000s this dynamic was derailed by the financialisation of the economy, which was facilitated by economic and monetary union and financial liberalisation in Europe. National political compromises built this financialisation into the structure of the public finances. The property and credit bubble was already deflating from 2007 onwards, but the international crisis of 2008 produced a particularly dramatic crash in Ireland's economy.

However difficult it was to solve, the origins of Ireland's economic crisis appear to be no mystery. The crisis was fivefold (NESC, 2009). The core was a *financial* crisis – an unholy combination of property speculation by developers, reckless lending by bankers and a lack of governmental oversight and regulation created a property and banking bubble that brought the Irish economy to its knees when the international financial system ran into trouble in 2008. The liabilities of these banks were guaranteed by the state in 2008 and developer loans and assets have been taken under state management. A *fiscal* crisis mushroomed as the public finances were burdened with the cost of bailing out failing banks, but also with a growing deficit as tax revenues associated with the asset bubble disappeared. One of the largest austerity policies in recent history was undertaken in response (Whelan, 2010).

This was reinforced by an *economic* crisis. Despite widespread emphasis on problems of competitiveness, major deficits in productive investment and collapsing domestic demand were more significant economic weaknesses. These three crises drove a major *social* crisis based on negative equity and mortgage arrears, cutbacks in public services and disastrous rises in unemployment. Finally, Ireland faced a *reputational* crisis, particularly evident in the reluctance of international lenders to finance the government debt – culminating in an EU–IMF bailout in November 2010. Ultimately these crises hastened and were reinforced by a sixth, broader crisis of *political* capacity, solidarity and action (Kirby and Murphy, 2011).

A myriad of books and articles have traced the disastrous consequences of developments in these different spheres of property, banking and the state. There is still much to be discovered here regarding the cultures, coalitions and decisions that shaped each of these spheres. However, the most significant questions relate to the conditions that allowed the crisis to emerge, the reasons why the crisis took the form it did in Ireland, and why it has been so deep and persistent. Social and political institutions and the ways in which they are worked into everyday economic life are crucial to understanding these issues. Although my analysis focuses on the Irish national crisis, that story is itself woven with a number of broader and recurring threads.

The first is the increasing tension between financial and productive capital – where Ireland's boom of the 1990s, rooted in public and private productive investments, was sidelined by an asset bubble rooted in financial and property speculation in the 2000s. 'Development' and 'financialisation' competed as projects within the political economy, resulting in financialisation winning out with disastrous results.

The second recurring strand running through this story is forged from the linked processes of economic globalisation and regional integration. The EU has been the paradigmatic case of the trend in recent decades towards the emergence of dominant regional blocs. However, the crisis has been in part produced and intensified by deep structural fault lines in the relationships between core and peripheral economies and states within the EU – fissures that were only papered over by the European effort to promote integration through liberalisation. The European project involved the integration not only of different economies but also of diverse 'varieties of capitalism'. Monetary union and the European Stability and Growth Pact of the late 1990s attempted to manage this integration through a combination of market- and rule-based disciplines. However, these disciplines proved unable to manage the speculative market activity produced by European and international financial integration.

The third thread is the perennial tense embrace of capitalism and democracy. In principle, free market capitalism and representative democratic national government are complementary components of liberal societies. However, the economic inequalities and concentration of power produced by market processes have always posed a significant threat to democratic governance. This tension has been further intensified in the recent decades of global economic liberalism, leading Dani Rodrik (2012) to argue that all societies face an inescapable trilemma where they can choose only two out of deep economic integration ('globalisation'), national government and democratic politics. The only way to save national democracy appears to be to halt economic globalisation, while politics in an era of globalisation appears to offer the choice of democratic international institutions or negotiating and competing national governments. However, this trilemma may pose the question too dramatically. In practice, the experience of liberalisation has produced both powerlessness and fatalism, as well as experimentation with new forms of governance. Much as development and financialisation competed as counter-tendencies within Ireland's economy, experimental public action competed with aggressive liberalisation within Ireland's economic governance even as they were intertwined.

These three threads are linked by a deeper theme that runs through the entire analysis – the question of the economic liberalism that has dominated the global political economy since the 1970s. Throughout the analysis, I examine the role that economic liberalism played in the emergence of the crisis itself and ask in the concluding analytical chapter why the crisis has reinforced economic liberalism despite seeming to herald its demise (Crouch, 2011).

Political debates regarding the crisis largely pushed the question of liberalism to the sidelines. In Ireland, continuing revelations about a catalogue of governance failures in the public and private sectors led to a focus on cronyism and corruption rather than on the systemic dynamics of the Irish model. In Europe, the focus was on the problems in the design of the euro and the profligacy of national governments – as well as on the disastrous interaction between them. The increasingly liberal character of the regional integration process disappeared from view as a source of the region's difficulties. At a systemic level, while the tensions between capitalism and well-being have never been as obvious as they are to current generations, the prospects of generating shared social and political solutions to these economic problems have rarely seemed so remote.

This book attempts to understand economic liberalism not as a theoretical concept or as a political idea or programme, but as a particular way of organising capitalist economies, involving character-istic forms of economic organisation, government, welfare and social protection, and other elements of the political economy. I examine 'actually existing economic liberalism' through the case of the Irish political economy over the past three decades.

All political economies are mixtures of the various 'types' that research has identified – liberal, social democratic, developmental, Christian democratic regimes and so on. Ireland too mixes these types together – with a liberal emphasis on economic globalisation and the rights of capital combined with Christian democratic emphases on family, social democratic elements of universal social benefits, Mediterranean clientelist political cultures and the active industrial policy of developmental states. Nonetheless, there is enough internal coherence within these 'types' and enough differences between them that it proves useful to continue to use such typologies. Furthermore, most comparative analyses suggest that Ireland's economy fits the 'liberal' mix of characteristics most closely, with some notable exceptions in the areas of wages and active labour policy (Amable, 2004), industrial policy (Ó Riain, 2004), pay-related welfare benefits (Ó Riain and O'Connell, 2000) and some others. To understand real-world examples of economic liberalism, it is necessary to analyse not only the process of marketisation but also the social structures, political dynamics and institutional forms that are most common in liberal political economies.

Accounts of the Irish political economy usually place its apparent or desired liberalism at the centre of their explanations. Most 'orthodox' economic analyses emphasise the 'convergence' of the Irish economy in the 1990s as Ireland removed a number of obstacles to the operation of a market-led economy (Honohan and Walsh, 2002; Lane, 2011). Key policies here included spending cuts that stabilised the government deficit, an emphasis on wage competitiveness, maintaining low infla-tion rates and the pursuit of foreign investment and trade-oriented policies.

However, the 2000s saw a departure from these fundamentals. Spending increased, wage competitiveness and export performance declined, and the economy was allowed to overheat, in particular through the creation of a credit and property bubble – in this view, largely due to the weakness of even simple prudential regulation. Crucially, poor financial regulation and poor fiscal discipline spread, at just the time when membership of the euro currency imposed severe costs upon such weaknesses, eventually fuelling the crisis (Lane, 2011). While public policies play a role, in this view the critical variable is the extent to which policy and economic practices enable the operation of market processes. Prudence and disciplined enforcement of market processes and conditions are the critical elements of policy. When such policy characteristics are weakened, liberalism is weakened by political failure or, worse, cronyism.

Similarly, critical accounts of the Irish political economy often also place the liberal character of Ireland's political economy at the centre of the explanation (O'Hearn, 2001; Coleman and Coulter, 2003; Kirby, 2010; Kitchin *et al.*, 2012). In these accounts, liberalism is at the root of structural weakness in the Irish economy, but, more import-antly, is also at the root of Ireland's social failures of income inequality, high poverty rates and weak structures of social protection. Ireland's political failures are associated with its liberalism in that cronyism is rooted in close ties to a dominant business sector, and the failure to develop a vibrant public sphere weakens the effectiveness and democ-racy of political institutions (O'Toole, 2009). Again, politics is present even in the liberal political economy, but primarily as a disciplinary mechanism that enforces market processes – acting as a 'competition state' (Kirby, 2002). The constraints of liberal forms of capitalism result in a variety of problems in Ireland that could be addressed through movement towards a different variety of capitalism (Kirby and Murphy, 2011) or through alternatives to capitalist organisation (Cox, 2011).

In keeping with these two competing perspectives, in this book I examine Ireland as a case of liberal political economy, an economy where market activity was taken to be the dominant and legitimate way of allocating resources and making economic decisions. However, rather than viewing liberalism as a fixed feature of Ireland's political economy, I analyse how that liberalism ebbed and flowed and how other political economic projects and tendencies contended with the overall liberal pattern of organisation. Specifically, I argue that developmental and corporatist institutions were critical in promoting growth in the 1990s, but were derailed by the property bubble of the 2000s fuelled by market liberalism and state boosterism.

Ireland is a fascinating, although surprisingly unusual, case of economic liberalism. It represents the clearest case of small country liberalism in Europe, perhaps the only case in Western Europe (with the possible exception of Switzerland). Even this classification of Ireland as liberal directs our attention to the historical specificity of liberalism as a form of national political economy. For, even though economic liberalism has had a sweeping and profound impact across the world, it is institutionalised in only a small set of advanced capitalist countries. Indeed, the subset of liberal political economies in advanced capitalism consists of the two historical hegemons (the UK and the US) and their former colonies and/or cultural and trading neighbours – Australia, Canada, Ireland and New Zealand.

Ireland's distinctiveness within this group is the result of certain characteristic features of economic liberalism. Apart from Ireland, these smaller variants of liberalism are distant from Europe. One of the ways in which the liberal world of capitalism is different from the others is that it is more geographically scattered. Unlike the social democratic, Christian democratic and Mediterranean versions, the geography of liberalism follows the footsteps of colonialism rather than the cultural clusters of European societies. This in turn reflects the close link between a policy and regime preference for liberal economic organisation and a country's power in the global political economy – the key promoters of a liberal trading regime have always been the hegemons of each era whose interests are favoured by the expansion of such regimes (Arrighi and Silver, 2000). While Ireland is among the most open advanced capitalist economies, this too is unusual as most of the liberal economies are more likely to operate as largely closed economies, despite a stated general policy preference for trade, financial and other market integration.

While Ireland is an exceptional case within actually existing economic liberalism, it is an important one. Countries that adopt liberal policy regimes in the contemporary economy are more likely to match Ireland's conditions as a small, open economy with significant legacies of post-colonialism and under-development (for example, see Mahoney (2010) for a discussion of Latin America's mercantilist and liberal forms of post-colonial development). Ireland's exceptionalism within the world of economic liberalism makes it a particularly significant case for the increasing number of countries across the world that pursue liberal policies.

Understanding liberal political economies

The following chapters explore the specific arguments offered from these perspectives in more detail. But in seeking to answer these empirical questions, it is necessary to tackle some profound conceptual issues. How should economic liberalism itself be understood? What kind of social structure and political programme is 'economic liberalism' and what are its key features?

In the field of comparative political economy, liberal countries occupy an unusual position. Liberalism is often the reference point from which others are seen to depart – with social democratic, Christian democratic or developmental states all seen as 'deviations' from the 'normal' state of lack of political intervention or social coordination. Partly as a result of this, liberal economies receive relatively little direct analysis compared to the other 'varieties of capitalism'. The economic dynamics, social institutions and political conditions of liberalism are perhaps less well understood and conceptualised than those of the alternative systems that seem more obviously 'social' or 'political'.

However, it still makes sense to talk about 'economic liberalism', both as a 'type' of national economy and as a transnational set of institutions and practices (Brenner *et al.*, 2009). There are clearly liberal political economies – a number of them have been listed above. The last three decades have also seen the international spread of what can be agreed is broadly a liberal economic order. The question is not whether liberalism should be abandoned as a category, but how the characteristic features of these liberal national and transnational social formations should be understood.[1]

I develop this understanding in the next three sections. First, I examine the 'non-liberal' foundations of liberalism itself, arguing that the social conditions of choice, individualism and rationality are such that the liberal individual and the institutions of liberal societies will always bear the stamp of the particular societies within which they are embedded and that make them possible. We should not simply postulate an ideal liberal economy and then critique most of the historical social and political deviations from it – many such 'deviations' are inevitable. More fundamentally, these 'non-liberal' elements prove to be essential to the functioning of the economic actor at the heart of economic liberalism – the rational, choosing individual. In the analysis of economic institutions, in recent decades economic sociology has also added significantly to our understanding of the non-market foundations of market structures and action.

Second, existing concepts of liberalism underplay the deep tensions between 'the market' and the social institutions and relations that sustain markets and market actors. Therefore, the section on the dynamics of markets and societies develops Karl Polanyi's discussion of the relationship between the market and society. Economic sociology has been built largely upon the foundations of Polanyi's central argument that economic life is 'always embedded' within social relations and social structures. However, Polanyi's body of work went well beyond this foundational but ultimately limited insight. Crucially, he posited an inherent tension between markets and the very social forms that sustained them – if markets came to dominate and create a 'market society', market relationships would undermine relations of production and social reproduction and would ultimately lead to counter-movements for social protection. How might this fuller Polanyian perspective be applied to understanding contemporary political economies?

---

[1] The reason for this conceptual blindness has an analogy in scholarship with the study of race. In recent decades, increasing attention has been paid by such scholars to 'whiteness' – once taken as the unspoken 'state of nature' against which blackness and other racial categories were held in relief, scholars began to explore whiteness itself as a racial identity with its own cultural meanings, political identities and so on.

Third, not only are there 'non-liberal' features to 'liberal' economies, but these are patterned in characteristic ways in liberal political economies. Certain forms of industrial policy, regulation, welfare states and political coalitions are more common in liberal economies than in the other worlds of capitalism (Esping-Andersen, 1990). These should be included as features of liberalism in order to be consistent with both the concept of liberalism as rooted in its social foundations and the empirical evidence as to the characteristics of liberal economies. 'Liberal' political economies have their own charac-teristic institutional and political forms – just like other 'varieties of capitalism' that appear, on the face of it, to be 'more social' and 'more political'.

Social foundations of liberal societies

In the classical notion, liberalism is defined by a set of institutions that is minimalist – individual choice and market mechanisms are domin-ant, reinforced by clear and limited legal frameworks and by represen-tative democracy in the government of state affairs. Liberalism is defined by the dominance of these institutions, which define clear boundaries around their own power and serve to define fields of action that are then shaped by patterns of individual choice and negotiation. The normative foundation of these arguments is the claim that such institutions secure human freedoms through creating the conditions for rational action, choice and bargaining. However, sociological research suggests that individual choice and rational action depend on a much more broad-ranging set of social and institutional conditions – and that there are many possible 'varieties of liberalism'.

In important ways, all advanced capitalist economies are 'liberal'. What are the constitutive elements of this liberalism? At the micro-interactional level, the liberal era is defined by the centrality of the rational decision-making individual and the bargaining and negoti-ation between such individuals. At the meso-level, institutions are to be designed to allow the maximum freedom to individuals to make their own rational choices according to their own judgments and preferences. The macro-level shape of society emerges from the aggregation of the various preferences and bargains of social actors through the key liberal institutions of market, law and representative democracy. Indeed, the implementation of these sets of institutions in such a way that they minimise restrictions on individual action lies at the core of liberal thinking.

In the study of markets, neoclassical analysis has claimed the liberal tradition and has also transformed it. Its focus is the operation of markets – law and politics are treated largely in terms of their role as conditions for market action. Furthermore, the normative claim of the analysis is related not only to freedom but also to efficiency – the decentralised decision making and negotiation of social actors is the most efficient manner of generating decisions, particularly in complex societies where the informational demands of centralised decision making are said to give markets a distinct institutional advantage (Hayek, 1973).

The strength of neoclassical economic analysis is in analysing the workings of markets in contexts where key assumptions are broadly met. These assumptions include full information among market actors, clear and well-ordered preferences among those actors, and a relative equality of bargaining power within market relations. In practice, of course, these conditions are rarely met. The information available to actors is often limited and the ability of actors to process full information is in any case bounded (Simon, 1957). This information and actors' preferences are often complex, contradictory and culturally shaped. Furthermore, there are often significant inequalities of bargaining power that make the operation of efficient clearing markets difficult. Many of the current innovations in economic analysis seek to deal with exactly these limitations on neoclassical analysis – for example, in informational and behavioural economics.

However, my approach, while sympathetic to these innovations in economic analysis, is based on a more fundamental critique. I argue that the very founding concepts of liberalism – rational choice by autonomous individuals – depend on conditions that can extend well beyond an individual's autonomous understanding of the world and the choices he or she makes in it. Choices, rationalities and the types of actors in markets are defined through relationships with other actors and broader social conditions beyond the individual (Granovetter, 1985; Beckert, 2002).

In a dispersed series of articles, sociologist Art Stinchcombe has provided a sociological account of some of the key categories of liberal thought and political economy. In particular, he shows that the classic liberal concepts of choice, rational decision making and the freedom of individuals are all unavoidably social phenomena. Crucially, he argues that in each of these cases it is not simply that liberal choice, rationality and freedom need to be guaranteed by social institutions, but that it is not possible to think of how any of these operate without understanding how they are constantly intertwined with the structure of the broader society.

Stinchcombe (2000) argues that choice by individuals in democratic market societies is always a choice from a particular set of alternatives. But the menu of alternatives is always collectively structured, not only through the operation of culture and social values but also through the power of collective actors to shape these menus of choices. If we focus on the choice process at the individual level, we ignore the many social processes that structured those choices. We cannot even consider the possibility of individual choice without thinking about the repertoire of choices that are made available at any given time to individuals making decisions in the economy. But this means that individual choice, even when it operates at the individual level in much the same way that classical liberal theorists proposed, is always a profoundly social process.

Similarly, rationality and reasoned decision making depends on the actions of others, and not only in the sense that actors need to take account of others' actions, as has been comprehensively explored in game theory-based research. Stinchcombe again extends the argument further here, arguing that any kind of social action depends on an interpretation of future conditions – and the possibility of this interpretation depends upon the future being 'solid enough' to permit a degree of planning and rationalist deliberation and decision making. For him, 'the social structures and processes that make parts of the future solid enough to plan on are, ordinarily, what we usually call institutions, and the process of creating solidity to the future is what we usually call institutionalization' (Stinchcombe, 1997: 391). 'Rational' individual decisions can only be made when the institutional context is sufficiently developed and stable to give actors 'solid enough futures' upon which to base their decisions. But these institutions always have a cultural content, meaning that 'rational individual decisions' are always both made possible by institutional structures and inflected with cultural meanings by them.

Finally, Stinchcombe (1995) argues that even freedom, perhaps the most fundamental liberal category of all, is inherently social. The analysis begins from the level of the individual, defining freedom as the ability to dispose of a resource or other element of social life as a person sees fit. However, if one person has the freedom to dispose over elements of his or her environment as he or she sees fit, others do not by definition. Freedom is then, at least in its liberal definition, a scarce resource to be struggled over through social relations and social institutions. Karl Polanyi (1944) argued that the liberal notion of freedom began from a false presumption of individual independence. Instead, for Polanyi, individuals are inherently interdependent and their freedom as individuals to make choices regarding the elements around them is always defined by and through these interdependencies with others. Polanyi argues that we should not ignore the importance of freedom, but need to understand that our individual freedoms are inherently developed through our relations with others.

Finally, Amartya Sen's (1999) work on development as freedom suggests that freedom requires the development of capabilities, allowing a person to live the kind of life that they value. These capabilities are formed through what in practice turns out to be inherently social processes. Indeed, Peter Evans (2002) argues that Sen does not go far enough. He suggests that many of the capabilities that Sen contends are crucial to both development and freedom are inherently collective capabilities that cannot be reduced to the individual level.

Sen extends his argument not only to an expanded definition of freedom but also to the various institutional forms that it takes. He identifies five institutional arenas in which freedoms are developed and supported. Each of these corresponds to a core element of classical liberal definitions of freedom. However, he expands the definition of each to argue that ensuring liberal freedom is a much richer but also more complex task than simply putting in place the minimalist institutional conditions that classical liberalism defines.

The first of these institutional arenas is the area of political freedoms, which in classical liberalism corresponds to the institutions of liberal democracy centred on the free choice of a representative government. However, Sen expands this greatly to incorporate a much wider range of participatory institutions and a greatly enriched degree of dialogue and participation on the part of civic society, as well as the need for a much higher degree of social equality to ensure a genuine political freedom. The freedom to play a part in choosing the system of rules – and the rulers – is only part of political freedom. In practice, political freedoms are about developing the full range of capabilities of all within the society to participate in political dialogue and decision making.

This is complemented by the second institutional arena, which Sen refers to as 'economic facilities'. Again, where classical liberalism focuses on the importance of the free market and the absence of constraints on economic action and choice, Sen expands this to argue that a fuller development of the ability of all within the society to participate in the economy is crucial to economic freedom. This necessarily involves a greater focus on distributive issues than is normally the case in classical thinking.

The final three institutional arenas relate in different ways to the structure of social relations within the broader society – social opportunities, transparency guarantees and protective securities. In classical liberalism, these correspond to equality of opportunity (achievements over ascription), free information and the rule of law. Sen re-interprets each of these in terms of the capabilities required to genuinely exercise these social freedoms. Social opportunities depend upon a wide range of social investments, including education in particular, and also the openness and fairness of a variety of institutions within the society. Transparency depends not simply on some availability of information on institutions in principle, but on systems of information provision and dialogue that allow even those with relatively few resources to understand and assess the operation of institutions. Finally, protective security depends not only on the rule of law but also on the degree of social trust (which also enhances transparency) and on social capital and a social safety net within the society. Overall, Sen argues that freedom, in the classic liberal sense, depends upon conditions which go far beyond the classic definition of liberal institutions.

As I argued above, this shows that even the most basic elements of liberal economic and social action – choice, rationality and freedom – are shaped by and, most fundamentally, made possible by social relations and structures. This poses a genuine puzzle for the analysis of liberal political economies. If all market activity is socially structured and embedded, can we still talk about some economies as being 'market societies'? Part of our argument has been that these market societies are just as socially embedded as other forms of political economy, including social democracies, Christian democracies and so on. Liberalism in the general sense is compatible with a wide variety of institutional, social and political arrangements.

Therefore, the presence of these key interactional and institutional elements is not enough to define a 'liberal political economy'. I therefore develop an account of liberal political economies along two separate, but connected, lines of analysis. First, liberal political economies are indeed characterised by the particular dominance of markets as institutions within those systems. I use Karl Polanyi's analysis of markets and society to examine what it means to say that markets dominate society within liberal political economies. Second, despite this dominant role of market institutions, I argue that liberal political economies are no less coordinated by institutional mechanisms than other forms of political economy. However, the institutions of liberal political economies are distinctive – partly in the central role of market institutions and related private and semi-private forms of regulation, but also in the characteristic forms of the welfare state, industrial relations, macroeconomic policy and even social and political organisation that characterise them. The next two sections explore these aspects of liberal political economies in turn.

The dynamics of markets and societies

Perhaps surprisingly, given the emphasis on the non-market foundations of liberal societies above, it is important to emphasise that one distinguishing feature of liberal political economies is indeed the importance of markets as proximate modes of coordination. It is clear that a distinctive feature of liberal political economies is the extent to which 'markets dominate society' (even though they depend upon particular social foundations). The place of 'the market' requires sustained attention, even at the risk of 're-centring' markets. In other words, we can try to understand what we mean when we say that liberal political economies are 'market societies', where markets dominate society, rather than the other way around (Polanyi, 1944).

The great sociologist and anthropologist of markets and their interaction with social relations, institutions and structures is Karl Polanyi. For our purposes, his main contribution is his exploration of when markets come to dominate societies, as developed most fully in his book *The Great Transformation*. In this book, Polanyi examines what he sees as the 'double movement' between the rise of markets to dominate society in the nineteenth century and the counter-movement from society to protect itself through the nineteenth and twentieth centuries. This counter-movement generated fascist, communist and social democratic alternatives to 'market society'. However, there is much that can be used from Polanyi's analysis, aside from his specific historical discussion.

Without delving too deeply into recent debates about whether analysts should focus on 'capitalism' or on 'market society' (Block, 2012), it is worth noting that Polanyi's main focus is clearly on the operation of markets, not on capitalism as a social system. Similarly, we learn more from Polanyi about the pressures placed upon social reproduction by the operation of markets than we do about the classic Marxist focus on the relations of production within capitalism. Indeed, Polanyi has relatively little to say about capitalism and corporations, focusing more firmly on markets rather than hierarchies. Polanyi, for example, has little to say about how corporations and their strategies and institutional structures might seek to offer their own solutions to the double movement – for example, through the construction of corporation-centred 'modern manors' of welfare capitalism (Jacoby, 1997). Similarly, Polanyi has relatively little to say about class, explicitly focusing on the different groups of persons within the broader society rather than on opposing classes within the realm of capitalist production itself. The counter-movements against market society may take many forms for Polanyi and may be rooted in many different social groups, not only exploited wage labour. Nonetheless, Polanyi's focus on the relation between markets and society makes his approach a particularly useful one for understanding those periods in human history when markets are the dominant institution organising social life – much as they have been in recent decades. In general, Polanyi's framework is particularly well suited for analysing those periods when markets and finance dominate society and production (Silver and Arrighi, 2003). If this is true, then for better or worse, Polanyi's time has certainly come.

Polanyi re-entered contemporary economic sociology and analysis largely through the revival of his key concept of 'embeddedness' (Krippner *et al.*, 2004). This concept allowed sociological scholars of the economy an entry point into understanding how economic action was shaped by social relations (Granovetter, 1985). Polanyi develops the useful concept of a 'market society', a society which is dominated by market relations, linked to a process of 'disembedding' of economic action from the social structure. However, the analysis of economic liberalism as a process of disembedding is unsatisfactory, even in Polanyi's terms. For Polanyi, as was argued above, the 'economy' is always embedded in the 'society'. But if markets cannot be disembedded from society, how can a society come to be dominated by markets to such a degree that it can be called a 'market society'?

Polanyi does in fact provide us with significant conceptual tools for understanding the process through which 'market societies' emerge. He analyses this process at the macrohistorical level. However, the same concepts can be applied at a variety of different scales – local, national, transnational – and across a variety of different time horizons – from macrohistorical shifts through changes in the business cycle down to the cycles of organisational and working life (Ó Riain, 2006). The key concepts for Polanyi are the twin notions of 'fictitious commodities' and the 'liberal creed'.

First, Polanyi provides an argument about the specific institutional arrangements that underpin a market society. He argues that it is not simply the presence of markets that is significant, but the transformation of intrinsic elements of natural or social relations into tradable 'fictitious commodities'. He identifies three such commodities – land, labour and money. Recent analyses suggest that knowledge might be added to this list (Ó Riain, 2006; Jessop, 2007). For Polanyi, marketisation is a process through which the social relations of real people are turned into a commodification of labour, the interaction within the economy is reduced to a market for money (which is ultimately simply the medium of economic relations) and the relationship between human beings and nature is turned into markets for land. Polanyi clearly distinguishes between the presence of markets and a broader market society, and he also clearly distinguishes between commodities which are products that have been produced from the cooperation and labour of individuals and those fictitious commodities which are themselves part of the essence of nature and society. This process for Polanyi is not a process of disembedding from social foundations, but the mechanism through which markets enter social relations. In liberal market societies, the commodification of land, labour, finance and knowledge is much more developed, and therefore market relations become a dominant institutional form in everyday interaction. This is the institutional mechanism through which liberal political economies operate and through which they are distinguished from other forms of political economy.

Polanyi also identifies a cultural dimension to marketisation as he argues that the spread of a 'liberal creed' is a key element of the growth of market society. The liberal creed is a set of beliefs or an ideology that supports marketisation. More importantly, it is a process through which market relations and institutions come to be seen as natural by members of the society. Somers and Block (2005) argue that this liberal creed is a crucial element of market societies and that it is this 'ideational embeddedness' that is the crucial feature of liberal political economies. It is worth noting that the liberal creed may operate in a number of different forms. For example, it may take the form of an aggressive ideological justification of the superiority of markets, but it may also take the form of a more pragmatic approach to markets which simply suggests that market mechanisms are matters not of intrinsic superiority but common sense (see, e.g., Fourcade-Gourinchas and Babb's (2002) analysis of ideological and pragmatic forms of neoliberalism). The liberal creed, in whatever form, is crucial in making invisible the social foundations of market action and therefore denying the importance of political choice.

However, Polanyi's analysis of this institutional and cultural power of market society should not obscure the dynamic vision of markets in society that is at the heart of his theory. Markets are not naturalised, self-reproducing institutions, a view which dominates orthodox economic analysis. Nor are they the static, stable entities implied in much of economic sociology, which tends to assume that the social embedding of economic action normally produces stable market relationships. It is also possible to interpret Polanyi as telling us that each phase of marketisation is met with an equal, progressive phase and counter-movements of social protection from within society itself. However, Polanyi's analysis of twentieth-century history suggests that it cannot be assumed that movements for the self-protection of society would always generate a 'progressive' outcome. In Polanyi's analysis, fascism, communism (in its Stalinist form) and social democracy were all reactions to the process of marketisation. Self-protection of society can result in both murderous and protective regimes (Berman, 2006).

Nonetheless, in making this argument, Polanyi defines a central place for politics within political economy. What all these counter-movements to market society have in common is their emphasis on 'the primacy of politics' (Berman, 2006). The interaction between markets and societies generates an inevitable space for politics. As

Burawoy (2003) argues, Polanyi's analysis of the double movement helps to explain where civil society and politics come from. However, as Burawoy also notes, the Polanyian framework does not provide us with particularly rich tools for understanding the political process and the outcome of this politics. The analysis of politics itself, and the factors that influence whether a country ends up with fascism, communism, social democracy or some other alternative form of economy, requires that we turn to other theories and lines of analysis.

As Bohle and Greskovits (2012: 14) argue, Polanyi provides a theory of politics and clearly shows how the operation of the double movement does not result in automatic movement and counter-movement, but opens up an autonomous space for political action, also recognising that this space is shaped by the structure of politics itself. This is a subtle analysis, more so than is often recognised, as Polanyi provides a set of structural dynamics through his analysis of the double movement, but also identifies within these structural processes how politics can play a crucial part in shaping contingent social outcomes. This analysis is further enhanced if it is recognised that Polanyi's dynamic analysis of the double movement can apply across different time and spatial horizons (Ó Riain, 2006).

Nonetheless, Polanyi is relatively weak on how particular outcomes are generated through the political sphere. What Polanyi does offer that is extremely significant is a way into the mid-range analysis of politics and comparative political economy which allows us to see them as embedded within market and society and shaped by the interaction of market and society, rather than as simply an autonomous political sphere. Where Polanyi is weaker is in allowing us to explain the distinctive particular form that the politics of liberal economies, and other forms of political economy, takes in particular times and places – a topic I will take up in the next section.

The distinctive institutions of liberal political economies

If Polanyi neglected the comparative political dimension, so too has much recent work on the sociological foundations of market economies. Despite its foundational contributions at the micro- and meso-levels, economic sociology has only rarely strayed into the territory occupied by comparative political economy – the analysis of the varying institutions of (typically advanced capitalist) economies and their effects on economic and social outcomes. Little is known, for example, of how the structuring of market action by institutions, networks and norms might vary systematically according to the type of political economy within which these markets are located. Team-based work practices may, for example, take on quite different dynamics and result in quite different productivity, innovation and employment security outcomes depending on whether those work teams are located in the US, Sweden or Japan (Cole, 1991). How are such micro-organisational social relations patterned differently in other realms of economic life?

Neoclassical approaches have dominated the study of capitalist societies, but have rarely been applied to comparative analysis that would set up liberal capitalism as just one variety of capitalism among others. Liberal market economies are assumed to be the baseline analytical model of the economy, while at the same time offering an ideal to be aspired to. This is in large part because neoclassical analysis is most fundamentally a theory of how marginal individual behaviour drives structural change in a market system. However, institutional and comparative analysis argues that, in practice, structures are often the drivers of marginal behaviour and are relatively (although not always) impervious to marginal pressures. Comparative political economy does not share the confidence of neoclassical analysis that marginal behaviour will 'clear' the institutions of the economy.

Similarly, Marxism, long the opposite pole to neoclassical analysis, has also had a weak comparative perspective given its focus upon the system-level workings of capitalism. Burawoy (2001) rightly criticises economic sociology and comparative political economy for ignoring such systemic 'commonalities of capitalism' (Streeck, 2011). What comparative analysis learns from Marxism is the crucial importance of understanding comparative cases as interacting within a broader system of relations. However, this strength of Marxism has often been undermined in specific analyses by a tendency to emphasise the final determining power of the capitalist system over political institutions (Block, 2012). Analyses of liberal political economies in particular are often framed as expressions of underlying capitalist logics (Jessop, 2002). In my analysis, I understand national political economies in terms of their commonalities, their most significant differences and the interactions among them that together form the complex of institutions that make up contemporary capitalism.

For example, Esping-Andersen's (1990) 'three worlds of welfare capitalism' was critically important in directing attention not only to different institutions of the welfare state but also to different types and constellations of ways of organising capitalism. More recently, for all its flaws, the 'varieties of capitalism' literature has similarly directed our focus to how different production regimes are organised within capitalism – including the organisation of employers, modes of competition and cooperation among capitalists, and the character of labour and its relations with capital (Hall and Soskice, 2001). The move towards identifying worlds or varieties of capitalism was a significant advance past the built-in liberal assumptions of modernisation theory or the determining power of liberal capitalism within certain strands of Marxist analysis.

The comparative approach argued that the operation of market capitalism depended profoundly upon the structure of institutions, social relations, and social and political governance – shaped through historical legacy and also political choice. Therefore, comparative political economy went some way towards refocusing the analysis of the economy from a focus on 'the market' as a baseline point of reference to looking at markets as one kind of institution that combined with others in different ways and in different times and places. Theories suggested that 'institutions mattered' and that various forms of economic organisation existed within liberal capitalist societies. Nor could it be assumed that liberal political economies inevitably experienced better levels of economic performance (Pontusson, 2005).

However, the central place of market and liberalism as an implicit 'normal' reference point sneaked back in, even where the political motivation was clearly an interest in alternatives to liberalism (Krippner, 2011). For Esping-Andersen, for example, the crucial distinguishing feature between different forms of welfare capitalism was the degree of commodification of social relations and the extent to which the welfare state decommodified labour and made workers less dependent upon the market for their survival and livelihoods. In practice, Esping-Andersen's analysis then revealed more about the non-liberal forms of the welfare state than countries within the liberal category, which were often seen as being simply 'market-led'.

Although Esping-Andersen's clusters of political economies made a great deal of sense, the distinction based on degree of commodification (or 'marketness') was less successful. For example, as well as non-liberal elements in liberal political economies, there were also significant 'liberal' elements in non-liberal systems. For instance, it is not the absence of markets that distinguishes the social democracies, but the embedding of those in non-market institutions so that workers and citizens become 'empowered market participants' who are both active in the labour market and protected from its greatest pressures (Huo *et al.*, 2008; Pontusson, 2011).

The 'varieties of capitalism' literature brought capitalism back into comparative political economy in some respects as it directed the focus onto production regimes and capital. However, it was a significant step backwards from Esping-Andersen's approach in its simple distinction between market and non-market political economies. This was particularly problematic in the distinction between *coordinated* and *liberal* market economies, implying strongly that while there might be markets in coordinated economies, there was little coordination in market economies. The market was firmly re-centred rather than problematised. In addition, while this literature argued that neither liberal nor coordinated market economies were inherently superior, the liberal economies were given the pre-eminent place in the drama of capitalism, being associated with innovation and the growing high-tech industry (Hall and Soskice, 2001).

This re-centring of the market was ironic given that at precisely the same time, economic sociology was revealing the 'always embedded' nature of market processes. While political economy, in the form of the varieties of capitalism, and economic sociology shared the view that economic systems varied significantly over time and space, there was in fact a deep tension between them. For Hall and Soskice, liberal market economies were non-coordinated, while arguably the main intellectual project of economic sociology was to show the social coordination behind market relations. This perhaps explains the surprisingly weak engagement between two literatures that appeared to share much in common. Each could have gained a great deal from the engagement – with the 'varieties of capitalism' analyses needing to focus more on the social construction of markets and economic sociology needing to link its micro-level analyses to national and global differences and interactions.

A different approach is the argument that neoliberalism does not mean the retreat of the state but the increasing importance of the state in a different form, operating in conformity with market rules. States are seen to be important actors promoting markets, but are converging on the form of a 'competition state' (Jessop, 2002; Kirby, 2002; Brenner, 2004). A competition state is a state that intervenes actively in the organisation of the economy, but only in ways that privilege enterprise over civic purposes and that promote competition and competitiveness (Cerny, 2000). The competition states theory runs into some difficulty, however. For a start, there seems to be a significant amount of activity that is undertaken by competition states that has a significant civic component and that could be turned towards social protection and/or egalitarian outcomes. Cerny himself argues that:

The outer limits of effective action by the state in this environment are usually seen to comprise its capacity to promote a relatively favourable investment climate for transnational capital – i.e., by providing an increasingly circumscribed range of goods that retain a national-scale (or sub national-scale) public character or of a particular type of still-specific assets described as immobile factors of capital. Such potentially manipulable factors include: human capital (the skills, experience, education, and training of the work force); infrastructure (from public transportation to high-technology information highways); support for a critical mass of research and development activities; basic public services necessary for a good quality of life for those working in middle- to high-level positions in otherwise footloose (transnationally mobile) firms and sectors; and maintenance of a public policy environment favourable to investment (and profit making) by such companies, whether domestic or foreign-owned. (Cerny, 1995: 611)

This is quite a list of tasks that the market-friendly state can still undertake.

More tellingly, the description of some of the specific features of competition states in practice fits quite closely with the kinds of activities undertaken by, for example, social democratic states. Jessop, for example, argues that advanced political economies are going through a transition from Keynesian national welfare states to Schumpeterian workfare post-national regimes (Jessop, 2002). But when we look at each of these dimensions, we find that the Nordic economies have long emphasised each of these aspects of the apparently new, liberal states. As will be seen later in this analysis, the Nordic economies have long been as Schumpeterian as they are Keynesian in their approach to macroeconomic management, favouring fiscal discipline and export competitiveness (Erixon, 2008). While they have not undertaken punitive forms of workfare, for the most part, they have had exceptionally high labour force participation rates and strongly emphasised labour market activation, including significant decreases in benefits for the long-term unemployed combined with very generous short-term replacement rates (Huo *et al.*, 2008). The Nordic and other small open economies of Europe have also long seen a close tie between their openness to the global economy and their national political institutions and social contracts, being globalised before many of the larger liberal political economies such as the US and the UK (Katzenstein, 1985). Finally, as will be seen in Chapter 5, the liberal political economies have tended to emphasise the power of central state and parliamentary politics while more decentralised mechanisms of government have been more prevalent in a social democratic economy.

If these are the key dimensions of the competition state and they are equally as compatible with social democracies as with liberal political economies, then there is a significant amount of political leeway attached to globalisation, much more significant than has been recognised by authors writing in this vein. It becomes difficult to argue, as Cerny (1995) does, that the structural demands of globalisation promote the need for a competition state and at the same time make social democratic strategies much more difficult to sustain. There are significant challenges associated with globalisation, particularly for social democracies, but these are not captured adequately within the theory of the competition state. It also follows that the competition state theories cannot provide adequate accounts of the institutions of liberal political economies, even if they have shed significant light on the specific practices of liberal policy regimes.

We turn then to a different strategy, seeking to identify some of the empirical regularities in how institutions are structured within liberal political economies in ways that are significantly different from those in other 'worlds of capitalism'. What are the characteristic ways in which finance, production, welfare and politics are organised in liberal political economies? And how does Ireland fit into these patterns?

Describing the distinctive institutions of liberal political economies is not as easy as it seems. It is assumed that what makes liberal political economies different is that markets are the dominant institutions. As mentioned previously, there is a certain truth in this. But markets themselves operate through a variety of their own organisations and institutions. For example, the rise of neoliberalism at a transnational level is associated not with the spread of textbook market processes but with the diffusion of corporation-friendly policy environments and private regulation. In part, this is because freer markets mean more rules (Vogel, 1996). But it is also because even 'free markets' operate through sets of organisations that, while private, do not necessarily conform to textbook market dynamics. So we have seen a growth, spread and increasing importance of a range of institutions that provide new forms of private regulation – such as credit rating agencies, investment analysts and a wide variety of market makers and arbitrators. I explore the importance of such 'institutions of the market' throughout this book.

We find, for example, that financialisation progresses faster and deeper in liberal than in other political economies, as do 'markets for governance' in corporate organisation (Davis, 2011). This has significant transnational effects since competition within the international financial sector tends to generate knock-on effects in non-liberal economies as their financial firms pursue the profits secured in the US, the UK and elsewhere.

More generally, the 'social compacts' in liberal political economies are typically narrower and much shorter in their time horizons – a fact reflected in the weakness of negotiated institutional agreements in liberal production, welfare and macroeconomic regimes. Given these patterns, liberal economies appear likely to experience more volatile economic cycles and to incorporate these into their macroeconomic policies. Greater reliance on policy tools such as interest rate changes and currency policy are linked to this tendency, as are the typically higher deficits in the public finances that are characteristic of liberal political economies – despite the perception of fiscal rectitude as a 'liberal' policy (Huber and Stephens, 2001). It appears that it is the liberal economies that may ultimately be more 'Keynesian'.

Other differences arise in considering the social and political institutions of political economies. It is widely, though not universally, recognised that states do not necessarily intervene 'less' in liberal economies. The competition to attract foreign investment is in practice a highly statist project, as well as a 'liberal' policy. Liberal political economies show some of the highest rates of public and quasi-public investment in research and development (R&D), alongside the social democracies (Pontusson, 2005). They are also more likely than other systems to make use of tax incentives to steer private action.

While liberal economies typically have smaller welfare states, they also often have a distinctive structure where public benefits are closely intertwined with private market resources – for example, in the 'pay-related' (Ó Riain and O'Connell, 2000) or 'wage-earner' (Castles, 1985) welfare state. In addition, both corporate organisation (Holm *et al.*, 2010) and parliamentary affairs (Döring, 2001) are more centralised in the apparently less coordinated market economies.

Many of these are 'non-liberal' elements, but are nonetheless relatively consistently associated with political economies (the US, the UK, Canada, Australia, New Zealand and Ireland) that we can sensibly call liberal. If we were to retain the 'liberal' label for only those elements that are closely tied to market mechanisms, this would provide conceptual elegance. However, it would fly in the face of the empirical evidence and, crucially, would lead to a misunderstanding of how liberal economies actually work. Analysing real-world economic liberalism as a set of social relations that are heavily influenced by market mechanisms but are not limited to them also allows us to examine in more detail how the 'liberal' elements interact with the many other features in a national political economy – including clientelist systems of patronage, welfarism, trade unionism, developmental statism and so on. It is better to identify these regular 'non-liberal' features of 'liberal' economies and treat them as characteristic features alongside market mechanisms, identifying the empirical regularities in how these interact and then conceptualising these interactions as part of how liberal political economies 'work' in practice. That is the strategy employed in this book in my interrogations of liberalism with an Irish face.

Structure of the book

This book explores these varied forms of organisation of liberalism in Ireland, how they intersected with other forms of economic organisation nationally and transnationally, and the ways in which they shaped Ireland's development and crisis. I use the perspectives of economic sociology and comparative political economy to understand both Ireland's experience of development and crisis, and economic liberalism itself. In the five chapters that follow, I trace each of the key plotlines identified at the start of this chapter – including Ireland's development, the tension between finance and production, between national and transnational, and between democracy and the capitalism it seeks to both promote and control – before ending with an account of the course of Ireland's crisis. In each chapter, I also trace one of the key elements of Polanyi's account of the creative tension between market and society, and identify the characteristic institutional forms of liberal political economy revealed in that chapter's analysis.

Chapter 2 traces the evolution of the Irish political economy in broad strokes, outlining a series of key periods during which the dynamic of the economy shifted. These periods included the decades between the crises of the 1950s and 1980s; a period of macroeconomic stabilisation from 1987 to 1994, followed by deepened development in the midst of the economic boom in the late 1990s; and, after a period of uncertainty from 2001 to 2003, the emergence of the credit and property bubble economy from 2003 to 2008. The chapter identifies a number of different 'Celtic Tiger' economies over the twenty years of growth, forming – as Polanyi would expect – multiple regimes of 'socially embedded market action'. However, the chapter argues that the conventional view of Irish 'convergence' on European levels of national wealth, driven by orthodox liberal economic policies, is mistaken. Much of the growth was driven by policies that were closer to the European model of social partnership and export-oriented industrial policy, but Ireland never completely 'converged' on this European model of political economy and society.

The following three chapters explore the origins of the crisis in Ireland in more detail, focusing upon the dynamics of the period between 2001 and 2008, and how the development dynamic of the 1990s was transformed into the crisis of the late 2000s. Each chapter traces one of the key plotlines identified at the start of this chapter – the tension between financial and productive capital, the transnationalisation of capitalism (and in particular the deep economic integration in Europe) and the dilemmas of the political management of capitalist growth.

Chapter 3 examines the politics of finance and investment in Ireland itself. The crisis of 2008 had its roots most fundamentally in the massive expansion of an asset bubble formed by the intersection of finance and property, enabled by weak regulation. However, the social foundations of this liberalisation of finance go well beyond the degree and kind of regulation. This 'social structure of liquidity' (Carruthers and Stinchcombe, 1999), facilitated by Ireland's position at the nexus of a 'triple financialisation' of the US, UK and European economies,

triumphed over an alternative social structure that channelled investment towards the development of high-technology production and
innovation. This was the triumph of Polanyi's 'market society' with
the hyper-commodification of land and money and the emergence of
finance as the enemy of production (Polanyi, 1944). The chapter traces
how a 'liberal creed' was normalised in 'market talk'. This was central
to the institutions of the market itself – such as bank management,
stock markets and credit rating agencies – which were given a particularly central role in liberal political economies and in the liberalising
financial sectors across Europe.

Chapter 4 examines how these conflicting modes of organisation of
capitalism were linked to globalisation, and particularly to the faltering
project of Europeanisation. Over the past fifty years, Ireland has
shifted, in the words of Joe Ruane (2010), from a 'simple periphery'
of the UK to a 'multiple interface periphery' located between the UK,
the US and Europe. This multiplicity of connections allowed the Irish
state and political economy some 'strategic flexibility' and was a
crucial element in the private and public investment during the 1990s
boom. However, financialisation in Europe combined with European
economic and monetary integration to restrict the range of policy tools
available to national states, even as the pressures for instability
increased. The policy incentives and constraints that accompanied
monetary union were much closer to the policy styles and broader
social compacts of the Continental core than of the European periphery. Uneven structural development and the fragmentation of 'Social
Europe' proved to be crucial fault lines along which the economic crisis
emerged.

Chapter 5 analyses how national politics was challenged by these
twin trends of financialisation and Europeanisation – managing these
processes for a time, but eventually building both into the fabric of the
political economy, with disastrous consequences. The neo-corporatist
processes of 'social partnership' were at the centre of the management
of the Irish economy from 1987 onwards and the analysis traces how
the early phase of an elite-led management of crisis was extended and
deepened in the 1990s, as state capacity to support development and
manage growth was enhanced. However, the 2000s saw a reassertion
of electoral and governmental politics as well as a narrowing of the
agenda of social partnership, even as government policy decisions and
partnership agreements built elements of the asset bubble into the

public finances. As Polanyi argued, 'laissez faire was planned' (1944: 147). However, the political dynamics went far beyond this, with the electoral and social politics of the period inflating the bubble further. These processes of political economic bargaining can only be understood in terms of the character of Ireland's fragmented production regimes, the pay-related welfare state, a hierarchical political system and a dualist system of public administration. All of these, I argue, can be understood as characteristic features of a liberal political economy.

Finally, having analysed the sources of the crisis, Chapter 6 traces the course of the crisis itself. I trace the narrative of the Irish crisis through various phases and dimensions of Ireland's deepening systemic crisis – how a financial crisis became a crisis of the public finances; how economic and social crises were mutually reinforcing and intensified the fiscal and financial problems; and how all of these together led most directly to a crisis of external creditworthiness, which ultimately resulted in a crisis of sovereignty and citizenship. I trace the national and international sources of the dominant policies of protecting the financial system and improving public finances through austerity, starting with Ireland's bank guarantee in September 2008 and running up to Europe's 'fiscal compact' in December 2012 and Irish negotiations with the ECB over debt repayments. Finally, the difficulties of forging viable alternative strategies from both within and outside the power structure are explored. These include the persistence of financialisation in Europe and elsewhere; the difficulties of combining economic policies and social politics that diverged profoundly across European economies; and the contradictions of Irish politics, public administration and social compacts. I argue that a distinctive 'European solution' to the crisis could have been developed, based on existing policy instruments and political coalitions, but failed to emerge for a variety of reasons.

2 | *Ireland: between development and crisis*

Ireland's development dilemma

The crisis of 2008 was far from Ireland's first Great Recession as an independent state. The 1950s had seen a largely agricultural, domestically oriented economy on the verge of collapse, with mass unemployment and emigration. A shift to a trade-oriented economy produced increased agricultural exports, the decline of protected domestic industries and a strong and persistent focus on attracting foreign direct investment (FDI). The 1960s and 1970s brought significant economic growth and some major social transformations – including the beginning of the 'modern' welfare state, the expansion of educational participation, changing family and gender relations, and the entry of Ireland into the European Economic Community (EEC) in 1973.

Nonetheless, the 1980s saw the arrival of a new crisis. Fuelled by government borrowing and cheap international finance in the late 1970s, Ireland's political economy shared in the international debt crisis of the early 1980s. With emigration and unemployment again sky-rocketing, the limits of Ireland's economic development and social transformation were clear. Female labour force participation remained extremely low and the overall employment rate within the economy was the lowest in the EU. Despite major inflows of foreign investment, the bulk of the Irish population remained dependent on the state for either employment or benefits – worse still, even in such an underdeveloped economy, inequality was among the highest in the Organisation for Economic Co-operation and Development (OECD) and was built into state policies (Breen *et al.*, 1990).

The 'Celtic Tiger' decades marked a dramatic and unexpected shift in Ireland's fortunes. The economy stabilised from 1987 to 1994, despite an international recession in the early 1990s. The mid-1990s brought a boom that lasted into the 2000s – foreign investment surged, indigenous Irish companies expanded, national income grew rapidly and, most strikingly, these combined to produce an 'employment miracle', with the Irish labour force almost doubling within fifteen years.

All this, as we know, came to a screeching halt in 2008 as the international financial crisis found one of its key transmission points in Ireland. Understandings of the Great Recession in Ireland are of course intertwined with how analysts understood the 'Celtic Tiger' era and, indeed, previous periods of crisis. Ireland's history of crises, most recently those of the 1950s and 1980s, suggests persistent dilemmas in the political economy and society. Many believed that, in one way or another, the Celtic Tiger period had delivered an escape from these dilemmas, while others warned that these underlying problems remained. In this chapter, I consider these understandings of the Celtic Tiger years that preceded the crisis, explore the patterns of continuity and change that run as threads through that history, and show the inadequacy of existing accounts of these crucial years. Ultimately, the chapter argues that the Celtic Tiger period was characterised by a number of 'embedded market projects' that sought in different ways to construct alternatives to the historical organisation of Irish underdevelopment and inequality. This period proves, in retrospect, to have been a period of possibilities – many of which were realised in part, but which were never fully institutionalised at the centre of the Irish political economy and society. These failures of transformation and institutionalisation combined with the destabilising effects of financialisation and liberalisation to produce the disastrous events of 2008 onwards.

Ireland and Western European convergence

Ireland missed out on Europe's post-war 'Golden Age'. But from the 1990s onwards, it caught up rapidly. Figure 2.1 shows growth in gross national income (GNI) per capita across the OECD in recent decades. It is particularly useful to compare GNI rather than GDP as there is a significant gap in Ireland between GDP and other measures of national wealth, since GDP is particularly strongly affected in Ireland by the financial activities of transnational corporations and over-estimates national income by 10–15 per cent. The figure compares Ireland to the OECD as a whole as well as to Denmark, another small open European economy, and Spain, which has undergone a similar trajectory of development to Ireland.

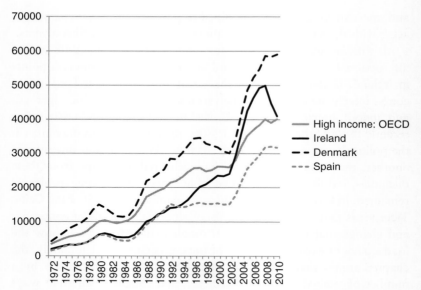

Figure 2.1 GNI per capita, selected European economies, 1972–2010
Source: World Bank

While income levels have grown across all these countries and across the OECD high-income countries, the relative place of different economies has stayed much the same. Ireland stands out for its dramatic increase in income until 2008. The increases in Irish national income per capita track those in Spain quite closely until 1994. However, from 1994 to 2000, Ireland makes a dramatic leap ahead of Spanish income levels, reaching the same level as the high-income OECD countries and even almost closing the gap with Denmark by around 2002. Ireland and the UK (not shown) shared a similar experience after Ireland's period of catch-up through the 1990s. Both increased national income rapidly through the 2000s, with Ireland's growth being even faster than the UK's. However, both also experienced by far the most significant falls in national income after the economic crisis.

Nonetheless, it is clear that Ireland's position within the hierarchy of comparative national income has shifted significantly. Until the early 1990s, Ireland was firmly in the European periphery alongside the Mediterranean nations. The 1990s saw it catch up with the average of high-income OECD countries and pull ahead through the 2000s.

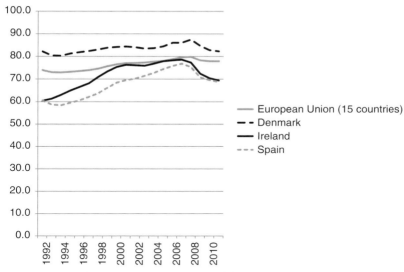

Figure 2.2 Employment rate, 25–54 year olds, 1992–2010
Source: Eurostat

However, the fall in national income in Ireland was particularly calamitous after the economic crisis.

Perhaps a better indication of economic progress is the employment rate within the economy as a whole, given that this, especially in liberal economies, is the primary way that the bulk of the population gain their income. Figure 2.2 shows the even more remarkable speed at which Ireland 'caught up' in the percentage of the population at work, although it remained behind most other European economies. The employment rate is preferred to unemployment as it captures the overall level of activity among the population and the focus is on 25–54 year olds to control for different educational and retirement policies and practices. The figures concentrate on the same countries, although they compare them to the EU-15 instead of the OECD.

In 1992 Ireland was once again alongside Spain in its exceptionally low level of employment among 25–54 year olds. Once more, we see a surge through the 1990s, with Ireland's employment rate increasing to that of the EU-15 by 2000. Through the 2000s, a period of significant immigration, Ireland's employment rate did not increase above the EU-15 average. Ireland never managed to close the gap on Denmark (or even the UK). From 2007 onwards, Ireland's employment rates dropped disastrously once more, falling well below the EU-15 average and once again to Spanish levels. Despite a spectacular growth in absolute employment, the Irish economy was still dependent on a relatively narrow base of employment to sustain the population as a whole.

Is it the case then that Ireland's growth and development has been an example not so much of an economic miracle, but of 'delayed' (and partial) 'convergence' on the Western European norm? Honohan and Walsh (2002) have provided what has become the standard economic account of the 'convergence' story. They point out that when Ireland entered the EEC alongside the UK in 1973, the major difference between the two countries was poor agricultural incomes, low labour market participation and a low percentage of advanced sectors in Ireland. The 'Celtic Tiger' economy was the outcome of adding a new 'layer' to the economy, which involved employing a new generation (including the women of that generation) in modern sectors. Honohan and Walsh split this thirty-year project into two parts. For the first fifteen years, policy was wrong. The governments of the 1970s adopted fiscal expansion as a response to the oil crisis, drove wages up and crowded out productivity growth – in turn leading to rapidly increasing debt, further depressing growth and resulting in the economic crisis of the 1980s. Ireland should have (more or less automatically) converged on European living standards, but policy mistakes delayed this convergence. However, when it did happen, the very lateness of Ireland's catching up meant that it was 'telescoped' and dramatic (Honohan and Walsh, 2002: 2). From the mid-1980s onwards, governments got policy 'right' with fiscal correction, macroeconomic stability and, crucially, wage moderation.

This has become in many respects the standard account of Ireland's success and is a key reference point for accounts of the crisis (e.g., Whelan, 2010; Lane, 2011). It mirrors other popular explanations of Ireland's long-standing under-development in its emphasis on the importance of the factors that impeded underlying tendencies towards progress, modernisation or convergence. Although Honohan (2004) is himself critical of it, Garvin's (2004) *Preventing the Future* similarly emphasises how institutions and policies obstructed the modernisation of Ireland in the 1940s and 1950s – although the villain in

Garvin's analysis is traditional nationalist institutions rather than fiscal and monetary policy.

Other accounts are more critical of the economic model that underpinned the Celtic Tiger economy, even in the 1990s. Some question whether the 1990s growth brought genuine development, pointing to the problems in understanding Irish growth figures due to transfer pricing and other financial flows associated with transnational companies. Where development did occur, it was largely simply down to Ireland's place within global production networks and financial flows with few indigenous roots (O'Hearn, 2001). Others see genuine elements of development, albeit in pockets (Kirby, 2010). Nonetheless, there are serious limits to the Celtic Tiger model from this perspective – development depends excessively on foreign investment, economic success combines with social failure (in the form of inequality and weak social provision) and the state favours its enterprise over its civic role (Kirby, 2010).

Such accounts share with the neoclassical analyses the view that the Celtic Tiger was a largely liberal political economy. However, where the neoclassical analyses see liberalisation as a crucial element in generating growth, critical analyses emphasise the limits of liberalisation in generating development. Where the neoclassicals see international market convergence, critical analysts argue that Ireland remains dangerously disadvantaged within the hierarchies of the international economy. The critical analysts see the bubble and bust of the 2000s not as a departure from the patterns of the 1990s, but as rooted in the weaknesses of the liberal model of that era, which only become fully evident during the crisis. Ireland's deliberately weak regulation of finance and low levels of taxation and expenditure left it particularly vulnerable to the financial crisis, particularly within a liberalising EU (Kirby and Murphy, 2011).

The account developed in this chapter shares elements with both of these perspectives. However, it begins from a somewhat different starting point. While Ireland's political economy was clearly liberal in many respects in the 1990s and 2000s, there were also a series of institutional and political projects within the society that made significant strides towards establishing other possible models, including a developmental approach within parts of the state and social democratic elements in neo-corporatist 'social partnership'. These were critical elements in the genuine economic and employment progress made in the 1990s. Ireland was not quite as liberal as analysts of various stripes have suggested.

If that is the case, then we need to rethink Ireland's 'convergence' with Europe. First, and most fundamental, is the question of what the Irish economy was converging upon. Honohan and Walsh cast the story in terms of Ireland finally joining the world of the 'modernisers' – defining modernisation as the removal of barriers to the operation of markets (2002: 4). However, this glides over crucial features of the Western European experience. Ó Gráda and O'Rourke (2000) also compare Irish and European economic growth patterns. They argue, however, that post-war growth in Europe was built on a grand bargain where wage restraint on the part of labour was exchanged for reinvestment of profits by business and the expansion of the welfare state, all helped along by European integration and aid from the Marshall Plan. They draw parallels with Ireland in the 1990s, where centralised wage bargaining promoted export success, helped along by a new wave of European trade integration and structural funds investments. Crucially, however, elements of the post-war grand bargain were missing – wage restraint did not turn into higher investment rates or build the welfare state, despite efforts by parts of the policy system in that direction.

Second, Honohan and Walsh pay relatively little attention to the interactions between different elements of the political economy and how they can generate virtuous or vicious cycles. They provide a very useful account of the kinds of factors that may or may not have influenced Irish economic growth over the 1990s, identifying a number of clusters of factors. First, they argue that a number of features of the Irish political economy were important 'slow burners', but were not crucial factors as they operated as background factors throughout the whole period. These include the education system, a falling dependency ratio across the 1990s, very generous tax and business environments for foreign investment, and a series of institutional and cultural factors. These institutional factors include the rule of law, the quality of public administration and the depth and efficiency of the financial system, and are seen as largely consisting of the basic institutional requirements of liberal democratic market systems.

Other factors were catalytic factors which were important but not quantitatively significant on their own. These include the EU structural funds from 1988 and the currency devaluations in 1986 and 1993, which were important at the time, but only had a transitory effect. FDI promotion had a positive but also a consistent effect. Equally, more liberal measures such as welfare retrenchment and weak employment protections are also dismissed as key factors, as welfare provision was always ungenerous and employment protections were always weak. Honohan and Walsh also mention a number of popular explanations that did play a role, including corporatism and social partnership and tax reductions. However, they argue that these measures were part of the 'wider normalisation' (2002: 52) of the economy, including the tackling of institutional sclerosis and fiscal normalisation. In short, where social partnership worked, it worked to remove the historical barriers to growth and market liberalisation in Ireland. However, by placing their focus firmly on the operation of markets in their 'natural state', Honohan and Walsh fail to examine the more complex inter-actions across the many factors they discuss and the variety of forms of coordination of these factors, typically through different patterns of socially embedded market action.

Third, and following on from this, the conceptual weakness of the focus on the 'removal of barriers' to markets is substantial. As this argument has been made in detail in Chapter 1, it is enough to say here that such a view ignores the creation of new capabilities and the variety of forms of coordination within an economy. 'Non-liberal' factors such as industrial policy, wage bargaining and international subsidies and investment are re-interpreted as part of 'normalisation' when in prac-tice they were critical 'heterodox' elements in building the new, modern economy that Honohan and Walsh identify as the core of Ireland's success.

Therefore, to examine Irish 'convergence' with Europe requires a different approach. It is indeed useful to examine Ireland's economic history through the lens of the Western European experience. This was a real and significant change in the Irish economy, but was a conver-gence not only on European living standards but also in part on elements of the European model of 'coordinated capitalism' or the 'social market' (Hall and Soskice, 2001; Pontusson, 2005). Further-more, this convergence was supported by explicit public interventions in Europe that provided investments to promote regional and social cohesion as countervailing forces to market integration.

A useful starting point in understanding this broader convergence is the work of Dieter Senghaas. In his book *The European Experience*,

Senghaas (1985) seeks to make sense of the history of Europe's political economy in terms of uneven capitalist development, social structural change and national political economic institutions. He argues
that the history of capitalism is a history not of the inevitable progress
of poorer countries towards the core of capitalism, but of a general
process of peripheralisation, excluding most national economies from
the core but punctuated by a significant number of cases where new
economies join the core. He defines development as the ability to build
an 'autocentric' national economy which can draw in resources from
the global economy and use them as the building blocks for the
circulation and enhancement of resources within the national society.

Perhaps the most significant of these successful cases is the European
economy itself, involving both a wide range of countries and the
formation of a distinctive form of political economy organised primarily around Christian democracy and social democracy. Mjøset (1992),
in a study that compared Ireland's economic performance to that of
other small open economies in Europe, develops these points in more
detail (see Figure 2.3). He argued that these comparison economies all
shared certain common features in terms of their patterns of growth
and development. Two particular features prove crucial: a national
system of innovation that can anchor a country's economic efficiency
and export performance so that it makes the most of its links to the
global economy, and a system of social welfare that generalises these

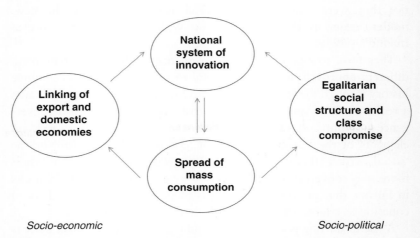

Socio-economic   *Socio-political*

Figure 2.3 The European Development Model (based on Mjøset, 1992)

gains from the global economy throughout the national economy and underpins a system of mass consumption. These economic features of autocentric development are also anchored by a political coalition, and in Europe this has taken a distinctive and generally more egalitarian form than in other advanced capitalist countries.

As the literature in comparative political economy tells us, there are many 'social worlds of welfare capitalism' (Esping-Andersen, 1990, 1999; Ó Riain, 2000, 2011). Nonetheless, each is built on these key elements of macroeconomic orders, production regimes, welfare regimes, and institutions of governance and socio-political coalitions. This then is the heart of the European model – a system that links together export performance through the national innovation system and social welfare organised through mass public and private consumption, all organised through a national socio-political compromise. How might this perspective shed light on Ireland's historical under-development?

Figure 2.4 shows the vicious cycle of Ireland's under-development prior to the Celtic Tiger era, represented in the framework outlined in Figure 2.3. It maps the dynamics of the Western European post-war political economies onto the Irish case. However, in Ireland's case the dynamic interaction between these different spheres of the

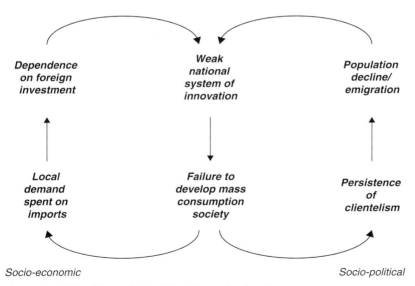

Figure 2.4 The vicious circle of Fordist under-development

economy and socio-political processes produced a vicious cycle of under-development rather than a virtuous cycle of development and upgrading.

This is rooted in large part in Ireland's failure to develop a system of innovation, a set of institutions and policies that could support a dynamic indigenous industrial sector (Lundvall, 1992; Mjøset, 1992). This was caused by a number of complex factors. Most fundamentally, Ireland failed to make a transition from an agricultural economy to an industrial economy. The reasons for this are, of course, controversial. Although colonial and post-colonial patterns of trade with the UK were important, so too were domestic factors. In particular, the specific way in which the transition from agriculture was resolved shaped much of Ireland's political economy over the past century or more. The critical conjuncture here was in the second half of the nineteenth century, when Irish tenant farmers struggled with their (mainly British and Anglo-Irish) landlords. Crucially, the tenants ultimately won rights as smallholder farmers, cementing the organisation of agriculture through small-scale, relatively conservative family farm units and creating a new class of small property holders and family businesses. State policies in the decades after independence in 1922 systematically favoured this smallholding farmer class over the urban working classes (Hannan and Commins, 1992). At the same time, agricultural policy and rural development policy were focused on maintaining the family farm rather than developing the agricultural sector or the rural economy. The kind of broad-based industrial development rooted in the upgrading of agriculture that was central to economies such as Denmark and later Finland did not occur in any significant way in Ireland. This may well have been aggravated in the middle decades of the twentieth century by a disjuncture between the business class, which was often Protestant, and the agencies of the new state, which was dominated by Catholics (Ó Riain, 2004). In any case, domestic industrial development lagged far behind Ireland's small open European neighbours in the post-war decades.

Poor industrial development weakened economic growth and living standards, in the process choking the spread of the mass consumption economy that was growing across the US and Europe. These weaknesses in supply of businesses and demand from consumers meant that a significant portion of domestic spending went on imports, further reinforcing the weakness of domestic industry. Over time, this reinforced Ireland's dependence on foreign investment, which became the cornerstone of industrial policy from the 1960s onwards. While Ireland was successful in attracting foreign investment, it proved exceptionally difficult until the 1990s to build a broad-based development strategy around 'industrialisation by invitation'.

Just as important was the socio-political dynamic that underpinned this vicious cycle of under-development. In place of the European corporatist systems that provided economic growth and social solidarity through negotiation among organised interests, Ireland developed a system of brokerage politics (Komito, 1992). The dominant force was Fianna Fáil, which constructed itself as a highly successful national catch-all 'party of government'. The party appealed across all classes (Hardiman and Whelan, 1994), but was particularly skilled at brokering the interests of the smallholder classes forged in the late nineteenth century (Hannan and Commins, 1992). Ironically, Mjøset (1992) argues that it was in part the very failures of this economic and political model that continued to reinforce it, as mass emigration at regular intervals acted as a 'safety valve' by allowing (or forcing) citizens to 'exit' the social and political system instead of staying to 'voice' their concerns and potentially drive internal socio-political and socio-economic transformation (Hirschman, 1970).

The shape of Ireland's political economy mirrors the kinds of regimes at work in the small open European economies, but the interaction between those regimes was significantly different. Given this perspective on Ireland through a European lens, how do we assess Ireland's performance since the economic crises of the 1980s and its apparent convergence with those same European economies?

The perspective developed above, drawing on Senghaas and Mjøset, suggests that 'convergence' with Europe would involve a great deal more than simply growing to similar levels of per capita national income. The structural dynamics of Ireland's economy were dramatically different from those in similar countries in Europe, and a deep and sustainable convergence would require change not only in the various individual elements of the political economy but also in the interactions between them. In this chapter I provide an analysis of the changes in the Irish economy during the Celtic Tiger years of boom and bubble, examined through the lens of the socio-economic and socio-political processes that underpinned economic growth and autocentric development in Europe. In light of this discussion, it is useful to take a more

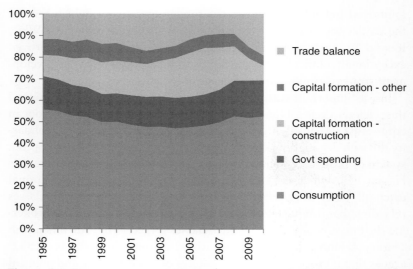

Figure 2.5 Percentage composition of components of national income, 1995–2010
Source: CSO, *National Accounts*

detailed look at Ireland's recent economic performance, once again through the twin lenses of national income and employment as outlined in Figures 2.1 and 2.2.

Having documented Ireland's dramatic economic growth in the 1990s and the 2000s, Figure 2.5 provides a closer look at the changing components of that growing national income from 1995 to 2010. In the late 1990s one of the key elements driving growth was the growing trade balance, reflecting booming exports primarily linked to foreign investment. The contribution of trade and exports relative to private and government consumption increased throughout this period. There were also some minor increases in the share of non-building investment. However, we also see the beginnings of the expansion of investment in construction, even during the 1990s 'export-led' boom.

Figure 2.6 provides a slightly different perspective, looking at the absolute amounts of income generated through each of these categories. The trade balance remains important and indeed persists further into the 2000s than is suggested in the figure on percentage composition. The growth of construction is illustrated dramatically, as are

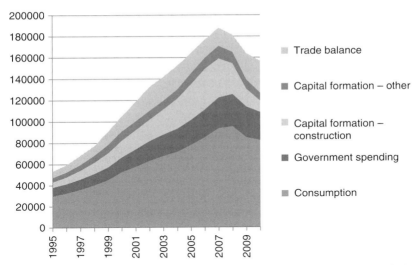

Figure 2.6 Absolute level of components of national income, 1995–2010 (€m)
Source: CSO, *National Accounts*

increases in government spending through the 2000s. Most dramatic of all perhaps is the crucial importance of private consumption, which increases steadily across the entire period until the crisis of 2008. Once again, our attention is directed towards the interaction between the system of innovation that supported exporting, the balance of productive and speculative investment produced by that system of innovation, and how this interacted with the dynamics of domestic private and public demand. Like autocentric development in Europe, Irish development in the 1990s was based on the interaction of innovation and exporting with constantly expanding consumer and government demand. But there are signs in these figures too of the growing dominance of construction over other forms of investment and capital formation as early as the 1990s.

National income provides only one perspective on economic development. Honohan and Walsh (2002) pointed out that economic convergence came through a structural change, with the addition of a whole new 'modern' economy on top of the existing one, largely involving a new generation of workers, firms and even public agencies. This structural change is captured more clearly in changing employment profiles than in national income statistics. Changing sectoral patterns in employment reveal the degree of structural transformation that may or may not underpin income convergence among European economies. This issue, while having been hotly debated during the 1990s and 2000s, has become even more critical in light of the current crisis and what it has revealed regarding the structural imbalances and unequal developments between the core and the periphery in Europe.

Earlier it was shown that the overall employment rate in Ireland remained significantly below similar small open economies in Europe. However, this only gives us the most general of pictures of the Irish economy's level of development. We can get a more detailed sense of the structure of the Irish economy and how it compares to small open economies in Europe by comparing the particular mix of sectors within the economy. Table 2.1 shows Ireland's employment structure compared to other European countries, classifying data by the countries' 'variety of capitalism' and by whether they are one of the 'small open economies' that cut across these varieties. The table focuses on employment as this presents perhaps the most reliable indicator of economic activity, given the well-known difficulties in Ireland in particular with measures of output, turnover and productivity.

There are of course significant differences between the various countries, but a number of key patterns can be noted. Ireland lagged behind other small open economies in (primarily public sector) social services and industrial employment. The figures also show that Ireland's share of employment in agriculture and construction remained relatively high, mirroring the Mediterranean economies. Finance, insurance and real estate (FIRE) was prominent within the employment structure, similarly to the liberal group of countries. Information and communications technologies, despite Ireland's high-profile and relatively successful growth, did not comprise an exceptionally large proportion of Irish employment. While Ireland had significant turnover in 'business services', most of these activities were linked either to foreign investment or real estate work, and employment in professional, scientific and administrative services was relatively low.

Ireland made some progress in 'leading-edge' sectors such as information and communications technology (ICT), but still clearly bore the imprints of having missed two key revolutions in European capitalism. The first was the manufacturing exports boom of the 'Golden Age', while the second was the major expansion in public social services through the post-war decades and beyond. Despite the evidence of

Table 2.1 *The sectoral structure of employment in European capitalisms (percentages)*

	Ireland	Small open economies	Social democratic	Liberal	Christian democratic	Mediterranean
Agriculture	5	3.3	3.1	2.1	2.8	6.3
Industry	13.2	14.9	14.7	13.2	16.1	17.9
Construction	7.9	6.8	6.7	7	7.1	9.5
Retail	25.4	22.8	21.8	22.1	23.1	25.7
ICT	3.8	3.4	3.9	3.3	3.1	2.3
FIRE	5.1	3.5	2.6	4.9	3.3	2.4
Real estate	0.5	0.8	1.1	0.9	0.8	0.6
Professional, scientific and administrative services	8.7	9.2	10.1	10.5	9.1	8.4
Public sector	25.1	28.1	30.7	27.3	27.7	20.2
Arts, leisure, other	4.9	5	5.1	5.7	5	6.7

Source: Eurostat
Small open economies: Austria, Belgium, Denmark, Finland, the Netherlands, Switzerland
Social democratic: Denmark, Finland, Sweden
Liberal: Switzerland, the UK
Christian democratic: Austria, Belgium, France, Germany, the Netherlands
Mediterranean: Italy, Portugal, Spain

'convergence' on European norms in income and, to a lesser extent, employment, this analysis suggests that under-development of manufacturing exports and social services over the decades has never been overcome in Ireland. The ICT and other leading sectors were asked in the Irish case to compensate for these missing historical 'leaps forward'. Even after the Celtic Tiger years, Ireland remained an incomplete model of development and of European convergence, running ahead of the Mediterranean periphery in terms of structural transformation and income, but remaining significantly behind the Continental economies and particularly the small open Nordic societies in terms of employment in key private and public sectors.

Ireland's Celtic Tiger decades were decades not only of boom but also of much greater variation and complexity than is often acknowledged. The 'Irish model' shifted over time, with different components of national income driving growth in different periods. Furthermore, Ireland's development was deeply ambiguous in relation to the degree of structural transformation, and therefore 'convergence', achieved. Ireland's employment structure bears the stamp of its export boom, its expanded domestic demand and its real estate and financial bubbles. However, it has also been shaped by missing out on significant elements of the two mutually reinforcing transformations at the heart of sustainable prosperity in Europe – the creation of a broad industrial base linked to a national system of innovation and the building of welfare state institutions and widespread social services. Ireland's partial progress towards economic development was ultimately a contributing factor to the crisis of 2008, although this was hastened along by financialisation, European integration and the pattern of national politics. However, before turning to a detailed examination of these factors in the next three chapters, the rest of this chapter explores in more detail the shifting patterns in the organisation of the Irish economy in the twenty years before the crisis – the years of the 'Celtic Tiger'.

Three Celtic Tigers

The 'Celtic Tiger' became an icon in discussions of the global economy, the label creating a single entity out of a beast that changed its stripes a number of times. In fact, the two decades of 'Celtic Tiger' consistent growth can be separated into three (and perhaps even four) periods

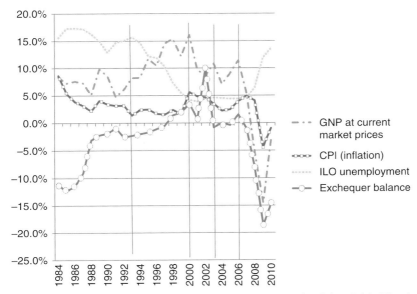

Figure 2.7 Macroeconomic trends across four time periods of the 'Celtic Tiger'
Source: CSO

(Figure 2.7). The year 1987 is conventionally taken as the turning point in Ireland's development – partly because a number of indicators began to turn in a more positive direction at that point and partly because the first neo-corporatist 'social partnership' agreement was agreed that year. The period from 1987 to 1994 was most significant for the macroeconomic stabilisation that was achieved, with reduced inflation and improving public finances, although dramatic inroads were not made into the unemployment and emigration problems of the 1980s. From 1994 to about 2000, the Irish economy grew rapidly and saw huge increases in exports and startling growth in employment. Net migration reversed as Irish emigrants returned and many new immigrants arrived, initially mainly from the US and the UK. Public finances went into surplus and inflation remained under control. This period ended with more difficult years in 2001–3 when the bursting of the dot-com bubble and overheating in the domestic economy appeared to pose some difficult choices in how to develop Ireland's economy after the boom years. However, the following years saw a third distinct period with a property bubble that drove new rounds of

high levels of growth in both incomes and employment. The rest of this
chapter briefly reviews the dynamics of each of these periods in terms
of the macroeconomic orders, production regimes, welfare regimes and
institutions of governance discussed above.

1987–94: macroeconomic stabilisation

The beginning of Ireland's exit from its position as *The Economist*'s
'sick man of Europe' is usually dated to 1987. This was the year in
which the first of a series of social partnership agreements was concluded, beginning a sequence of deals that would continue unbroken
until 2008. A three-year deal between employers, trade unions and the
state provided wage restraint and industrial peace in exchange for tax
cuts and acceptance of significant cutbacks in public expenditure in
1987–90.

Crippled by a debt/GDP ratio which had risen through the 1980s
to 117 per cent in 1987, the period from 1987 to 1990 in particular
saw a major emphasis on tackling the deficit in annual budgets (see
Table 2.2). Total current spending fell by over 10 percentage points in
real terms between 1987 and 1989. Total current spending fell from
57 per cent of GNP in 1985 to 42 per cent in 1990 and to 41 per cent in
1995 (Ó Riain and O'Connell, 2000).

One popular explanation for the growth in the years following 1987
was that the fiscal contraction, or spending cuts, of those years
had ultimately proved expansionary, as the stabilisation of macroeconomic conditions improved entrepreneurial and investor confidence (McAleese, 1990). However, others have argued that such
explanations are greatly overblown, with the role of investor confidence being greatly overstated and the importance of other conditions
for economic growth being neglected (Bradley and Whelan, 1997;
Kinsella, 2012).

A number of crucial features came into play during these years, with
fiscal consolidation proving to be only one part of an overall package.
The recovery in spending levels was fairly rapid. Furthermore, it
proved possible to concentrate many of the cuts in administrative
resources and to protect education in particular from the worst effects.
Real spending on education fell by about 2.5 percentage points
between 1987 and 1990, and health expenditure fell only marginally
during this period. However, by 1991, the real value of spending in

Table 2.2 *Public finances in Ireland, 1987–2007*

Year	GNI (€bn)	Debt/GDP ratio (%)	Exchequer balance (€m)	Total tax revenue as % of GDP	Public spending as % of GDP
1987	26.1	117	−2268	35.6	51.4
1988	28.1	113	−786	36.8	48.2
1989	31.0	102	−608	33.3	42.5
1990	33.7	94	−587	33.1	42.8
1991	35.1	96	−634	33.7	44.4
1992	36.8	92	−905	34	44.8
1993	39.6	95	−876	34	44.6
1994	42.8	90	−853	34.6	43.9
1995	47.7	82	−796	32	41.1
1996	53.0	74	−437	32.1	39.1
1997	60.3	65	−372	31.4	36.7
1998	69.2	54	984	31.3	34.5
1999	77.6	48	1,603	31.5	34.1
2000	89.0	38	3,137	31.7	31.5
2001	97.5	35	334	29.5	33.3
2002	104.7	32	95	28.2	33.6
2003	119.1	31	−980	28.8	33.4
2004	126.8	29	33	28.8	33.7
2005	137.5	27	−499	30.2	33.7
2006	150.5	25	2,265	30.6	33.8
2007	162.1	25	−1,619	31.7	35.4

Source: Department of Finance, *Economic Statistics*

each of these areas had been restored, and real expenditure levels in health were almost 20 per cent above the level in 1987 (Ó Riain and O'Connell, 2000). In addition, as will be seen further in Chapter 4, the availability of EU structural funding enabled significant amounts of government capital spending during these years and into the 1990s, counterbalancing some of the other cuts.

External conditions were also important, with growth in the international economy between 1987 and 1990, and Ireland's recovery was already underway by the international recession of 1991. The resumption of growth was driven by a boost in foreign investment and exports in the late 1980s which increased consumption in the following years, with investment also rising subsequently (Honohan and Walsh 2002). Ireland's production regime was dominated by the estimated 40 per cent of US electronics FDI in electronics in Europe that it secured from 1980 to 2000. Firms were attracted by corporate tax rates of zero to 12.5 per cent at different time periods, a supply of young (and increasingly skilled) labour, a supportive state and, increasingly, improved technological and innovation capacities (Gunnigle and McGuire, 2001; Ó Riain, 2004). In the process, Ireland came to have one of the highest proportions of foreign capital stock in the OECD and to be among the most open trading economies in the world.

Changes in the IT industry and the international recession resulted in the closure of a number of major high-tech employers in Ireland – most notably Digital's manufacturing operations in 1991. However, overall in this period the strategy of attracting FDI became somewhat more sophisticated, as interview evidence suggests that multinational corporations locating in Ireland were now attracted not only by the tax concerns that had been almost their exclusive incentive in the 1970s (Young and Hood, 1983) but also by the additional availability of skilled labour (Gunnigle and McGuire, 2001). State agencies were central to this. The attraction of FDI is, after all, a state project as much as it is a market. The 'market for corporate location' is a somewhat unusual market, based as it is on the locational decisions of large corporate hierarchies which respond largely to the conditions put in place by hierarchical state agencies. It is best seen as a system of competitive bargaining between corporations and states than as a market in the conventional sense.

Domestic industry remained weak, however, with some improvements in links between multinational firms and Irish sub-suppliers, but relatively few Irish-owned firms emerging in key sectors until the mid-1990s (Ó Riain, 2004). Nonetheless, some significant investments were made through the 'welfare regime' in the 1980s that started to bear fruit – in particular, in third-level education. The most critical factor of production for a learning industry is educated labour and the Irish education system expanded rapidly from the 1960s onwards, with public expenditure on education growing from just over 3 per cent of GNP in 1961/2 to 6.3 per cent in 1973/4 (Breen *et al.*, 1990: 123). Free post-primary school education and free school transport were introduced in 1967. The reforms which would most directly affect the high technology sector would be at the third level, however.

Absolute numbers in third-level education more than tripled between 1963/4 and 1984/5, largely because of increased participation rates (Breen *et al.*, 1990: 129). The catalyst for the change in the education system was the 1965 OECD report *Investment in Education*, which drew on the increasingly influential human capital theory of education to argue that 'manpower' training would be essential to a growing economy like Ireland's.

The state was also willing to use its newfound capacity to influence labour supply more directly. In particular, the expansion of engineering and computer science education undertaken in the late 1970s was accomplished through increased state funding earmarked specifically for those disciplines – including 1.725 million Irish pounds of extra funding put aside in 1979. In general, then, 'it could be argued that in Ireland over the past two decades the provision of higher education has been supply-led rather than demand-led. The huge growth in the non-university short-cycle sector reflects more the decisions of government than the nature of client demand' (Clancy, 1989: 129). Indeed, the goal of policy was to create demand by increasing supply. While assessments of the Irish education system and its standards are often overblown, this rapid expansion in educational participation was certainly an essential condition for growth.

Ireland's economy shifted significantly during these years away from a path of recession and growing unemployment and emigration in the 1980s. Nonetheless, the recovery of this period largely consisted of jobless growth as employment growth and the reversal of emigration did not kick in until the mid-1990s. For orthodox accounts, the crucial explanatory factors of the boom of the 1990s are to be found in the stabilisation of this earlier period when the fundamentals of the boom were put in place and barriers to growth were removed. However, this explanation over-estimates the achievements of this era as the employment boom (and much of the export dynamism) only followed later and under a complementary set of additional conditions. Furthermore, the argument under-estimates the heterodox elements in the recovery of the late 1980s, where cutbacks were counterbalanced by significant public investment (with heavy EU support) and where state agencies proved highly successful in attracting foreign investment and building exports.

Overall, the recovery of 1987–94 was a mixed affair. While Ireland had stabilised its macroeconomy in the late 1980s and weathered the recession of 1991 to see resumed growth between 1992 and 1994, progress in employment had been much more limited, with an upturn in unemployment once more towards the middle of the 1990s. While investments in education had been maintained relatively well in the face of cutbacks, this was in the overall context of continuing weak domestic demand and comparatively poor welfare state provision of social protection and services. While the recovery of the years between 1987 and 1994 was welcome, few could anticipate the boom that was to follow.

1994–2000: deepening development

While the Irish economy and in particular the public finances had stabilised by the mid-1990s, there were few signs of the dramatic improvements that were to follow. The international recession in 1991 combined with the departure of mid-range computing firms such as Digital chastened many observers of industrial development and innovation. The weakness of the Irish currency in the face of speculative attacks in 1993, ultimately undergoing a 10 per cent devaluation, reminded observers of the vulnerability of Ireland's macroeconomy. However, in the years that followed, Ireland's economic performance was spectacular, with booming economic and employment growth. Ireland was one of a number of small open European economies (such as Denmark and the Netherlands) to do particularly well in the latter half of the 1990s. Where the 1987–94 period had been characterised by an improvement in government finances and control of inflation and wage costs, the most dramatic changes in the later 1990s related to the real economy, with GNP growth running at over 10 per cent per annum and unemployment falling from 15 per cent in 1994 to 4 per cent in 2000. All this occurred in the context of an increasing population, with very significant return migration from about 1996 onwards. Throughout all of this, wage pressure and inflation remained relatively subdued.

While deficits continued, they were greatly reduced and steady growth allowed a more manageable servicing of the interest on the debt (Table 2.2). However, to pay down the debt significantly, more rapid growth was required, with progress made from 1994 to 1997 and the boom from 1997 to 2000 allowing the paying down of the debt to 38 per cent of GDP in 2000, with continuing steady reduction during the 2000s. As receipts of government increased across the late 1990s, a massive proportion of public spending went on restoring the government finances. In 1999, 40 per cent of government spending was on redeeming securities and making loan repayments, with another 4 per cent going on repaying the national debt interest. This was double the amount spent on transfers, twenty times the amount spent on capital grants to enterprise and over six times the amount spent on gross physical capital formation by government. While fiscal discipline had been crucial to restoring more balanced budgets in a structurally weak economy, growth – and the improvement of the capabilities of the economy – was crucial in tackling the debt issue. Ireland grew its way out of the debt crisis through the late 1990s; the question is how that was achieved.

At the core of this economic and employment performance was a boom in exports, driven largely by American foreign investments in the high-tech sectors. Ireland's wages and overall costs were highly competitive within Europe at the time, but an explanation focused entirely on wage competitiveness misses key elements, including the significant expansion in production capabilities within the economy during this period. Although foreign firms in Ireland engaged extensively in 'transfer pricing' and other forms of creative accounting, there was also a boom within the bubble. Employment in multinational companies in Ireland became more professionalised and expenditure on R&D per employee increased quite significantly in a number of sectors, including in the growing domestically owned software industry. State agencies played a crucial role in supporting and promoting this upgrading, especially in the Irish-owned sectors, through grant aid, soft supports, promoting associations and networking, and providing and incentivising the financing of businesses – working through a network of agencies to form a 'developmental network state' (Ó Riain, 2004). This stopped short of the transformation of the national system of innovation that Senghaas and Mjøset had argued was central to development. Nonetheless, it did represent a significant upgrading of industrial capabilities, public supports and export potential.

However, there were limits to the 'developmental network state' project in Ireland. While state agencies were effective in supporting more productive investment among domestic firms, the overall pattern of investment and the institutions that supported it remained relatively unchanged. This was a missed opportunity – as Honohan (2006) notes, the role of finance in promoting growth during the Celtic Tiger years was minimal. Productive investment in Ireland in these boom years was primarily driven by foreign private investors such as multinational corporations, foreign public investors such as the EU, and the Irish state. As will be seen later in the analysis, this investment and developmental project was accompanied by a 'growth machine' in property development. Indeed, the property sector was also starting to boom during this time, but was arguably still broadly in line with levels of demand until around 2000. In any case, in these years, it expanded alongside and not instead of the export sector. Therefore, the experience of the late 1990s saw Ireland make partial progress towards the development of a national system of innovation that could support a sustainable export base.

Also crucial during these years, particularly for employment growth, was the growth in domestic demand. This was the flipside of the wage competitiveness story as gradual increases in living standards generated a momentum in the domestic economy for increased spending on goods and, crucially, services, which in turn drove an expansion in employment that extended well beyond the export sectors. Public spending as a percentage of GDP decreased from 43.9 per cent in 1994 to 31.5 per cent in 2000 (see Table 2.2). This was in fact a much greater percentage decrease than in the period from 1987 to 1994. The 'welfare effort' of the Irish state declined significantly during these years of very rapid growth even as spending increased in real terms. Much of the decline in social spending was due to the significantly improved employment picture, which meant that spending on unemployment benefits and associated supports declined very rapidly. Those resources that were 'freed up' by this change were not diverted into other social investments, however, but were channelled into ongoing reductions in taxes, particularly after 1997. Overall public spending was nonetheless very low during this period, with one of the lowest rates of spending as a percentage of GDP in the OECD. This is all the more striking given that such a high proportion of public spending went to repay the government debt during the 1990s, such that even when spending increased in the 1990s, real spending on public services and social protection increased much more slowly and only really began to grow again after 2001.

The Irish welfare state therefore faced some of the same contradictions as its national system of innovation – making progress in some areas and significantly supporting private activity with public resources, but only weakly developing a sustainable set of national institutions that could underpin innovation and/or welfare. Where this was enabled in the case of the innovation system by major inflows of foreign investment, in the case of the social welfare system it was facilitated by a significant 'social bonus' in Irish society in the 1990s (Larragy *et al.*, 2006). Labour supply was highly elastic and the size of the labour force increased from 1.34 million to 2.01 million between 1987 and 2005. Between 1997 and 2005 alone, labour force participation rates for both sexes aged 15–64 increased from 54.7 per cent to 61.5 per cent. Ireland had access to new sources of labour supply as the economy grew. Key factors in boosting labour supply included a young population, a reservoir of untapped potential among married women, other reserves of highly educated and experienced people among emigrant Irish, and a mix of skill and labour supply among the unemployed.

Furthermore, Ireland was able to make up some of the welfare gaps in social investment (compared to the Continental European and especially the Scandinavian economies) by drawing on established social structural supports, which had yet to come under significant challenge from the socio-economic changes associated with the Celtic Tiger. The socio-demographic structure that fed the labour market was also a reservoir of informal care, welfare and protection for young children and older people. For much of the 1990s, for instance, labour market inflows of women with children were facilitated by informal arrangements for childcare, such as with grandparents, other relatives or neighbours. It is also well established that over many years, extensive voluntary community input was critical to the provision of various types of formal care and welfare services, such as meals, home help, daycare centres and transport.

While this will be discussed in more detail in Chapter 5, it is also worth noting at this point that social partnership itself changed during the latter half of the 1990s. Where the macroeconomic stabilisation of 1987–94 had been negotiated primarily through close network ties among union employer and state elites, in the late 1990s social partnership agreements began to develop a richer institutional structure around themselves. These included a variety of agencies and

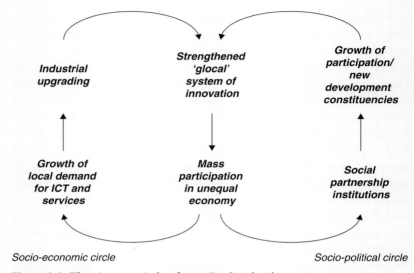

Figure 2.8 The virtuous circle of post-Fordist development

institutions focused on tackling local poverty and promoting community development, as well as a series of policy committees and the
expansion of the central institutions of social partnership to include
the community and voluntary sector and to establish the National
Economic and Social Forum in 1993.

Figure 2.8 shows how all these features operated together with a
strengthened system of innovation underpinning an export boom,
driven by foreign investment, and increasingly boosting domestic
demand. Industrial upgrading and significant supports for the growing middle classes supported the development of the new 'modern
economy' that Honohan and Walsh (2002) argue was the distinctive
feature of the development of the Irish economy between 1970 and
2000. While the 'convergence' associated with the emergence of
this modern sector is real, it is also associated with public subsidies
and development of the innovation and welfare systems. However, as
has been noted, these developments were beset with challenges
and contradictions. At the end of the Celtic Tiger boom of the late
1990s, Irish society had resources available to it that were hitherto
unimaginable, including economic, institutional and cultural resources.
Yet, it also faced major challenges and contradictions in its model

of development. A significant debate seemed certain to ensue, possibly shaping the future direction of Irish development.

2001–3: challenges at home and abroad

As it turned out, this discussion barely occurred. At the end of the 1990s, the massive burden of repaying a huge national debt left since the 1980s was about to be lifted. The Irish economy had been stabilised and significant developmental gains had been made. Opportunities presented themselves for reconstituting the Irish political economy to put the relationship between economic upgrading, social reproduction and public finance on a new footing.

But by the end of the 1990s, a number of years of rapid growth had also created significant pressures. The boom of the 1990s lost its momentum between 2001 and 2003 as growth rates declined, inflation increased and unemployment stabilised at around 4 per cent. The industrial and export growth of the late 1990s also came to a dramatic halt between 2001 and 2003 when the dot-com bubble burst in the US. This severely affected the high-tech sector, where computing manufac-turing employment never recovered from the losses of this period, while growth in software did not resume until 2003. Nonetheless, in the macroeconomy there were significant signs of overheating, with increases in inflation for the first time in ten years or more and signifi-cant wage pressure building in the economy. Industrial upgrading and innovation became all the more important in the face of this cost pressure. However, the trade-offs within the wage agreements created a squeeze on public investment and services, which were straining under the twin pressures of accumulated under-investment and increased population and economic activity. These pressures were obvious in the increasing difficulty in negotiating a social partnership agreement in 2001 and in the pressure from within the public sector for a 'benchmarking' exercise to enable public sector workers to 'catch up' with wage increases in the private sector.

Nor could the Irish economy rely as heavily upon the 'social bonus' as it had in the 1990s. The concentration of female labour force participation in younger cohorts remained very marked, so that there continued to be a supply of informal care in the community from the higher age cohorts. Over time, this 'free' resource was drawn into the formal economy. As this process accelerated in the late 1990s, new

challenges for policy makers emerged. In the 1980s too many community services depended on the employment of community leaders
through programmes such as Community Employment. These community leaders too would be drawn into market employment as the
economy grew – with implications for the opportunity cost of informal
care and possibly for the fabric of social and community support
(Larragy *et al.*, 2006).

Other countries have gone through a similar labour market transition – usually in the context of the post-war expansion – in which a
range of support services was built up in conjunction with the growth
of the welfare state. In the Irish context, however, the inflow came
about quite rapidly in a period when welfare state mixes were being
adjusted towards more market provision in such areas as childcare and
the care of older people. In the past the economic expansion could to a
limited extent draw on existing infrastructure where labour supply
was indigenous. However, changing household patterns towards
more numerous and smaller households, together with the swing
from emigration to immigration in the 1990s, multiplied the infrastructure implications – most obviously for housing, local transport and
environmental services (Larragy *et al.*, 2006).

The growing population, the increased economic activity and the
shift of those outside employment from the unemployed to single
parents and those with disabilities posed significant challenges. Serious
deficiencies in infrastructure in education, transport and health, among
other areas, were significant issues in the 2002 election. During this
period, the politics of Ireland's economy seemed caught between a
desire to continue with the growth model that had provided such
dramatic improvements in employment and migration, and creeping
concerns about its limitations in terms of weak social investment and
the problems of sustainability of infrastructure and social reproduction
in the medium term.

This sense of contradiction and uncertainty in the midst of growth
and expansion can be seen in the shifting governance arrangements
of the time. Social partnership agreements faced a shortening
of time horizons, while it began to be more difficult to reconcile
different sectoral demands. In addition, the government of the day
reasserted the power of party and governmental politics over
social partnership negotiations between interest groups. The Fianna
Fáil/Progressive Democrat coalition government elected in 1997

combined a long-standing 'growth machine' approach of the populist Fianna Fáil dynasty with the neoliberal economic policies of the 'modernising' Progressive Democrats. In 2003 it was quite unclear how these various tensions might be resolved, even if the Fianna Fáil/ Progressive Democrat coalition was re-elected in 2002.

2003–8: the bubble economy

As late as 2003, Ireland faced these contradictions and challenges with a relatively open field of policy choices, at least in terms of direct economic constraints on policy options. However, it was over the following four to five years that the crisis of 2008 was produced. While many of the factors that produced the crisis were in place before 2003, it was in these crucial five years that the key factors interacted to produce the dramatic financial, economic and fiscal crises of the late 2000s.

At the macroeconomic level, government spending increased significantly and in a pro-cyclical manner which further boosted economic growth, in the process contributing to further apparent 'overheating'. Wages also increased quite significantly during this period. Most importantly of all, entry into the euro in 2001 and financial deregulation across Europe made cheap money easily available in Ireland and the rest of Europe. Credit expanded greatly and, as will be explained in more detail in the following chapter, resources were increasingly allocated to speculation and to trying to keep up with rapidly increasing prices on the property ladder.

The major driver of the economy became domestic demand. The expansion of demand through improved living standards was a vital (and under-recognised) aspect of the 1990s boom. However, this expansion had been supported by booming exports, which flatlined through the 2000s in the wake of the dot-com bubble. Instead, construction and public spending became the anchors of expanding employment. Ireland's macroeconomy therefore came to resemble what Colin Crouch (2009) has called the hidden policy regime of 'privatised Keynesianism' (Figure 2.9).

In the area of innovation and industrial development, the flat export figures masked a significant recomposition and restructuring of industry in Ireland. In particular, computer manufacturing and associated sub-supply and assembly industries declined rapidly,

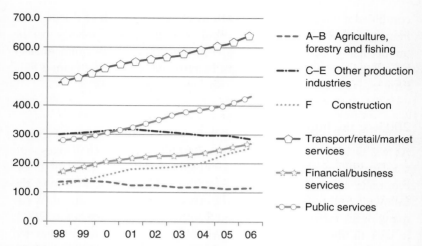

Figure 2.9 Sectoral employment, 1998–2006
Source: CSO, *Quarterly National Household Survey*

shifting eastwards towards the post-socialist economies that were now joining the EU (Barry and Van Egeraat, 2008). Medical devices and pharmaceuticals replaced these on the manufacturing side, albeit with less employment, while software and financial services became increasingly important as drivers of export growth as the decade went on. Indeed, once it recovered from the bursting of the dot-com bubble, the software sector added as many jobs per annum in the mid-2000s as it had in the celebrated boom years of the late 1990s.

Most significantly, all of these sectors were overwhelmed by the massive growth of the property bubble, driven by the construction and financial sectors. This bubble not only dominated the resources used in the economy but also had a number of knock-on effects on unrelated sectors – influencing, for example, student choices about third-level degree subjects, the availability of finance and credit for different activities, and even decision making about priorities and investments within particular sectors. Tourism, for example, was profoundly affected by the financial bubble, with investment increasingly centred on property-related tax incentives and re-sale opportunities rather than on product development within the industry itself (O'Brien, 2011).

In the welfare regime, the period saw a modest percentage increase in 'welfare effort', with social spending increasing from 15.8 per cent of GDP in 2003 to 16.7 per cent in 2007. However, given growing GDP, real public spending increased significantly over the period. Nonetheless, the period was associated primarily with increases in private incomes and the significant expansion of private services. Even as numbers in the public service and public spending increased, historical gaps in social service provision and in social infrastructure remained. As unemployment had fallen to 4 per cent in the early part of the decade, immigration provided a major source of labour supply, particularly after 2004, when Ireland was open to immigrants from the accession states of the EU.

The conflicts of the early part of the decade regarding public and private sector pay and the coordination of social partnership agreements were significantly muted by this new wave of economic growth. Indeed, this happened to such an extent that by 2006, the social partners were able to agree a deal with a ten-year time horizon, *Towards 2016*. However, this settling of tensions and conflict came at a price. Social partnership was once more strongly focused on the cash benefits of the wage and tax agreements, and the agenda of the late 1990s to expand and deepen partnership was weakened, even as

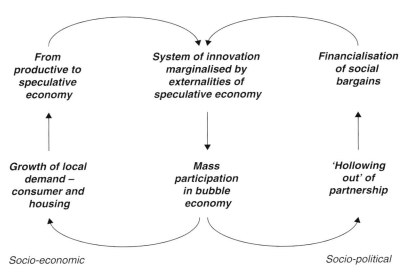

Figure 2.10 Dynamics of the Irish economy, 2003–8

more and more policies were loaded into the text of the agreements themselves. Arguably more importantly, party politics was increasingly in the ascendance and was particularly closely tied to electoral cycles (see Cousins, 2007).

The dynamics of the Irish economy in the 2000s were significantly different from those in the 1990s, even as key aspects of the 1990s model remained (Figure 2.10). There were a variety of controversial changes in the support system for industry in the 2000s. These complexities of the system of innovation were simply overwhelmed, however, by the degree to which innovation and productive investment and activities were marginalised by the growth of a speculative economy based around a property bubble. The loosening of credit within the Eurozone and within the Irish financial system became the central dynamic of the economic system during these years. This bubble economy drew in more and more of the population through cheap credit, property investments and the knock-on effects of the property bubble. Attempts at managing domestic demand or at combining expanding living standards with wage restraint and managed competitiveness were simply overwhelmed by the dynamics of the bubble economy. On the socio-economic side, booming local consumer and housing demand, driven by a reckless financial sector, drove the economy from productive investment to speculative financing.

This bubble even reached into the socio-political domain as social partnership agreements were 'hollowed out', focusing increasingly on the cash nexus. Even as the public sector expanded, and despite initiatives from within social partnership institutions themselves (NESC, 2005), movement in the direction of more universalistic social welfare systems was stalled. As will be seen in Chapter 5, these social bargains and the political arrangements that governed the society were themselves financialised in the 2000s. While the virtuous circle of the 1990s and the institutions that sustained it were largely still in place, they were either marginalised or incorporated by the booming bubble economy.

Conclusion

In this chapter the overall development of Ireland's political economy across the past three decades has been reviewed. Table 2.3 summarises the four key periods along each of the dimensions which

Table 2.3 *Changing socio-political projects in the Irish political economy*

	1960s–80s	1987–94	1994–2000	2001–3	2003–8
Regime	*FDI and indigenous patronage*	*Macroeconomic stabilisation*	*Upgrading development and boosting demand*	*Tension and contradiction*	*Boosting the bubble*
Macroeconomic order	Populism	Stabilisation through coordinated social pacts	Managing growth and inflation	Instability	Growth machine Lower taxes, domestic consumption
Production regime	Attracting FDI with tax	Attracting FDI with tax and labour	Developmental statism and deepening of innovation system	Dot-com bubble bursts	Narrowing development strategy and institutions
Welfare regime	Two-tier welfare state	Cutbacks and stabilisation	Increased spending but declining welfare effort Social bonus	Distributional conflict	Reassertion of central state control Erosion of social bonus

have been discussed – the macroeconomic order, the production regime and the welfare regime.

The table begins with the period of 'modernisation' in the 1960s and 1970s, book-ended by major national crises. Here the focus was on attracting foreign investment, with the domestic economy character-ised by structural weakness and under-development. The macroecon-omy was governed largely on pluralist terms, mixed with Fianna Fáil's broadly populist approach. The production regime was dominated by the pursuit of FDI, largely based on tax incentives, while the welfare state saw expansion through the 1960s and 1970s, albeit remaining at much lower levels of welfare spending than was the case in all Contin-ental European societies.

From 1987 to 1994 the main focus was on macroeconomic stabilisa-tion. This was organised largely through national social partnership institutions, which became crucial to the management of political tensions and the ability to partly transcend the demands of electoral cycle politics. FDI remained crucial to the production regime, but became somewhat more sophisticated, with an increasing focus on investment in more skilled labour. While the period began with signifi-cant cutbacks in welfare spending and public services, the welfare regime was stabilised by the mid-1990s. In most orthodox accounts this is the key period that provided the conditions for the private sector to lead the boom that followed.

However, when we look more closely at the period of the late 1990s, we find a key role for the state and more broadly for an upgrading of the development process, and an extension of the gains in the export sector into the domestic economy. At the macroeconomic level, there were significant efforts to extend social partnership into the commu-nity and voluntary sector and new areas of policy making, as well as to manage the wage and inflation effects of growth. The period saw the beginnings of indigenous industrial development and a significant sector of Irish-owned technology firms, promoted by Ireland's agencies of the 'developmental network state' (Ó Riain, 2004). This network statism extended into the welfare regime through a network of local area partnerships and increased participation of the community and voluntary sector in service delivery (albeit often at the cost of forgoing protest or more democratic forms of community development).

The period between 2001 and 2003 was one of great uncertainty, with growing inflation and wage pressures combined with the bursting of the dot-com bubble to create significant tensions within the Irish political economy. This was a period in which Ireland appeared to face significant choices about the model of economic development which it was to pursue. Mary Harney, then Minister for Enterprise, most famously posed the apparent choice in 2000 when she argued that Ireland needed to choose whether it was closer to Boston or Berlin – and that it should unambiguously position itself closest to the liberal model of the US. However, these choices and challenges were largely ignored in the midst of the credit bubble that fuelled renewed economic growth in the 2000s. Economic growth resumed from 2003 onwards, with significant growth in employment that was now driven not by exports and sustainable domestic demand, but by a growth machine driven by a credit and property bubble. The production regime in exports was now dominated by a speculative economy in the property sector. While public spending increased significantly and public employment expanded, the structural basis of the public finances and of public services was in fact weakening as the tax structure itself came to depend upon the bubble economy. We can now see that the question of where Ireland's crisis came from is best seen as a question of how the economy of the 1990s, which needed significant additional developmental supports, was instead sidelined by the growth machine bubble of the 2000s. The rest of this book examines these and the other dynamics that led to the multiple crises of 2008.

3 | Capital: the triumph of finance *

Ireland's political economy shifted from the 1990s to the 2000s. But who did the shifting and how? The following chapters explore the role of the dynamics of the EU and of national politics. However, our story starts with the key actor in the global political economy in the past two decades of liberalisation and financialisation – capital.

On one reading, Ireland's financial crisis was a very local crisis. The subprime mortgages and securitised mortgage products that were central to the triggering of the US crisis were much less important in the Irish case, where lending to developers and inflated property prices were much more significant (Connor *et al.*, 2012). While mortgage lending practices loosened in the 2000s, the crisis was not caused by mortgage defaults (although these became significant elements of the evolving crisis).

However, other features of the Irish crisis were shared more broadly. As Connor *et al.* (2012) point out, Ireland shared with the US features such as 'irrational exuberance' among market actors, a 'capital bonanza' (easy access to cheap capital for banks – in the Irish case through international borrowing) and failures of regulation and 'moral hazard'. In addition, the various crises of the current period are linked through increasingly close financial integration, with the US crisis in 2008 acting as the tipping point for the Irish banks' collapse as inter-bank liquidity dried up very rapidly. This financial integration itself was closely linked to a broader project of economic liberalisation in recent decades.

Ireland proved to be a world leader in the financialisation of the economy: 'the increasing role of financial motives, markets, actors and institutions in the operation of the domestic and international

* Parts of this and the following chapter were previously published in my article (2012) 'The Crisis of Financialisation in Ireland', *Economic and Social Review*, 43(4): 497–533 and are reproduced with kind permission of the *Economic and Social Review*.

economies' (Epstein, 2005: 3; Kus, 2012). While there are many potential indicators of this process, Krippner (2011) takes the share of profits within the economy going to financial activities as her central measure of financialisation, arguing that this measure reflects both the sectoral growth of finance and the accumulation of power within the economy. Figure 3.1 outlines trends in the profits of the 'financial intermediation' sector (banks and other financial institutions, but not including insurance, real estate and other business services) for the years for which OECD statistics are available.

The statistics reveal some interesting variations in Irish banking profits. Despite their lack of contribution to economic development (Honohan, 2006), Irish banks were comparatively profitable in the mid-1990s. Their share of total Irish corporate profits grew somewhat alongside the export boom of the late 1990s, but surged dramatically from 2003 to 2007. Ireland's financial expansion was, however, only one leg of a 'triple financialisation', also including Anglo-American financial systems and the financialisation associated with European integration and the euro in the 2000s. While the US was always more financialised than the European core, this gap widened

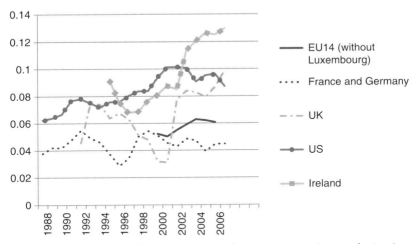

Figure 3.1 Proportion of all corporate profits (gross operating surplus) going to the 'financial intermediation' (banking) sector, 1988–2007
Source: OECD STAN Database
Note: EU14 and the France and Germany measures are an average of national rates, not a total of all profits across those countries.

significantly during the 1990s, and financialisation is most closely associated with 'liberal market economies' (Hall and Soskice, 2001) such as the US, the UK and Ireland. However, the EU economies closed the gap somewhat from 2001 onwards – with France and Germany showing a small surge in the 2002–4 period. The next chapter examines the transnational dimension of Irish financialisation and shows that the German banking system was highly segmented, with internationalisation and trading of financial instruments strongly concentrated among the commercial banking sector. Since the proportion of Irish banks' liabilities derived from foreign sources grew dramatically in the 2000s (Lane, 2011), these were very significant trends.

Therefore, the Irish financial crisis has both distinctive and more widely shared elements. It is both a national and a transnational phenomenon. The division of responsibility for the crisis between national and international factors is a matter of not only academic interest but also profound disagreement and controversy in terms of shaping policy responses, particularly in Europe. In this chapter, I focus on the local dynamics of the crisis. At the heart of Ireland's financial crisis were close ties between domestic banks and a small group of property developers in both residential and commercial property. Together, they misallocated capital in Ireland on a grand scale. This 'misallocation' can be thought of as the increasing dominance of a particular 'social structure of liquidity' (Carruthers and Stinchcombe, 1999) – where a lending and investment coalition focused on domestic property was able to secure the lion's share of available capital, to the cost of competing sectors (most notably the medium- and high-tech sectors).

Understanding financialisation

Connor *et al.* (2012) draw attention to the tension between the universal and specific features of financial crises. They contrast Reinhart and Rogoff's (2009) analysis of the universal features of financial crises with their own focus on the specific features of the Irish credit bubble, linked in particular to issues of governance and national business culture. These factors, they argue, are intrinsically context-specific, whereas the market dynamics that are the focus of Reinhart and

Rogoff's analysis are more generalisable. Market dynamics operate at a universal level of analysis, but are mediated by national organisational and political cultures.

There is a similar split in sociological analyses of finance in the macroeconomy and of social action by financial actors and in financial markets. The first strand tends to emphasise relatively consistent and widespread patterns of the expansion (and contraction) of finance in the economy. For some, historical surges in the importance of finance arise from the search of a declining economic and political hegemonic power for new sources of wealth and dominance (Arrighi and Silver, 2000). In the current era, the financialisation of the US economy since the economic crises of the 1970s and stagnant real incomes in the following decades is the classic case of such a process (Krippner, 2011). For others, financialisation is linked to the emergence of new technologies and, more broadly, new techno-economic paradigms, as capital rushes to gain the exceptional returns from the commercialisation of new technologies – most recently in the dot-com bubble and bust of the late 1990s and early 2000s (Perez, 2002). Most generally, Polanyi (1944) linked the rise of finance in the economy to a broader process of the rise of market society, where markets came to dominate the social structures within which they were embedded.

While the macrosociological literature on financialisation emphasises the ebb and flow of finance over time, the second strand in social studies of finance explores the microconditions or 'social structures of finance' (McKenzie, 2006). While patterns of capital allocation are produced by many individual investment decisions, these decisions themselves prove to be rooted in broader investment communities, with shared notions of value, risk and rationality in the market. Increasing attention is being paid to the dynamics of financial markets, including research on behavioural finance in economics and in sociology on how participants in financial markets contest and dispute the fairness and dependability of prices and the standardisation of financial instruments (McKenzie, 2006, 2012). These studies have yielded insight into the cognitive and interactional foundations of financial markets, but have relatively little to say about how such markets vary from context to context, or how they connect to broader processes of financialisation.

How are these universal and specific features of crises linked? To understand this, it is necessary to break down the separation between universal market processes and context-specific social and political processes. Action in financial markets is shaped by the social and political contexts within which these markets are embedded. Where broader patterns of the expansion of finance in the economy are observed, this must be linked in turn to the expansion of contexts that enhance the role of finance in economic life. Particular social contexts create the conditions that make 'financial action' more likely. The specific form this takes may vary even as the conditions for the increased importance of finance spread. As these various forms of action emerge and are institutionalised, together they form the macro-trends that come to be seen as 'financialisation'.

Carruthers and Stinchcombe (1999) develop the useful concept of a 'social structure of liquidity' as a way of understanding how such processes of action and interaction are linked to the social structures within which they are embedded. This is a bold attempt on their part as they seek to show the 'embeddedness' of the most marketised forms of economic organisation – highly liquid settings where assets can be disposed of without significantly transforming the structure of markets and pricing. Social structures of liquidity consist of a set of actors including buyers, sellers and intermediaries, and, crucially, a set of instruments that actors agree are easily tradable.

Carruthers and Stinchcombe take as one of their cases the very securitisation of mortgages that later proved so central to the US financial crisis. Theoretically, they emphasise the importance of liquidity as a problem in the sociology of knowledge, where it is critical to explain how market actors come to have a shared belief in the reliability and value of tradable assets – whether these are mortgage-backed securities, futures and options, shares in high-tech companies, commercial property development loans or other assets. Stinchcombe argues that 'social transformation ... has some of its most profound effects by changing the nature of the future that people are working on' (1997: 389) and trust in these various assets enables specific forms of this 'future work'.

The concept of 'social structures of liquidity' deserves a fuller treatment, but it directs our attention to a number of key points (Ó Riain and Rhatigan, 2013). First, any liquid asset depends upon a shared set of definitions of value and tradability, definitions which are themselves somewhat illiquid in that they are rooted in specific institutions, sets of buyers and sellers and national, occupational and other cultures (McKenzie, 2012). Financialisation transforms national economies and business cultures, but also works through and is mediated by them. There may be multiple 'social structures of liquidity', with different definitions of rational investment and tradable assets, shaping the patterns of capital allocation. Second, as 'liquid' finance seeks out investment opportunities, it links together these multiple 'social structures of liquidity' – which may in turn compete, interact, reinforce or undermine one other. Third, this linking process involves important elements of 'translation' of the varying definitions of what are sensible investment opportunities, with the growth of institutions and organisations whose function is largely to provide this translation, including in particular the growth of 'markets for governance' (Davis, 2011) and certification, regulation and arbitration by private agencies (Sassen, 2006). Institutional contexts prove to be vital elements in generating these social structures of liquidity. The rest of this chapter explores how such processes shaped financialisation in the Irish context.

Investment and development: the social structure of financing business in Ireland

Irish banks have historically played a relatively insignificant role in financing development in Ireland. Honohan (2006) documents the very limited role that the financial system played in the economic boom of the 1990s. Private venture capital, while active during the boom years, was often led by state programmes rather than driving economic recovery through early state investments in difficult times (Ó Riain, 2004).

Transnational corporations have been the primary source of private sector investment in Ireland. In addition to expanding production and employment, many of them used Ireland as a centre for transfer pricing and related financial activities. In many respects, this expansion in 'entrepôt' activity in Ireland (Honohan *et al.*, 1998) was the equivalent of the financialisation of non-financial corporations documented in the US by Krippner (2011: Chapter 2). Nonetheless, this was a negotiation with industrial capital whose dominance of investment in Ireland favoured production, at least from the perspective of the domestic economy.

The role of foreign corporations is only partly driven by market mechanisms. Although the state has used tax incentives to promote industrial development, the focus of public policy has been on direct engagement with firms. The policy emphasis on FDI involved significant organisational interaction with major international firms. As noted previously, it is perhaps best to think of the competition to attract mobile capital not as product market competition, but as competitive bargaining between governmental providers of how public goods are provided to private capital. Ireland's success in providing these public goods to transnational corporations is well known.

Furthermore, White (2010) has documented the private sector failure to turn liquidity into investment at the national level. He finds that from 2000 to 2008, investment in housing stock increased by 156 per cent. Productive capital investment increased by 66 per cent, or €70 billion. However, of this €70 billion, road building made up €13.5 billion, another €20 billion was invested in retail infrastructure (building shops, etc.), public buildings took up €9 billion and investment by semi-state companies and energy/utilities companies took up a further €10 billion. Ultimately, in an era when bank lending increased by three to four times, inflation-adjusted productive capital stock expenditure by private enterprise increased by 26 per cent between 2000 and 2008. Productive investment in Ireland has largely been driven by foreign private capital and domestic and EU-funded public funding and supports.

Public funding has also been crucial to R&D. Universities were strengthened in the late 1990s as funding and hiring picked up again after many years of neglect. The Programme for Research in Third-Level Institutions began in 1998 and put some €604 million into third-level research infrastructure from 2000 to 2006, largely through the funding of a series of research institutes within universities and institutes of technology around the country. Research Councils were set up for both the sciences (2001) and the humanities and social sciences (2000), providing funding for research sabbaticals and research projects. At the same time, Irish-American philanthropist Chuck Feeney donated 'several hundred million dollars' to the universities, which acted as quasi-public funding for university development. This was linked to the significant new investments in research noted above and in particular to the formation of Science Foundation Ireland, with massive funding for research in ICT and biotech, and a focus on the attraction of international scientists into the university system. The Irish science budget was one of the fastest-growing in the OECD from 2002 to 2006, but still lagged behind the EU-25, let alone the EU-15, in 2007. Ireland narrowed the gap with other countries in terms of science and R&D in a process that was largely driven by the public sector.

The 1990s also saw the development of new strategies for industrial upgrading and particularly the support of indigenous enterprise. Grant aid was comparatively small but was an access point for a network of supports that included R&D grants, management development, employment grants, mentoring networks and more. State agencies sponsored the activities of industry associations and technology centres. As such, the state played a critical role in constituting the social world of production within the industry (see Ó Riain, 2004 for a fuller account).

In addition, the 1990s saw the expansion of the capacity of state agencies in supporting and developing indigenous firms (Ó Riain, 2004; Girma *et al.*, 2008). The most successful firms benefited as much from public subsidies and supports as from private investor interest. Research into software firms in Ireland shows that a 'developmental network state' boosted economic performance as those firms that received the most state grant aid exported more, employed more people and grew faster (Ó Riain, 2004). These positive effects of state aid have also been found in manufacturing companies in the 1980s (O'Malley *et al.*, 1992) and the 1990s (Girma *et al.*, 2008).

However, our focus here is on the role of the state in directly mobilising investment. Under the Seed and Venture Capital measure of the EU Operational Programme 1994–9, Enterprise Ireland (the state agency charged with promoting Irish-owned industry) committed €44 million to venture capital – just over a third of a total venture capital investment during the period of €129 million. A total of 72 per cent of that investment was in Dublin and 70 per cent was in software (Enterprise Ireland, 2007). The importance of the state in providing financing and in stimulating private investment is indicated in Table 3.1, which provides data on private equity investments between 1997 and 1999, the period when private, increasingly international, investment took off in Ireland. These investments are concentrated in computer-related sectors, electronics, 'other manufacturing' and (in 1999) communications. The Irish share of European private equity investment increased from 0.3 per cent in 1995 to 0.8 per cent in 1998 and 1.2 per cent in 1999.

Table 3.1 *Trends in private equity investment 1997–9 (thousands of Irish pounds)*

	1997	1998	1999
Total funds	27,713	163,626	316,232
Total state funds	10,048	20,775	12,151
Selected major types of investor			
Government	36.3%	12.7%	3.8%
Private individuals	13.7%	26.2%	21.7%
Banks	17.1%	3.7%	25.0%
Pension funds	7.3%	8.2%	26.8%
Geographical breakdown of private equity raised			
% Domestic	100%	44.7%	42.8%
% Other European	0%	35.7%	19.6%
% Other non-European	0%	25.2%	32.0%

Source: European Venture Capital Association, Annual Reports

In 1997 all investment was from domestic sources and one-third of that was from the state. A significant portion of the remaining investment was stimulated by the state through 'matching funds' arrangements – perhaps up to an additional 25 per cent. In 1998 domestic investment increased, but, more importantly, international investors flooded into the increasingly successful Irish economy. The primary source of funds was private individuals as institutions such as pension funds, banks and insurance funds lagged behind. In 1999, however, institutional investors finally took the lead in funding. Non-European sources accounted for fully one-third of funds in 1999, up from a quarter in 1998. By 1999, Ireland was well integrated into international institutional investment circles and the state withdrew from its previously dominant role as a source of funds. However, individual and institutional investors largely followed rather than led the growth of the high-tech industries in which most of this funding was concentrated. Ironically, the risk taker here was the state. After the dot-com bubble burst in 2001, the state was crucial to the continuation and recovery of the venture capital sector.

Table 3.2 shows that the bursting of the dot-com bubble was followed in 2001–2 with a drying up of almost all except the publicly provided funds and the continuing prominence of public funds in the

Table 3.2 *Venture capital investment in Ireland, 2000–5*

	Total venture capital	Enterprise Ireland venture capital	Enterprise Ireland funds as % of total venture capital
	€m	€m	
2000	111.6	13.2	11.8%
2001	37.6	41.9	111.4%*
2002	27.4	20.8	75.9%
2003	32.9	14.5	44.1%
2004	27.8	16.2	58.3%
2005	36.1	8.1	22.4%
Total	273.4	114.7	42.0%

Source for total venture capital: Félix, 2007
Source for Enterprise Ireland venture capital: Enterprise Ireland Annual Reports
* Note: the 2001 statistics suggest that Enterprise Ireland provided over 100 per cent of all venture capital invested that year. It is likely that there will be discrepancies among these different data sources, particularly arising from any lags in the disbursement of Enterprise Ireland monies to venture capital funds, and from those funds to client companies. Nonetheless, the general trends and orders of magnitude hold.

recovery of venture capital investment as the decade went on. Given that much of the state investment continued to be provided through mechanisms that encouraged matched private investment, the majority of venture capital funding was publicly provided or stimulated, even if privately administered through a series of funds. However, the capacity for public action was weakened from the late 1990s. ICC, a profitable state-owned industrial investment bank, was sold and ultimately largely withdrew from business lending (NESC, 2012).

State agencies were also important repositories of business lending expertise, which built up over the previous two decades of extensive engagement with small domestic firms. The weak historical role of banking in Irish development and the focus on property lending went so deep that the organisational capacities of banks to lend in support of other sectors and, more generally, business development was weak. As one fund manager told me: 'The skills of cash flow lending have been lost in Ireland, because people have been doing asset-backed lending for so long.' Indeed, this was significant enough that in late 2008 and 2009, the state industrial development agency Enterprise Ireland sent some of its business development officials to the major banks to advise them on commercial lending and business development – transferring business lending and development expertise from the public to the private sector (NESC, 2012). Banks were marginal to enterprise development, but nonetheless proved crucial in the bubble years that led to the crisis.

The social structure of property investment

As we have seen, the dynamic of economic growth in Ireland shifted firmly from an export-led expansion of employment and domestic demand in the 1990s to an economy fuelled by domestic consumption and, particularly, construction in the 2000s. During the 2000s, the growth strategy increasingly took the form of a 'growth machine' where land-based elites 'profit through the increasing intensification of the land use of the area in which its members hold a common interest ... Governmental authority, at the local and nonlocal levels, is utilized to assist in achieving this growth at the expense of competing localities' (Molotch, 1976). The long-established connections between property developers and political elites were significant in reinforcing this model of growth. However, where past incarnations of the growth machine had relied heavily on state funding (through social housing expansion in the 1930s and through state office expansion in the 1970s), the property growth machine of the 2000s was linked to a booming private market in residential and commercial property.

Construction has long been a crucial plank not only in the Irish economy but also in the electoral calculations of both of the leading political parties (McCabe, 2011). It offered the opportunity to appeal to business through the promotion of a housing-based growth machine, to appeal to the middle classes through offering home-ownership and to the working classes through a mix of employment, social housing and the transition to private home-ownership. Fianna Fáil in particular developed close ties with developers during its long tenure in government. In the 1970s and 1980s, these ties were fully institutionalised as key developers benefited enormously from state contracts for both development of properties and re-leasing of the developed properties as state offices.

As the state was the dominant customer for commercial property and the residential markets were dormant, the politicisation of property markets was intense. A series of corruption scandals around rezoning decisions eventually emerged, involving large numbers of Fianna Fáil representatives, but the ties extended to more general policy measures such as the property development incentives that were extended from the 1980s and the retraction of efforts to calm the housing markets in the early 2000s. Records of political donations show close ties between property developers and Fianna Fáil during these years (Byrne, 2012). More generally, this link between property and Fianna Fáil was wrapped up in a broader sense of the worth of a rising class of entrepreneurs and a sense of nationalist hubris in the rise of these large-scale developers, extending in some cases into new projects in the UK and the US.

This bubble was rooted in a changing national and investment politics. The Fianna Fáil–Progressive Democrat coalition government elected in 1997 combined a long-standing 'growth machine' approach of the populist Fianna Fáil dynasty with the liberalising economic policies of the 'modernising' Progressive Democrats. It also shifted the dynamics of investment politics.

The financial sector was a target of industrial development, identified as a priority sector, with the main instrument for delivering this growth being the International Financial Services Centre (IFSC) in Dublin. As one supporter wrote in the *Irish Times* in 2006: 'In the early days the value proposition for the IFSC was simple: low corporation tax, a light touch regulatory regime – as little red tape as possible – and an English speaking workforce located in the EU. It was a value proposition that appealed to the international financial services community as attested to by the rapid growth of the IFSC' (*Irish Times*, 20 January 2006). Others viewed the light regulation less benignly, describing the international reputation of the IFSC as part of the 'wild west' of financial (de)regulation (O'Brien, 2006). With a weak regulator, little ability to steer long-term investment using taxes and the removal or marginalisation of public agencies shaping capital allocation, the field of domestic investment was ripe for banking dominance. With little historical role in productive investment and business development, a booming economy and the long-standing property-based 'growth machine', the banking sector was never likely to resist investing in a property boom.

As was noted at the start of the chapter, there is strong evidence that the state was more effective than the private sector in allocating capital (White, 2010). This does not mean that the role of the state was the same at all times and in all sectors, or that it was always channelled at the productive rather than the speculative sectors. Indeed, state agencies played quite distinctive roles in each sector. Although there were overlaps, it is striking that the state was most directly involved in funding the high-tech sector and relied much more heavily on tax incentives in the property sector. The regulatory issues will be addressed later, but first I explore some of the details of particular modes of state shaping of investment – the specific ways in which state agencies became part of the various social structures of liquidity.

The state has played a significant direct role as producer, consumer and investor in shaping private sector actions. In the property sector, this direct role diminished from the 1970s and 1980s, when the state was a major developer in its own right. By 1983, the Industrial Development Authority (IDA) had been associated with the development of nearly one-third of the factory units developed in Dublin since 1960 and was the largest owner of industrial space in the city. Furthermore, the second- and third-largest owners of Dublin industrial space were a bank and an assurance company which were both owned by the state (MacLaran, 1993: 159). Similarly, the state was associated with a significant amount of activity in the development of office space – sponsoring developers to build the office space and then renting it back from them, a relationship that was largely organised through close ties between developers and political parties (especially Fianna Fáil). In the period discussed above, these relationships were mediated through private sector development activity and the state featured much less prominently as a market for property. Similarly, state involvement in social housing was increasingly oriented towards facilitating private ownership and encouraging developers (with minimal success) to build social housing as complements to their market developments (NESC, 2004).

However, from the 1990s onwards, the Irish state influenced the property market less directly through the use of tax incentives (or 'tax expenditures') (Collins and Walsh, 2010). In property, these were extensive and are well documented. The waves of particular property incentives also appear to correspond to the major bubbles within the housing and commercial property sectors. A series of urban-focused tax incentives were introduced in the 1990s, particularly around inner-city residential development – corresponding perhaps to the early detachment of supply from demand in urban areas. MacLaran and Murphy warned as early as 1997 that, while these schemes did help to boost the inner-city population, they had also been used by developers in a way that created new communities distinct from the existing population. In a highly prescient warning, they cautioned that: 'Notwithstanding the problems associated with the social and physical homogeneity of the developments, the very character of the incentives possesses negative implications for property values in the longer term and these will have important implications for the behaviour of financial institutions and of individual occupiers in the future' (1997: 36).

Norris and Gkartzios distinguish between the period from 1986 to 1998 and a later period from 1998 to 2006, arguing that:

in the years immediately following their introduction, the incentives were successful in drawing residential development and higher income residents into target areas and addressing dereliction. However, the decision to extend their lifespan and their geographical focus during Ireland's economic boom of the late 1990s was problematic for several reasons. Although take-up of these incentives has remained high, over time they have become less effective in achieving their stated aims. In addition, in the context of a strong economic and construction boom, it is likely that a substantial proportion of the developments the scheme subsidized would have gone ahead in its absence; these developments have resulted in over-supply of housing leading to high vacancy rates and have displaced investment away from manufacturing into an already overheated construction sector. (Norris and Gkartzios, 2011: 263)

Similarly, Section 23 tax incentives encouraged over-development by allowing developers to hedge development costs against taxes on other activities. O'Brien (2011) documents how one consequence of this was an over-supply of hotels and hotel rooms, leading to a crisis in the hotel industry when the crisis hit tourist and business demand – and also orienting the development of the tourist sector away from the development of new products and upgrading and towards speculative activity.

Clearly, state tax incentives have had a major effect on the property sector. The precise extent to which these incentives altered developer logics is unclear. In many cases, developers welcomed the incentives and might indeed have acted in similar ways in the absence of the incentives, as Norris and Gkartzios (2011) argue. However, there also appear to be clear structuring additional effects of incentives on over-supply and the spread of that over-supply.

It is important to note that the impact of the schemes was not entirely negative – they may well have contributed to stemming loss of population and other desirable outcomes (Gkartzios and Norris, 2011; Norris and Gkartzios, 2011). However, the focus of this analysis is on their contribution to over-supply, which itself was closely tied to their largely undifferentiated design – where the constraints on developer behaviour were primarily in terms of location of development rather than any other considerations of housing or other policies.

Capital decides: favouring speculative construction over productive investment

In the new government's budget of 1998, capital gains tax was reduced from 40 per cent to 20 per cent with a view to releasing pent-up capital into the economy. This goal was rapidly achieved – in the decade after the reduction of capital gains tax to 20 per cent, bank lending in the economy grew by 466 per cent. However, that capital flowed primarily and rapidly into property investment.

The number of state agencies involved in regulation grew rapidly during this period (MacCárthaigh, 2012). However, for all their activity, these regulatory agencies varied greatly in their power and effectiveness. While some agencies dominated their constituencies, others were less immune to 'capture'. The financial regulator was designed as a relatively weak institution in terms of its official powers, its range of action and its personnel. The Regling–Watson report of 2010 details a series of additional failings in the regulatory system. To add to the difficulties of regulation, the state dealt with both finance and construction not only as regulator but also as promoter of industry growth. Capital was to decide the investment priorities and development paths of the Irish economy, choosing which social structure of liquidity to support.

Ireland's boom in the 1990s almost inevitably included elements of 'overheating' and even 'irrational exuberance'. The damaging effects of such tendencies were likely to be weakened as long as they were balanced by the marshalling of newly available resources for productive purposes. However, the vast bulk of these monies went into the property sector, with construction, real estate development and

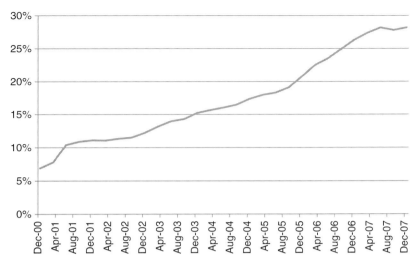

Figure 3.2 Percentage of total credit going to construction and real estate activities, 2000–7
Source: Central Bank of Ireland, multiple years, *Sectoral Distribution of Credit*
Note: These figures do not include personal mortgage lending.

housing finance accounting for the vast bulk of the increase and of total lending by 2007. Despite rapid increases from a very low base in lending for R&D, lending to computer services firms remained a tiny proportion of lending and lending to hardware firms declined, as did the industry. Construction and real estate lending increased from 7 per cent to 28 per cent of total lending over the period (Figure 3.2). In contrast, the high-profile high-tech sectors attracted less than 2.5 per cent of credit[1] (Ó Riain, 2009).

Figure 3.3 shows in absolute terms how, although non-construction investment increased, the vast bulk of the capital available for investment in the economy went into construction. The growth in construction investment was large in the 1990s, but further sped up in the 2000s. Of course, it may be that the figure for productive investment is understated as 'non-material' investments become more important (e.g., R&D, marketing and so on). Figure 3.4 provides

[1] Data on lending from Central Bank of Ireland, multiple years, *Sectoral Distribution of Credit.*

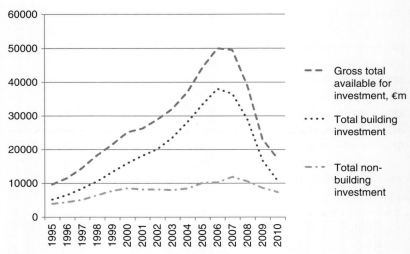

Figure 3.3 Capital availability and investment, 1995–2010
Source: CSO, National Accounts – Institutional Sectors

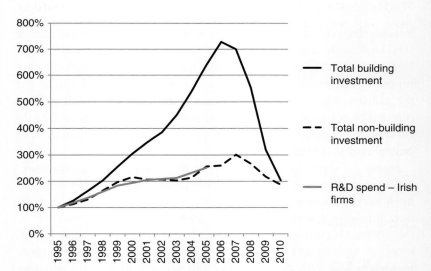

Figure 3.4 Relative growth of different forms of capital investment, 1995–2010
Source: CSO, National Accounts – Institutional Sectors; Forfás (multiple
years), *R&D in the Business Sector*

some information on this, as well as a clearer picture of the relative growth of the different forms of investment. Non-building investment grows substantially and steadily until 2007. The relative growth of R&D spending of Irish-owned firms is also plotted in this graph as an indicator of the kinds of productive investments made in non-material factors of production during this time. For the years where data are available in a consistent series (1995–2005), the R&D investment tracks the non-building investment trends very closely. Construction investment of course increases much more quickly until 2006, with the same even more rapid increase from 2003 onwards showing up in the data on relative growth rates. In short, while the construction boom began in the 1990s, the dominance of construction over other productive forms of investment was dramatically consolidated in the 2000s.

Shifting logics within the property boom

Figure 3.5 indicates that house prices began to rise rapidly in 1994–5 and continued on a steep, almost linear trend until 2007. However, Whelan (2010) suggests that Irish house prices could be explained by rising incomes and changing demand linked to demographic and

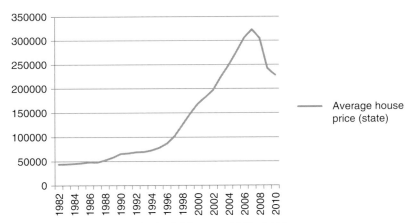

Figure 3.5 House prices in the Irish state, 1982–2010
Source: Department of the Environment, *Housing Statistics*

Table 3.3 *Correlation between vacancy rates and new housing stock in local authority areas, 1996–2009*

Counties included (N)	1996 with 1996–9	2002 with 2002–5	2006 with 2006–9
All areas (34)	−.32	.14	.36
Non-USRS (29)	−.23	.04	−.09
Urban and environs (15)*	−.22	.07	−.41
Urban (8)**	−.03	.05	−.91

* City areas plus county areas attached to cities (e.g., Limerick County) and Wicklow, Kildare and Meath (surrounding Dublin)
** City areas only
Source: data provided by All-Ireland Research Observatory, NIRSA, NUI Maynooth. Thanks to Rob Kitchin and Justin Gleason

family change until at least 1997 – and possibly later if the low interest rates of the period are taken into account. By 2007, however, Irish houses were overvalued by at least 30 per cent.

We can take a closer look at these shifting dynamics by examining the link between demand and supply in residential housing markets. Table 3.3 shows the correlations between the vacancy rate in dwellings (excluding holiday homes and uninhabitable buildings) at the time of the three censuses of the period (1996, 2002 and 2006) and the percentage increase in new housing stock in the following three years (April 1996–December 1999, April 2002–December 2005 and April 2006–December 2009) (see also Kitchin *et al.*, 2010). Since a high vacancy rate implies a relatively low level of demand, we would expect that high vacancy rates (low demand) are negatively correlated with a high percentage of new housing stock (i.e., high supply). We are able to examine these relations by using data on vacancy rates and housing stock and completions in the 34 local authority areas in the state (including major urban areas and the 26 county areas).

The top row of the table provides the results for all areas. The second row provides the results for all counties except the five counties of the Upper Shannon Renewal Scheme (USRS). This scheme started in 1998 and provided generous incentives for investment in property in the declining rural counties of Cavan, Leitrim, Longford, Roscommon and Sligo. These counties accounted for 5.1 per cent of completions in 1996–9, 7.2 per cent in 2002–5 and 9.8 per cent in 2006–9. The last two rows provide the results for the city areas and their contiguous counties, and finally for the city areas alone.

Care should be taken with the small numbers of cases in some of the categories, but the results are nonetheless interesting. A negative correlation suggests that high vacancy rates depressed the increase in new housing stock in subsequent years – as common sense about demand and supply might suggest. However, the data suggest that overall supply of housing became increasingly delinked from demand, particularly between 2002 and 2005.

In the 1990s, high vacancy rates suppressed subsequent supply in most areas, although the relationship was weakest in the urban areas. All areas broke the link with demand in the early 2000s, although the break was strongest in the five USRS counties (as shown in the gap between the correlation for all counties and for the non-USRS counties). In the period from 2006 onwards, supply in the USRS counties continued to go against demand, and rural areas in general remained largely delinked from demand (see the difference between non-USRS and Urban and Environs). Supply and demand were closely linked once again in urban areas.

Overall, the data suggest that a boom in the 1990s was only detached from demand in the urban areas, but that completions in the early 2000s were increasingly detached from demand across the country. This suggests a broadening boom that was turning into a widespread bubble. A total of 89 per cent of all ghost estates in 2010 (or those with dates assigned to them in the dataset) were granted planning permission in 2002–8 (based on analysis of data provided by the All Ireland Research Observatory, NUI Maynooth). The volume of transactions also increased during the 2000s (Figure 3.6), suggesting an increasing 'liquidity' of housing as an asset.

In the late 2000s the residential bubble weakened significantly, except for the tax incentive areas of the USRS. In the late 2000s, demand reasserted itself as a factor in developers' logics in urban areas. However, they appear to have continued to search for opportunities in rural areas (most clearly in tax incentive areas, but also much more broadly) even as developer behaviour in urban markets returned to

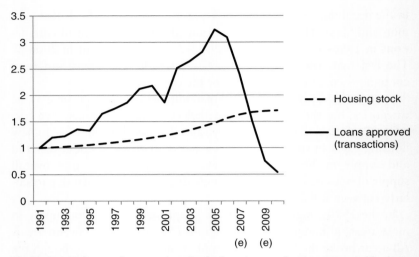

Figure 3.6 Volume of transactions in the housing market (as measured by loan approvals) and housing stock – growth relative to 1991 base year
Source: Department of the Environment, *Housing Statistics*

some semblance of normality, albeit at highly inflated prices. Small local developers also appear to have helped drive this continuing expansion of construction in rural areas as local builders were tempted into moving into development.

Taken together, these patterns suggest that a housing boom turned into a widespread housing bubble that was then aggravated by the property-based tax incentives provided in certain areas. This is also reflected in trends in the granting of planning permissions that allow the construction of various buildings (Figure 3.7). Residential planning permissions grew strongly from 2002 to 2005, as the correlational analysis suggested, but then began to decline with an increase in extensions to existing homes. The residential market seemed to cool somewhat from the mid-2000s.

No such cooling took place for commercial development, with planning permissions increasing rapidly until 2007. Whereas residential planning permissions in 2007 were 17 per cent higher than in 2001, commercial planning permissions were 132 per cent higher. Figure 3.8 traces the evolution from 1991 to 2011 of the office construction market in Dublin, the largest market for non-residential

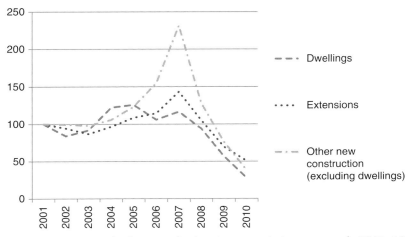

Figure 3.7 Rate of change of planning permissions granted 2001–10 (2001=100)
Source: Department of the Environment, *Housing Statistics*

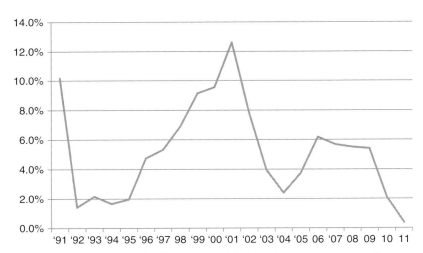

Figure 3.8 Percentage of office space added in the previous year, Greater Dublin Area, 1991–2011
Source: data generously provided by Andrew MacLaran, TCD. Further details in MacLaran (2012)

development.[2] The market shifted over these decades in a number of significant ways – including massive expansion and suburbanisation (MacLaran, 2012). However, our focus is once more on the link between demand and supply and the shifting logics of developers over time.

Figure 3.8 shows the percentage of office space in any given year that was newly added since the previous year. It shows that between 1995 and 2001 there were significant increases in the proportion of new office space added each year, reaching a peak of 12.6 per cent in 2001. The rate of increase dropped rapidly in the downturn of the following two years, but then increased again to remain between 5 and 6 per cent between 2006 and 2009. This suggests that a major bubble in the late 1990s was followed by a smaller bubble in the mid- to late 2000s.

However, a closer look at the underlying logic of demand and supply across the period reveals a quite different picture. As in residential construction, we can track how closely vacancy rates affected office space supply (i.e., how responsive developers were to demand) by looking at the relationship between office vacancy rates in a given year (demand) and the percentage of new office space in the following year (supply). Figure 3.9 plots the percentage of new housing stock in a given year on the y-axis, with the vacancy rate in the previous year on the x-axis.

In the early 1990s, the market was stagnant, with vacancy rates of around 10 per cent, but growth through the 1990s soon took off, with the percentage of new office space climbing steadily each year. What is striking, however, is that vacancy rates fell during the same period as underlying demand was strong. A sudden spike in development in 2000–1, combined with a stuttering economy, led the vacancy rate to spike and this increase in vacancy rates continued as the economy struggled from 2001 to 2003. After a spike in the area available for rent in 2001, the rate of supply of new office space reduced rapidly. However, from 2004 to 2008, the supply of office space increased again to an additional 5–6 per cent per year. At a time when there was a great deal of office space vacant in Dublin, development activity continued at a level that maintained and even increased these vacancy rates.

---

[2] The data were kindly provided by Dr Andrew MacLaran. There is an analysis of broader trends in Dublin commercial real estate in MacLaran (2012).

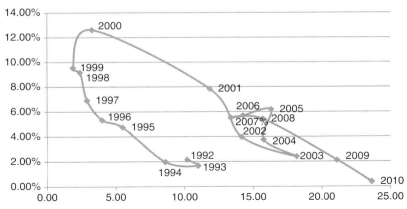

Figure 3.9 Office space vacancy rate and new housing stock in the subsequent year, Dublin, 1991–2011
Source: data provided by Andrew MacLaran, TCD. Further details in MacLaran (2012)

The time horizons of property deals were shortened as developers at the height of the boom were building housing estates that had already been sold off the plans, or where urban renewal and other development tax incentives had greatly reduced the financial risks involved. The practice of 'flipping' properties – building properties that were sold to investors for more or less immediate re-sale to other buyers – became quite widespread (MacDonald and Sheridan, 2009; Kelly, 2010). In addition, first-person accounts suggest that developers were increasingly tied into the bubble through inter-locking deals and interests, making it difficult for them to exit the complex network of contracts that sustained the highly leveraged market (Kelly, 2010). A whole range of actors were tied into the dynamics of the bubble through booming land values, housing and office space prices and rent, and property flipping (Kitchin *et al.*, 2010).

In short, the property market moved from a highly liquid market in property development assets to a market in real estate development liquidity itself – in the 'flipping' of deals with relatively low levels of uncertainty over short periods of time. However, these short-term 'solid futures' were increasingly built on futures that were remarkably fragile in the medium to long term.

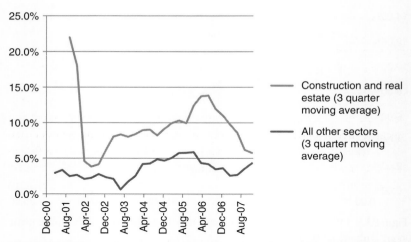

Figure 3.10 Quarterly percentage increase of credit to: (a) construction and real estate activities; and (b) all other sectors (three quarter moving average of quarterly increases)
Source: Central Bank of Ireland, multiple years, *Sectoral Distribution of Credit*

Finally, we can turn to credit itself. Here again, it is instructive to examine the broadly linear pattern of increase in credit outlined in Figure 3.2 in more detail. Figure 3.10 indicates trends in the speed at which the volume of credit increased in the economy, measured on a quarterly basis (and reported as the average of the previous three quarters' increase). It shows that the rate of increase of credit provided for construction and real estate activities ran ahead of all other sectors at all times from 2000 to 2007. During the middle of the boom, the rate of increase in development credit and all other credit went broadly in the same direction. However, there are also interesting variations. In the period from early 2002 to mid-2003 (the bursting of the dot-com bubble) credit to non-development sectors grew slowly and barely at all in the first half of 2003. However, real estate development credit grew rapidly. Again, in 2005–6 property and construction-related credit in the economy grew increasingly rapidly even as the rest of the economy saw a slowing of credit growth.

The origins of the property and credit bubbles lie in the late 1990s, when economic growth was driven primarily by exports and an increase in domestic demand (including, but not limited to, housing). Construction and real estate investment and lending grew faster than the rest of the economy, even during this period. However, investment in both housing and commercial real estate largely tracked the increasing demand and declined in 2002–3 as the economy slowed. However, from that period on, while the rest of the economy was much slower to recover, property lending and investment expanded very rapidly and became increasingly detached from demand. Buyers and sellers chased the market in an increasing volume of sales while credit grew rapidly – most of the long-term damage to the economy was done in a relatively short number of years between 2002 and 2008, even if the conditions for a bubble had been put in place before the 2000s.

Translation over time: property lending becomes more rational

How did the developers and banks themselves make sense of this bubble? Looking at the construction sector, the press releases from four major companies identify almost no risks until 2008. McInerney, a major residential builder, suggested in 2005 that: 'Strong market demand for Irish housing shows no sign of diminishing. It is expected that this demand will continue, boosted by employment, demographics and inward migration. We remain well positioned to capitalise on these trends' (McInerney Holdings plc, 2007). Treasury Holdings reported from its 2007 annual conference that 'the sun is not ready to set on Ireland's rapidly growing global property empire' (2007).

While there was some recognition of slowing growth and market pressures in late 2007 and 2008, these risks were discounted based on 'a very strong indigenous economy and a strengthening international environment' (Treasury Holdings, 2007), ongoing strength in the non-residential construction market (Kingspan Group plc, 2008) and a 'resilient income producing portfolio and its well timed long-term development pipeline' (Treasury Holdings, 2008). McInerney observed in 2007 that 'the fundamentals of the Irish economy and housing market remain strong although consumer caution became more evident as the period progressed, impacted by the tightening of interest rates'.

Banks' optimistic assessments of asset quality, capital position and economic growth also evolved over time, becoming more confident even as the conditions of the banking boom became less sustainable.

Table 3.4 *Key business issues – years mentioned in bank annual report opening statements, 2000–7 (eight years)*

	Risk management	Capital position	Asset quality	Operational efficiencies	Market position
Anglo	3	3	5	0	2
AIB	6	4	5	4	4
BOI	2	1	6	6	2

Here it is instructive to examine the annual reports of the banks and the risks and mitigating factors they identify in their chairman's and introductory statements.

Table 3.4 classifies the major business issues mentioned in the opening statements of the annual reports of the three major banks from 2000 to 2007. Although there are broad similarities between the banks, there are also interesting differences. The retail focus of the Bank of Ireland is evident in its focus on operational efficiencies and weak focus on capital and risk management. What is not clear from the table is the lack of detailed content in the reports of Anglo Irish Bank and the general and formulaic character of many of the statements. The issues raised are considered in more detail in the reports of the other two banks.

In a 2006 issue of *About Banking*, the journal of the Irish Banking Federation, two solicitors argued that Ireland needed to prepare for the end of the bubble by securitising more asset classes so that it was poised to take advantage of the recovery. Similar articles in trade magazines and the national press also interpreted the crisis in terms of the US difficulties with subprime mortgages and securitisation, and minimised the possibilities of contagion from the US and the importance of commercial rather than residential property lending to Irish banks.

Two key elements connect bank rationalities to a belief in market organisation. The first is the concept of *economic or market fundamentals* – underlying aspects of the economy which allow the discounting of specific or localised risks. This concept extended across a range of institutional actors, often used in quite similar ways. This allowed the discounting of warning signs in the economy through the bubble period:

Economic fundamentals remain firm – demographics, job creation, income growth and the government's fiscal position all remain positive while the interest rate outlook is now more supportive. These fundamentals support ongoing demand for housing, although below the exceptional levels seen in recent years. Buyer and seller expectations are realigning and prices are likely to settle with a measured reduction in supply. This will support a more stable house price environment, important to the long-term growth and competitiveness of the Irish economy. (Anglo Irish Bank Annual Report, 2007)

While short-term economic prospects for AIB's [Allied Irish Bank's] main markets are somewhat mixed, the medium term outlook is more positive. Irish GDP is forecast to slow to 2.5 per cent this year, reflecting the slowdown in the housing sector and a weaker global economy. However, economic fundamentals remain solid and growth is expected to pick up again in 2009 and beyond. (AIB Annual Report, 2007)

A second dimension is the reliance on the *self-correcting* properties of the market, obviating the need for extensive political management of economic tensions:

After a decade of such strong price growth it was always inevitable that the market would peak and that prices might start to come back at some stage. (*About Banking*, 2007)

New Dublin office supply in the next two years will be very modest as output has been reduced significantly in the last 12 months, helping the market move towards equilibrium ... House prices have been falling in Ireland now for 19 months, longer than in many other countries, and this, combined with falls in interest rates, means that Irish housing is now significantly more affordable than it has been for some years and in 2009 is expected to drop to 1997 affordability levels. (Source: AIB Economic Research). (Treasury Holdings, 2008)

The set of circumstances that could result in a sudden sharp correction to the market are not in place and it is unlikely that they would come into place for the forecastable future. (Friends First, 2006)

These two elements came together in the varying trends in each bank's assessment of the macroeconomic environment. This proved crucial, as many of the positive assessments of the asset quality of banks and of sectoral trends were justified in terms of their underlying value and the percentage of performing loans – factors that were increasingly dependent upon, and justified by, ongoing economic growth. For example, the chief of Danske Bank argued in *About Banking* in 2006 that Ireland did not have a bubble because of the presence of low interest rates, financial innovation and liberalisation that was still

Table 3.5 *Assessments of the macroeconomic environment – positive and negative mentions in bank annual report opening statements, 2000–7*

	2000	2001	2002	2003	2004	2005	2006	2007
Anglo								
Positive		X	X			X	X	X
Negative	X							
AIB								
Positive						X	X	X
Negative		X	X		X			X
BOI								
Positive	X	X	X		X		X	X
Negative		X	X	X				

reducing the cost of borrowing, and the trend towards urbanisation driving high-end demand as elites desired city centre living.

Table 3.5 examines trends in macroeconomic assessments more formally. Anglo Irish Bank's reports indicate some concerns in 2000, but throughout the 2000s are almost exclusively positive in their assessment – and particularly at the height of the bubble in 2005–7. By contrast, in the uncertain years of 2001–3, its evaluations were negative, while those of Bank of Ireland were mixed. However, these concerns disappeared at the height of the boom, with all three banks offering uniformly positive assessments. As the bubble grew, the banks that had expressed concerns in the earlier years converged on Anglo Irish Bank's lack of concern about the bubble.

Competition between the banks appears to have been a factor in 'crowding in' the two leading banks, AIB and Bank of Ireland, into property lending. Figure 3.11 shows trends in profits among the 'Big 3' banks in Ireland and the surge in Anglo Irish Bank's profits, to the point where it had significantly closed the gap with Bank of Ireland by 2007. Executive compensation followed suit – including, as became apparent in 2008, secret loans to executives and directors of as much as €70 million. AIB in particular responded with a shift into real estate and development lending, with a corresponding surge in profits and subsequent collapse.

If market competition could not provide the discipline required, perhaps managerial authority could. In practice, however, the

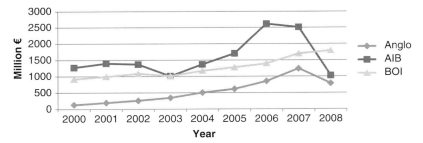

Figure 3.11 Bank profits, 2000–8
Source: Annual Reports

centralisation of executive authority in the banks further reinforced the convergence of optimistic assessments of asset quality, capital position and economic growth. Bank executives faced few challenges to their perspectives. Authority within the banks was highly centralised, as the Anglo Irish Bank report of 2006 notes: 'The Bank's centralised business model enables quick decision making, ensuring consistent delivery of service to our customers and effective management of risk. It also allows us to operate in an efficient and streamlined manner, as reflected by our cost to income ratio of 27%.' Senior bank executive salaries rose rapidly in all banks during the 2000s, with bonuses that were in practice increased by corporate strategies that inflated the bubble (TASC, 2010).

Furthermore, bank executives, and especially key figures like Seán Fitzpatrick at Anglo Irish Bank and Laurence Crowley at AIB, were at the very centre of interlocking directorates in the Irish business world. Cement Roadstone had a director on each of the banks' boards, while Anglo Irish Bank had directors from McInerney and Dublin Docklands Development Authority, Bank of Ireland had directors from the Dublin Docklands Development Authority, and Irish Life and Permanent had directors from Kingspan and the Grafton Group. In general, the most intensively networked executives were bank executives or property investors and developers (TASC, 2010: 10, Table 3). Internal centralisation of authority and close external networking of executives are likely to have minimised the opportunities for alternative perspectives to establish themselves and to have reinforced the property-based social structure of liquidity. Relatively autonomous managers failed to provide the organisational mechanisms to ensure financial prudence.

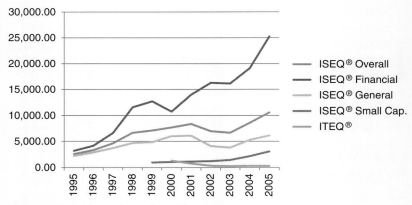

Figure 3.12 Irish stock market indices, 1995–2005
Source: Irish Stock Exchange, online indices

Shareholders were the other candidates for providing sufficient external oversight from within the private sector as a 'market for governance' (Davis, 2011). However, the stock market itself reinforced the tendencies towards financialisation. Figure 3.12 shows the progress of a variety of Irish Stock Exchange indices from 1995 to 2005. The General Index showed strong growth in the late 1990s, but dipped from 2001 to 2003 and only recovered in 2005. However, the financial stocks surged from 2000 onwards after strong growth in the 1990s. The stock market was also a weak mechanism for distributing investment to the productive and innovative, rather than speculative, sectors. The technology-based ITEQ index never recovered following the bursting of the dot-com bubble in 2001, while the financial stocks increased rapidly in value. The stock market rewarded the lending patterns that were summarised at the outset of this chapter.

Translation over space: lending to Irish banks becomes more rational

So far, our analysis has focused on domestic processes. However, a crucial element in the transformation of this property-based growth machine into an engine of national crisis was the rapid increase in international lending to Irish banks through the 2000s. This facilitated the increase in scale of activity during the 2000s that turned bank debt into a national catastrophe in 2008. While in 2003, 20 per cent of Irish banks' net liabilities were owed to international lenders, this rose to almost 80 per cent by early 2008 (Lane, 2011). Most of the growth in international funding appears to have come from the UK, although the Eurozone was also exposed through direct lending to Irish banks and, particularly, through the heavy reliance on the inter-bank lending system for raising these funds, creating interdependencies far beyond the immediate lenders and borrowers. The bubble in property and finance in Ireland was primarily funded through UK, US and European lenders. Access to international lending broke any automatic limits that a national economy might place on credit bubbles within its own borders. The social structure of liquidity that underpinned the asset bubble was not only local but also transnational.

The Irish financial crisis was intertwined with this transnational financialisation and particularly with the increasing reach of French and German banks in international financial markets. Figures 3.13 and 3.14 show that while domestic credit expanded in the French and German economies over the past two decades, the growth in international lending by domestic banks was the most striking change in each financial system. In addition, while the changes in domestic credit vary between the two countries, the trends in international lending are strikingly similar. The loosening of credit in the German domestic economy was greatest in the 1990s, with recovery after unification, but slowed in the 2000s. In France, by contrast, domestic credit grew more rapidly in the 2000s and tracked the growth in international lending at the time. International lending by both financial systems went from below 40 per cent of GDP in 1990 to around 160 per cent at the peak of the 2000s credit boom. Together, these represented a massive expansion of credit – and an expansion that was concentrated increasingly in international operations. The following chapter explores some of the conditions that enabled this internationalisation of European finance, but for the purposes of this chapter, I focus on how this intersected with Irish processes to produce the credit bubble in Ireland.

Where did the international lending of French and German banks go? Table 3.6 shows the location of the foreign claims of banks from France, Germany, the UK and the US. The Irish statistics are

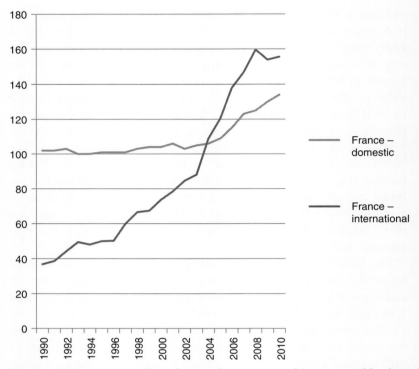

Figure 3.13 Domestic credit in the French economy and international lending by French banks, 1990–2010 (% of GDP)
Source: BIS Consolidated Banking Statistics, Table 9; World Bank, *Financial Statistics*

provided for indicative purposes only as they include both lending to domestic banks and to the IFSC. These statistics only begin in the first quarter of 2005, understating the surge in international lending that began in earnest in the 1990s and grew dramatically from 2003/4. The growth in international lending is much broader than the inter-action with the European periphery, even though for German and French banks the SPIIG countries (Spain, Portugal, Italy, Ireland and Greece) figure more prominently over time. Nonetheless, lending into SPIIG countries accounts for one-quarter of German and just under one-quarter of French international lending at the peak of the credit boom. The international lending boom found an outlet in the European periphery; however, it was not driven primarily by

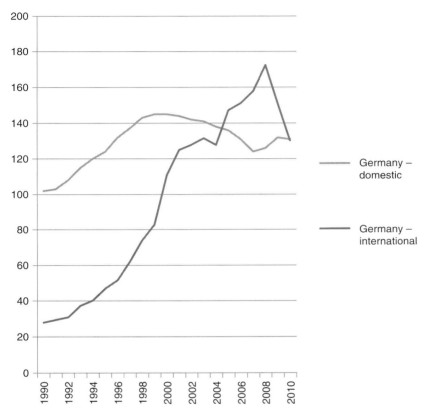

Figure 3.14 Domestic credit in the German economy and international lending by German banks, 1990–2010 (% of GDP)
Source: BIS Consolidated Banking Statistics, Table 9; World Bank, *Financial Statistics*

developments in peripheral countries but by the broader dynamics of financialisation.

Not surprisingly, this overall increase in lending contributed substantially to a credit boom in the SPIIG countries in the 2000s (see Figure 3.15). By 2007, domestic credit in these two economies was at 200 per cent of GDP, while it accounted for 125 per cent of German and French GDP.

Ireland's story is a particularly dramatic national pattern of credit expansion, but this is embedded in a broader transformation in

Table 3.6 *Foreign claims of domestically owned banks, 2005–8: proportion of foreign claims in the European periphery of German, French, UK and US banks*

	Germany		France		UK		US	
Total increase in international lending 2005–8	35.0%		127.1%		79.9%		63.3%	
	2005Q1	2008Q3	2005Q1	2008Q3	2005Q1	2008Q3	2005Q1	2008Q3
Ireland	3.3	5.4	1.7	2.5	4.2	4.6	1.0	2.4
Spain	4.0	6.7	4.5	4.9	3.0	3.1	2.2	1.9
Greece	1.3	1.0	1.2	2.3	0.4	0.3	0.8	0.5
Italy	5.8	5.6	7.6	12.8	2.8	2.0	3.7	1.6
Portugal	1.0	1.1	0.9	0.9	0.6	0.6	0.3	0.2
Total SPIIG	15.3	19.8	15.9	23.4	11.0	10.6	8.0	6.6

Source: BIS Consolidated Banking Statistics, Table 9

Notes: the Irish statistics are provided for indicative purposes only as they include both lending to domestic banks and to the IFSC

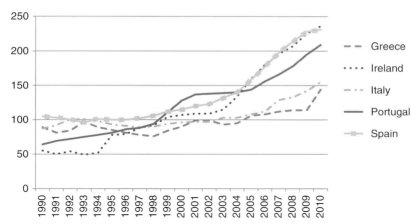

Figure 3.15 Domestic credit in the European periphery (% of GDP)
Source: World Bank, *Financial Statistics*

financial systems in the European core and periphery. The question then becomes how it was possible that the banking systems of the core and periphery could become so enmeshed, given historically weak relations and the apparent bubble character of their property booms in the 2000s.

A crucial role here was played by the credit rating agencies, private regulatory organisational forms that provide ratings of the quality of a wide variety of privately issued and sovereign financial instruments. They offer a market in regulatory monitoring and have also become crucial in creating the informational basis for markets in financial products and assets. The ratings provided by agencies are in many cases what is effectively being traded as the character of the underlying asset is of less value than the re-sale value of the asset and the possibility of repackaging and/or securitising it (or part of it).

International lenders did not lend to specific business development projects provided by Irish banks. Instead, the funds were raised through various offerings of bonds, commercial paper and other instruments associated with the banks (Killian *et al.*, 2011: Appendix 4). Investors' decisions to invest in these instruments depended heavily on the rating of the funds and the banks. Although credit rating reports are largely proprietary, the press releases of Moody's ratings agency are publicly available on its website. It is possible to obtain from these releases the major changes in the credit rating of Anglo Irish Bank from 1998 to 2008 and to analyse the summary comments provided by Moody's outlining the reasons for changes in ratings (see Table 3.7).

Anglo Irish Bank's credit rating climbed steadily through a period when the bubble was growing and then inflating rapidly. The OECD (2012) finds that more intense competition in the credit ratings market loosened credit rating standards and increased the overall level of ratings. The comments in the years up to 2003 exhibit a degree of caution that largely disappears in the later bubble years. In addition, the reasons for raising the credit rating are specifically those issues that came to be the downfall of Anglo: asset quality, poor underwriting and operations, cash flows from bubble operations and securitisation. Not surprisingly, this gave reassurance to Anglo itself. Anglo commented regarding similar upgrades by Fitch: 'We are delighted that the Bank received yet another upgrade of its credit ratings, most recently in February this year by Fitch Ratings, the international rating agency. The Bank's long and short term ratings now stand at A and F1 respectively. This provides further evidence of the Bank's underlying strength and follows the upgrade last year by the international ratings agency Moody's, of the Bank's long-term deposit credit rating' (Annual Report, 2002).

Rather than monitoring the market, the rating agencies were firmly embedded within the rationalities of the property and credit bubble – in the process reproducing and deepening it. They 'translated' the Irish banks' activities into a homogenised metric of asset quality that enabled international funders to purchase bonds issued by Irish banks. The agencies played a critical role in translating the specificities of the Irish social structure of liquidity around property into a set of defined, standardised instruments that could be traded alongside other instruments from other social structures of liquidity around the world.

Anglo-American and European financialisation became enormously consequential for countries like Ireland. The triangle of Irish banks, international funders and credit rating agencies connected the Irish social structure of liquidity based on personalised property development lending to the international trade in securitised financial instruments through the standardising effects of credit ratings. In the process, it weakened the ties between financial and industrial capital in both the European periphery and the core.

Table 3.7 *Moody's credit rating changes and summary comments regarding Anglo Irish Bank, 1998–2008*

Date	Long-term deposit rating (LTD) Financial strength (FS)	Comment
Various, 1998–2001	Baa1 (LTD) D+ (FS) Increase to: A3 C	'In the context of 20% banking growth rates in 1997/98, which is not sustainable longer term, a key challenge will be to preserve acceptable asset-quality indicators.' 'The rating agency added that asset quality remained sound and that profitability has been reasonable, constrained in part by the costs associated with the bank's acquisitions.' 'Anglo Irish's credit quality is constrained by its reliance on middle market corporate lending. Furthermore, the bank is reliant on market funding and has a limited retail deposit base.' 'Moody's has maintained a stable outlook on First Active's ratings, noting that the bank's financial condition was sound, even after the effects of margin compression, and that the mortgage and savings business offers predictable earnings with a lower risk of credit losses than many other sectors.' 'Moody's added that the bank's profitability could be

Table 3.7 (*cont.*)

Date	Long-term deposit rating (LTD) Financial strength (FS)	Comment
		affected by an economic slowdown in Ireland but the agency sees this risk as manageable, short of a less likely "hard landing".'
		'Moody's added that the bank's profitability could be affected by an economic slowdown in Ireland.'
2002	–	–
2003	Change from stable to positive outlook	'Loan-loss provisions are likely to increase in 2003, but underlying asset quality remains sound.'
		'Liquidity levels in the sector are good (underpinned by Central Bank requirements).'
		'Moody's said the changes in the rating outlook reflected the continuing progress Anglo Irish has made in strengthening its funding profile despite strong lending growth, whilst maintaining the quality of the loan book.'
		'The ratings agency expects that the weakening of property markets in the UK and Ireland will put pressure on profitability going forwards.'
		'Moody's notes that Irish banks have limited exposure to troubled sectors overseas such as high-tech, telecoms and aviation.'

Table 3.7 (*cont.*)

Date	Long-term deposit rating (LTD) Financial strength (FS)	Comment
2004	A2 C+	'The upgrade takes account of the AIBC's ongoing success in maintaining and indeed growing its position within the highly competitive Irish and UK commercial property lending markets. Importantly this growth has not been at the expense of asset quality which remains good, built as it is on precise underwriting standards. In particular we note that AIBC's lending for investment property lending is on pre-let properties and that its exposure to larger high profile properties is limited. Further most loans are secured on a portfolio of property cash flows.'
2007	A1 C+	'The Cover Pool comprises a relatively concentrated pool of commercial mortgage loans. In particular, the borrower and property diversity is lower than for other Cover Pools. Moreover, properties securing the Mortgage Loans comprise of a significant portion of specialty and operating assets. These assets bear a relatively high operational risk resulting in relatively

Table 3.7 (*cont.*)

Date	Long-term deposit rating (LTD) Financial strength (FS)	Comment
		challenging servicing, especially in case of a Mortgage Loan's adverse performance or default. Moody's has taken property quality, property diversity and borrower diversity into account when determining the required over-collateralisation.'
		'The A2/P-1/C+ ratings of AIBC reflect the bank's stable market position and proven strategy as a secured lender to medium-sized corporates, professional property investors and high net worth individuals. The ratings also take into consideration AIBC's sound profitability, good credit quality and rigorous lending approach. AIBC is somewhat reliant on short-term wholesale funding, mitigated by the ongoing diversification of funding sources and by the institution's successful deposit-gathering strategy. Moody's noted that, whilst the issuance of extendible notes provided a further degree of diversification to the group's funding base, it nevertheless regards the

Table 3.7 (*cont.*)

Date	Long-term deposit rating (LTD) Financial strength (FS)	Comment
		instruments as a less robust form of long-term funding given their 13 month tenure.'
2008 (pre-guarantee)	A1	'The Covered Bond investors benefit from
		1) the credit strength of the Issuer, rated A1/Prime-1.
		2) a pool of assets securing the Issuer's payment obligations under the terms of the Covered Bonds (the "Cover Pool"). The Cover Pool comprises of UK commercial mortgage loans that have been originated by the Issuer and has a weighted average LTV of approximately 75%.
		3) Securitisation style techniques designed to i) mitigate the risk associated with the possible deterioration of the credit profile of the Cover Pool; ii) ring fence the Cover Pool in the event of the insolvency of the Issuer; iii) mitigate the risks associated with the credit deterioration of the swap counterparties and of the Cover Pool; and iv) mitigate refinancing risk, through the extension features contemplated in the terms and conditions of the Covered Bonds.

Table 3.7 (*cont.*)

Date	Long-term deposit rating (LTD) Financial strength (FS)	Comment
		As is the case with other covered bonds, Moody's considers the credit strength of the transaction to be linked to that of certain parties, mainly the Issuer in particular from a timeliness of payment perspective. Should such credit strength deteriorate, all other things being equal, the rating of the Covered Bonds may be expected to come under negative pressure. However, the Issuer has the ability, but not the obligation, to increase the over-collateralisation of the transaction in order to reduce the linkage to the credit strength of the Issuer.'

Conclusion

The excessive and foolhardy lending to the property development sector in Ireland was produced by a number of social and institutional shifts. The property-based 'growth machine', linking developers and political elites, especially in Fianna Fáil, has long been a feature of Irish society. However, it could only become the force that derailed the national economy through three crucial steps.

First, it sidelined alternative 'social structures of liquidity', most notably the export-oriented industries that had been the primary drivers of economic development in the 1990s. These sectors were dominated by foreign investment, but were also shaped by public agencies supporting the development of indigenous firms (Ó Riain, 2004). Private banks were notably absent from the process of indigenous industrial and business development. When capital gains tax was cut and financial regulation weakened in the late 1990s, private capital was given the institutional power to decide the destination of investment and favoured property over technology (or indeed other potential productive industries, such as food).

Second, the banking sector itself came to see property lending as a rational investment strategy, despite warnings regarding the risks of a bubble. More specifically, the banking sector promoted property even after the slowdown in growth in the 2002–3 period and as property development became detached from demand. Justifications for this support relied heavily on notions of strong economic fundamentals and self-correcting markets. Competition between banks 'crowded in' the banks that were late to property lending into an enthusiastic pursuit of the profits enjoyed by Anglo Irish Bank and others. Neither managerial authority nor markets for governance through the stock market provided the necessary check on this risky activity. Instead, property lending was translated over time into a rational investment.

Third, the expansion of this activity to a scale that was disastrous in terms of the national economy was dependent on the willingness of international lenders to fund Irish banks. This occurred most dramatically between 2002 and 2007, and was encouraged by the liberalisation and internationalisation of significant sections of the German and French banking systems. The specific ties between international and Irish banking were made possible by the translation over space of Irish lending into an internationally tradable asset through the work of the credit rating agencies.

These steps together linked the general process of financialisation and the specific features that characterised it in Ireland. The existence of a broader process of financialisation facilitated its expansion in Ireland. However, this broader process itself is constituted out of the interaction of a variety of national systems of finance – for example, the early financialisation of the US encouraged banks in Europe to pursue strategies based on trading in international financial markets in place of patient lending to domestic business, which in turn enabled the expansion of Irish property lending.

The Irish case also shows the importance of market liberalism as a force promoting the financialisation of the economy. In Ireland this had three major dimensions. The first dimension was the *institutional power of capital markets*, as legal, institutional and taxation changes made private capital the primary arbiter of investment in the economy and sidelined the public agencies and private enterprises that supported productive investment and export-oriented firms.

The second dimension was the fact that the market-based financial system in Ireland (and elsewhere) does not operate in practice only through sets of buyers, sellers and rules, but through a *network of market institutions*. However, while these institutions – competitive markets, stock markets, managerial authority and credit rating agencies – were crucial aspects of a liberal market system, they did not enforce prudence and discipline, but in practice encouraged speculation and indiscipline.

Finally, the third dimension consisted of the various rationalities and justifications of action that actors draw upon in making and interpreting conditions and decisions. In a liberal market system, these rationalities rely heavily on *market talk* – justifications that give a central position to the autonomous effects of market processes. Chief among these in Ireland were the appeal to economic fundamentals and the belief in the self-correcting properties of markets.

Krippner (2011) documents that liberalising financial markets was initially seen in the US as a political strategy that could discipline inflation and socio-political demands. However, policy makers soon discovered that financial deregulation and low interest rates resulted in the opposite – a significant loosening of economic discipline. However, this unanticipated policy failure quickly proved attractive to policy makers. Similarly, in debates about the EU capital liberalisation directive of 1988, Germany wished to remove the possibility of capital controls even as France and the UK wished to retain that option, at least for bargaining leverage (Abdelal, 2007: 69). Hans Tietmeyer, the senior German official dealing with the issue, explained the German position in terms that echoed the US policy makers' belief in the market as a source of discipline: 'We saw in full capital liberalisation the possibility for a test of the stability of the Exchange Rate Mechanism – a test by the markets of policy credibility. We wanted a test by world markets, not just European markets … [that] would demonstrate that we had in Europe a stable fixed exchange-rate system with market-proved stability, rather than artificial stability provided by controls' (quoted in Abdelal, 2007: 70).

However, just as in the cases of the US and European integration, financial markets in Ireland promoted indiscipline rather than the discipline that many had hoped for. The lesson of the Irish case may be that markets are not the overarching disciplinary institution that keeps the other institutions in a society 'honest', but that they are simply one institution among many to be used for various purposes, for better or worse. The necessity of social and political regulation, decisions and debate cannot be avoided with an appeal to the arbitration of markets, which proved so disastrous in the crisis of financialisation in Ireland.

4 | *Europe: between market and diversity*

Introduction

The Irish banking crisis was produced at a variety of levels. Most narrowly, it was a local crisis, produced primarily by Irish banks and developers who were largely oriented towards the domestic economy. Most broadly, it was one case of a broader crisis of economic liberalism. Many of the conditions that made the local crisis possible were intrinsic elements of market liberalism – the limiting of public regulation and the rejection of political guidance of the economy, the weaknesses of private regulation in securing the common good, and the structural importance and discursive privileging of markets and particularly finance.

The previous chapter touched on a further crucial element in the Irish crisis that links these specific and universal features of crisis together. These are the transnational organisational and institutional connections that translated the local and global features of the crisis into one another. Most crucial in the Irish case were the set of connections that allowed Irish banks to raise massive amounts of funding internationally from 2001 to 2007, the period in which the property bubble was largely funded from external funds channelled through the main Irish banks. The role of the credit rating agencies in making this relationship possible has already been discussed both in terms of their role in making bubble-era development loans into 'investable' or increasingly 'liquid' entities and their own reliance on broad assumptions about market efficiencies to underpin their judgments. More broadly, these agencies were important in the connection they made possible between the Irish banking and property-based growth machine and the broader regional processes of financialisation and Europeanisation.

However, the credit rating agencies formed only one thread in a broader canvas of intertwined European and Irish trajectories of economic development and change. Ireland is famously one of the most 'globalised' economies in the world, with high levels of investment, trade, migration and financial flows. It is the changing form of Ireland's relationship with the global economy – and particularly with Europe – that is the focus of this chapter. Ireland's historical links are firmly within the Anglo-American 'Atlantic economy' (O'Hearn, 2001). However, these relationships became more complex over time as Ireland located itself in the global economy, retaining close ties to the UK but now brokering significant elements of the relationship between the US and Europe – particularly by providing a 'gateway to Europe' for US corporations. It became a significant hub for US investment networks and associated trade from the 1970s to the 2000s. International lenders from across the UK, the US and Europe were significant in funding Ireland's boom, as each of these economies in different ways formed part of a 'triple financialisation' of Ireland's external economic environment. However, it was the integration into the European financial system and the threat posed to the euro by both private financial debts and public sovereign debts that loomed largest in the politics of Ireland's crisis.

This chapter first traces Ireland's road to this 'triple financialisation', showing how Ireland came to be located within multiple international networks, becoming a 'multiple interface periphery' (Ruane, 2010). Like the rest of the European periphery, Ireland's relationship to the EU and the European core was transformed in the 2000s by the financialisation of the process of economic integration and monetary union.

The next section of the chapter explores the distinctive form of the financialisation of the European economy. The creation of the euro and capital market integration promoted financialisation, but of a different form than in the US or even the UK. The European financial system remained bank-centred despite trends towards marketisation of governance (Davis, 2011). However, these banks were significantly transformed, breaking with their historical ties to industrial corporations and largely abandoning their strategic orientation as 'patient capital' for greater involvement in markets for financial instruments. While the expansion of credit as a whole was slower in the European core than in the periphery, this masked a fundamental shift in banking that deeply entangled the once-prudent large European banks in the bubble of the 2000s.

However, the crisis in Europe is not only a crisis of financial bubbles but also of the failure of national government finances to cope with the shocks posed by the bursting of those bubbles. As is well known, the establishment of the euro removed most if not all of the monetary tools available to governments to respond to such shocks – interest rate changes and currency devaluations were no longer available as policy tools to countries within the Eurozone. Policy makers had foreseen this potential difficulty and sought to introduce some degree of discipline to government finances – in part through the budgetary criteria for euro membership and in part through a series of loosely coordinated institutional changes, including central bank independence and corporatist wage bargaining.

This chapter traces those changes in the 1990s, showing that economic and monetary union involved significant institutional changes. Furthermore, despite first impressions, those changes should not be interpreted as simply 'neoliberal' as they mimicked key features of Europe's 'social market' economies (Pontusson, 2005). However, the chapter also shows that additional key elements of the social compacts in those social market economies were missing from Europe's Mediterranean and liberal economies. The EU consisted not only of diverse places within European markets but also of deeply institutionalised and very different social compacts which were never well integrated within the European project and its institutions. Europe's excessive integration of finance and the incomplete integration of social bargains generated huge pressures – particularly in the liberal and southern economies.

Behind these dynamics lies a fundamental transformation in the European political economy – with financialisation trumping development, structural divergence even as national incomes converged, and a shift from EU Commission bureaucratic leadership to intergovernmentalism allied to Stability and Growth Pact criteria and the euro. Before moving on to the analysis proper, I briefly review existing debates on three crucial dimensions of European economic integration.

European integration: between uneven development and capitalist diversity

The emergence of regional blocs for both trading and governance is one of the major developments in the organisation of global capitalism in recent decades (Solinger, 2009). Europe is a particularly fascinating and important case as it is the most ambitious of all such projects – in terms of its historical origins in preventing world war, its global ambitions and the degree of its internal integration. How do we understand these new social orders? Most fundamentally, economic integration creates new 'fields of action' (Fligstein, 2008), incorporating not only market action but also a wide range of relationships and possible modes of cooperation and competition. This chapter examines the international conditions of Ireland's crisis through an analysis of the emergence of this new field of action in the EU – particularly along three dimensions: the incorporation of different countries with highly uneven development into a single economic bloc; the dominance of finance in the 2000s as the primary mode of action in a field that had been shaped primarily by the combination of trade and intergovernmentalism; and the extent to which significantly different 'varieties of capitalism' interacted and were (or were not) integrated within a single field of action. Let us briefly examine the issues arising along each of these dimensions in more detail.

Uneven development

This is not the place to rehearse the many debates on European integration. It is a process, however, that is increasingly recognised as riven with tensions that the once-dominant functionalist understanding of European integration ignored. The neo-functionalist approach argued that integration in one realm (for example, the economy) would drive further integration in other areas (for example, the political) through spillover effects across sectors and spatial levels (Haas, 1958). Its main rival theory, intergovernmentalism, viewed integration as a process of self-interested negotiation between national states. More recent theories of multi-level governance retained this emphasis on the negotiated character of European development alongside the neo-functionalist emphasis on the changing character of the actors and levels within the governance process. While this approach directs us towards the changing authority patterns within the EU, it has relatively little to say about the deeper socio-economic and socio-political transformations occurring across Europe.

The European project is intimately connected to issues of uneven economic development, particularly as it has spread ever further beyond the Continental European 'core'. Most approaches to integration expect economic convergence over time. However, Chapter 2 showed that this perspective only weakly explained the Irish experience. In particular, it was clear that while Ireland 'caught up' in terms of income, major structural problems remained in its model of development that were only partly resolved in the growth years of the Celtic Tiger and were manifested once again in the years of crisis.

Why is it necessary to think of the European crisis in terms of uneven development? First, as Senghaas (1985) argues, the 'European experience' forms a distinctive model not just of social organisation but also of capitalist development, with the social compacts and political institutions of these European societies crucial to their modes of capitalist development. Second, the European project has gradually extended across the continent, incorporating additional sets of countries, increasingly with significantly lower levels of income and facing major challenges of structural socio-economic transformation.

This raises the issue of how we should understand the relationship between these newly incorporated peripheries and the historical core of Europe, which was the empirical basis of Senghaas' analysis of the European experience. Analysts have linked the experience in the periphery to classic analyses of dependency and dependent development. Some argued that unequal exchange within Europe perpetuated patterns of core and periphery within the region despite relative geographical proximity (Seers, 1979). Michael Hechter (1975) analysed the structure of the Northwestern European periphery in terms of a core–periphery relationship between the southeast of England and the remainder of the 'Celtic fringe'. Mouzelis (1985) has argued that the Mediterranean societies of Greece, Portugal and Spain experienced under-development due to their semi-peripheral location within European capitalism and that this in turn facilitated the growth of populist and, particularly, fascist and/or military regimes. The success or failure of the European project in tackling problems of uneven development would have political as well as economic and social consequences.

Finance and the field of action

The European crisis has been formed through the interaction of structural problems of uneven development with the process of financialisation that has dominated global capitalist change in recent decades. Financialisation seems to respond to a relatively general set of dynamics, even if differing in scale and in the substance of content and social structure that underpins them. Clearest are the dynamics of the financial crisis itself, where Minsky has outlined the various stages through which a bubble builds and sustains itself, but is less successful in explaining the origins of such bubbles (Krippner, 2011). As Reinhart and Rogoff have argued, market actors dismiss these well-recognised features of financial bubbles by regularly concluding that 'this time is different' (2009). Nonetheless, there may be different 'types' of financialisation underway at the same time, leading to the possibility of misidentifying different types or that in practice the different types are entangled even in financial decision makers' own understandings of the situation. While financialisation is clearly a general process in the global economy, it has developed in ways that are both uneven in volume and scale and also qualitatively different in their characteristics. The general trend of financialisation is composed of a number of different 'social structures of liquidity', which interact with one another over time and across space to produce this complex overall trend.

Temporally, finance and production capital seem to dominate over the other in (highly contingent) cycles of capitalist growth. For Arrighi and Silver (2000), financialisation typically follows the exhaustion of a growth model as a hegemonic economy searches for new rounds of growth that can sustain its power in the world economy. With access to capital and dominant market position as resources, this leads it historically towards the promotion of financial bubbles – whether this is the Dutch trading empire, the British Empire or the US economic domination of the twentieth century. The bubble represents the death of the old order and precipitates a crisis out of which will emerge the new order, typically very painfully and violently. Arguably, this is the process that has underpinned the general liberalisation of the US economy since the 1970s.

However, for Perez (2002), financialisation is typically linked not to the debt of the old national and international order, but to the emergence of new technologies and sectors or 'techo-economic paradigms'. The new technologies and economic arrangements that periodically emerge become the basis of a new growth model and attract vast amounts of speculative finance in the early rush of enthusiasm regarding the new technologies and the profits to be gained from them.

The classic recent case here is the dot-com bubble of the late 1990s. When the bubble bursts, Perez argues that we expect a period to follow of a more rational approach to investment in the new technologies and a further period where new models of growth and techno-economic paradigms are institutionalised.

It may be that these theories are not so much competing explanations as descriptions of different types of financialisation that may emerge at different times and in different ways, with their own distinctive cyclical patterns. When both such financialisations are underway at the same time, as has been the case in recent years, it seems likely that each can only promote and encourage the other towards greater heights of speculation. In practice, recent decades have seen a financial system in pursuit of a crisis – whether in the Nordic economies in 1991, the East Asian economies in 1997 and 1998, the dot-com bubble in 2001, the commodities bubble of the mid-2000s or, most disastrously, the real estate and credit bubble of 2008.

Spatially, these processes of globalisation and financialisation are uneven. From a comparative perspective, there are many national forms of financialisation. Nonetheless, these national histories of financialisation also have distinctive cross-national patterns linked to their 'variety of capitalism'. The most dramatic financial booms and busts have been in those political economies that are generally clustered together as 'liberal' (the US, the UK, Ireland and others). More importantly still, the liberalisation of financial flows has intensified an already-growing interdependence between political economies of different sizes and types and at different levels of organisation (regional, sectoral, national and so on).

In the European case, finance became one of the providers of the rules of action in the new social field of the EU (Fligstein, 2008). The financialisation of European economic action was partly deliberately designed and partly had very significant unintended consequences. It took a distinctive form that I will explore in this chapter. But it was clearly closely linked to a broader political project of market integration – in particular in the European case to the formation of a new currency, the euro. Where the euro was supposed to provide a mechanism for managing tensions between different markets and different societies, in practice it has ultimately intensified the rupture between market and society across the EU as a whole.

Integrating diversity

However, economic integration and financialisation in particular raise yet deeper issues. Dani Rodrik (2012) identifies a core tension between 'deep' globalisation (understood as genuine factor mobility) and national democracy (understood primarily as the power of political institutions and popular opinion). This also became clear in the European integration process. Economic and monetary union promoted a radical programme of internal capital mobility that was driven largely by elites. At the same time, national worlds of welfare capitalism (Esping-Andersen, 1990, 1999) remained largely intact, with significant differences between them.

For critics of European integration as a neoliberal project, these national worlds of welfare are overwhelmed by the European market-building project. For others, the problem is that the euro allowed national governments very little flexibility in handling the imbalances and disruptions of capitalist growth. As Lane (2011) notes, the loss of monetary and exchange rate flexibility meant that financial prudence (to avoid bubbles and busts) and fiscal discipline (to withstand their effects) were crucial.

At the same time, the popular legitimacy of the European integration process faced new challenges. Fligstein (2008) argued that a deep fault line or 'Euroclash' was emerging between three groups: elite and younger groups with strong European ties; older and working-class citizens whose social ties are national and who have benefited far less from Europe; and a crucial swing group of the 50 per cent or so of middle-class citizens who sometimes think of themselves as Europeans and sometimes primarily in national terms. Hooghe and Marks (2009) identify a similar divide and argue that it is increasingly a barrier to further European integration. They contend that mass opinion regarding Europe has become a major factor in shaping European integration – the once-silent masses that provided a 'permissive consensus' for the elite project of European integration have become restless, creating a 'constraining dissensus'. As Schmitter (2003) argues, where neo-functionalism expected the masses to drive further integration in the face of the reluctance of national elites, in practice the dynamic has taken precisely the opposite form, with national elites promoting integration in the face of scepticism at home.

These analytical developments are welcome and push significantly beyond functionalist theories of integration. However, they skip too quickly over the structure of existing societies in Europe, as documented extensively in comparative political economy and sociology (e.g., Esping-Andersen, 1990, 1999; Amable, 2004). It is not necessary to essentialise national societies to recognise that a number of durable social formations have taken hold in countries across Europe, held together through social compacts of different types. These compacts are institutionally located within nations for the most part but also cluster in mini-regions within Europe – the social democratic Scandinavian countries, the Christian democratic Continental core and so on.

These debates – and the study of the EU in general – have largely been focused on economics and political science. The study of Europeanisation has, for example, involved a fairly narrow definition of the process – examining how the evolution of European institutions has shaped national politics (Favell and Guiraudon, 2009). 'Social factors' have been incorporated largely by adding the study of norms into the existing frameworks through the constructivist paradigm in political science. But this is a narrow basis for dealing with the more profound social transformations involved in European integration. More recent sociological approaches have focused on the question of whether a 'European society' is emerging. A sociological approach defines the EU and the degree of integration in terms of the extent to which it has created a common field of action across Europe – or at least the extent to which fields of action at the European level are superseding those at the national level.

Sociological approaches are well placed to examine the spatial and political-cultural remaking of these 'fields of action' (Parsons, 2010). However, this must involve the study of how these different national and transnational social formations interact with one another and are transformed within that interaction. A sociological approach must take seriously the middle range of analysis – seeing European integration as neither simply the negotiations of elites nor only the formation of new European social forms, but as the interaction and transformation of existing societies within Europe and the unsettling, reformulation and potential integration of their social compacts (as is suggested but not made explicit in Favell and Guiraudon's (2009) agenda for a sociology of the EU). This suggests that the interaction within the

European field of the institutionalised social compacts in national societies is a critical feature of the current impasse and this chapter explores some of the deeper reasons why that proved to be the case.

Ireland, Europe and the multiple interface periphery

We have seen that Europe is at its core a development project and Ireland occupies an unusual position within this. Peillon (1994) asked where Ireland sits within a comparative frame of reference in Europe. Should it be compared to the historical core of Europe, with which it shared certain key characteristics – a small open economy and durable liberal economic institutions? Or should it be compared to the Mediterranean periphery, with which Ireland shared a history of under-development and key structural characteristics of less developed economies, including a reliance on agriculture and weak industrial development that depended heavily on foreign investment? Ireland did not sit easily within either of these groups. Arguably, it was closer to the Mediterranean economies economically, given its structural under-development, and politically closer to the European core, given its durable liberal democratic institutions. However, even this distinction over-simplified the Irish case. Economically, Ireland faced major structural problems of development similar to those of the Mediterranean economies, but had a significantly higher national income (Peillon, 1994). Politically, it had durable liberal democratic institutions, but also shared a populist (although not militarist) political culture, with strong elements of 'brokerage' (Komito, 1992). The question is particularly crucial since in the 1990s Ireland was often compared to Spain, Portugal and Greece (Barry, 2003), but after the Celtic Tiger years seemed to have entered the world of small open advanced capitalist European economies. This came to a screeching halt in 2008, however, as Ireland was cast back into the company of the other European peripheral economies, collectively disparaged by some as the PIIGS (Portugal, Ireland, Italy, Greece and Spain).

Analysing the Irish case in terms of dependency and under-development, Denis O'Hearn (2001) argues that Ireland has functioned as a semi-peripheral node within the nexus of the British and American economies, particularly in recent decades as a platform for American firms exporting into Europe. The Irish economy experiences the classic features of a dependent semi-peripheral economy, including fragmentation and disarticulation of the export economy and the domestic economy. Most specifically, Ireland relies exceptionally heavily on foreign investment from the US. The weaknesses of this model of industrial development are relatively well known – weak local links with domestic firms, poor diffusion of technological know-how through the broader economy, and high levels of transfer pricing and significant financial flows through the Irish economy that, while providing some additional tax revenue to the Irish state, have little relationship to the real productive economy.

Ruane (2010) argued that while Ireland is certainly a semi-peripheral economy, the nature of its peripheral status has changed over time. In particular, he argues that Ireland has shifted from a 'simple periphery' of the UK to a 'multiple interface periphery' located between the UK, the US and Europe. In contrast to O'Hearn, Ruane argues that this new peripheral position has been adopted strategically by the Irish state and has allowed Ireland greater opportunities to manoeuvre and reposition itself within a more diverse set of international connections – even if all these connections are in themselves unequal. This analysis is largely in keeping with the discussion in Ó Riain (2004), which, while recognising the relations of unequal exchange and industrial weakness in Ireland, argues that there are strategic possibilities within international connections that states and other economic actors can use to promote various forms of economic development.

However, in Ó Riain's analysis, the focus is at the sectoral level and in particular on high-technology industries. Ó Riain (2004) finds significant sectoral differences within Ireland in the forms of globalisation that are pursued and the relative developmental success of those sectoral globalisations – in terms of high-quality employment generated, R&D spending per employee and local links, including the growth of indigenous Irish firms. O'Hearn's analysis operates primarily at the national level, as does Ruane's. In practice Ireland has sought to manage, and possibly escape, its peripheral position along both the national and sectoral paths. Industrial policy has sought to promote some sectors over others and to move up the value chain within those sectors, with the goal of producing industries that allow Ireland to break out of its historical pattern of unequal exchange in agricultural trade, particularly with the UK. There is a complex set of links between the sectoral and national levels of development, and of analysis.

Developments in some sectors can be generalised to others or may operate in isolation from broader national dynamics. Policies developed to promote particular sectors may cause tensions at the national level – for example, tensions with Germany and France regarding low corporate tax in Ireland. Furthermore, shifts in the importance of particular sectors – from agriculture to industry to finance – have transformed relations between nations.

Nonetheless, this simply adds a layer of complexity to Ruane's basic perspective. As O'Hearn argues, Ireland positioned itself as a gateway to Europe for US firms. But Ruane is correct to argue that this both locked Ireland into a set of international connections and allowed it some strategic space for manoeuvre within these connections. How did these connections combine to form the Irish 'multiple interface' strategy during the Celtic Tiger years?

At the national level, Ireland's engagement with the international economy was historically primarily through its relationship with Great Britain, both as colony and as a post-colonial economy dominated by unequal exchange with the UK. The Irish economy was deeply connected with, and dependent upon, the UK. This relationship was not completely one-sided – Ireland remains the sixth-largest trading partner for the UK. Ireland deviated both from the Continental small open economies and the Mediterranean periphery in its history as a colony. The historical conflict was with Britain, which was itself on the periphery of the European historical compromise and only weakly committed to the European project. Compared to the Continental core, Ireland was a late-developing but also 'liberal' political economy. This too was linked to a history as part of the British Empire – the 'liberal' political economies of the advanced capitalist world are largely those which fell under its influence (the US, Canada, Australia and New Zealand).

However, the Irish economy was closely tied to a declining hegemonic global power. Where US and UK national wealth was almost the same entering the Second World War, the US exited the war with a much higher GDP per capita and the gap between the US and the UK grew significantly over the following 50 years (see Figure 4.1). Perhaps not surprisingly then, Ireland sought to turn outwards towards the international economy more broadly. This policy shift is typically dated to the late 1950s, when Ireland apparently began its pursuit of 'industrialisation by invitation', although in practice the politics of this shift are located well before in the 1940s (O'Hearn, 2001; Ó Riain, 2004).

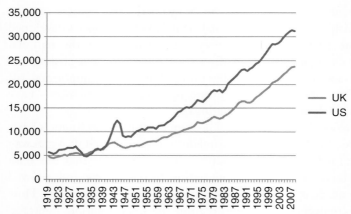

Figure 4.1 GDP per capita in the UK and the US, 1919–2009
Source: OECD, *National Accounts*

Furthermore, the turning outwards initially involved a deeper engagement with the UK. The key document that launched the outward
turn in Irish economic policy, *Economic Development* (1958), was
heavily focused on the promotion of agricultural exports, which themselves were almost completely destined for the UK. Furthermore, even
the first decade of foreign investment was dominated by the link to the
UK, with UK firms accounting for the bulk of foreign investment in
Ireland and in practice significantly crowding out domestic firms
as these UK investors largely sought access to the Irish market, rather
than using Ireland as an export platform (Barry *et al.*, 2005).

Over time, however, the Irish economy became increasingly
Americanised. The first significant US investment came in 1971 when
Digital Equipment Corporation set up a factory in Galway. However, in
the 1980s the flow of investment from the US ran at around $100 million
per annum, whereas the UK and rest of Europe accounted for approximately $70 million each (see Figure 4.2). US investment stayed stable
through the late 1980s, dipping slightly in the recession of 1990 with the
departure of a number of mid-range computer firms including Digital.
During this time, investment from the UK and the rest of Europe declined
very significantly. While investment from the rest of Europe, primarily
Germany, recovered somewhat in the early 1990s, this declined again as
the boom got underway. The most dramatic pattern in the figures,
however, is the massive increase in US investment in the 1990s, rising to

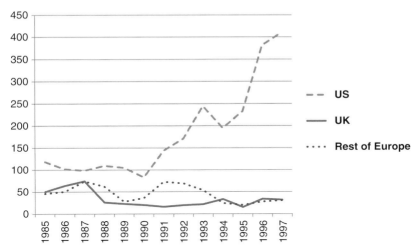

Figure 4.2 Foreign investment into Ireland from the US, the UK and Europe, 1985–97 ($m)
Source: OECD, Dataset on FDI Flows by Partner Country

approximately $400 million per annum by 1997 (when this data series breaks). This Americanisation of the Irish industrial structure was rooted in long-term patterns, but took a dramatic turn in the 1990s boom.

Nonetheless, Ireland's Europeanisation was also crucial along a number of dimensions. This included significant emigration flows and visitors for both business and tourism from the rest of Europe, which grew faster than intra-European flows of capital. However, by far the most significant development in terms of Ireland's relationship with Europe was its entry into the EU in 1973. While ultimately loosening its ties with the UK, this initial move towards Europe was at the time heavily influenced by the UK decision to join the 'Common Market'. Table 4.1 shows that Ireland was the first of the peripheral European countries to enter the EU. Indeed, when Ireland joined the EU, the Greek military junta still had a year left in power (from 1967 to 1974), Franco was still to rule for a year in Spain, and Portugal was to undergo revolutions in 1974 and 1975, with elections in 1976. Nevertheless, the European expansion into the periphery continued over the following decade after Ireland's entry, with Greece entering in 1981 and Spain and Portugal entering in 1986. Furthermore, these new entrants were relatively enthusiastic participants, all joining the euro in the late 1990s.

Table 4.1 *Waves of expansion of the EU*

	EU membership	Euro membership
The Continental core		
Germany, France, Italy, Belgium, the Netherlands, Luxembourg	1951	1999
Austria	1995	1999
The Northwestern and Mediterranean peripheries		
The UK	1973	–
Ireland	1973	1999
Greece	1981	2001
Spain, Portugal	1986	1999
Central and Eastern Europe		
Cyprus, the Czech Republic, Hungary, Latvia, Lithuania, Malta, Poland	2004	–
Cyprus, Estonia, Malta, Slovakia, Slovenia	2004	2007–11
Bulgaria, Romania	2007	–
The Nordics		
Denmark	1973	–
Sweden	1995	–
Finland	1995	1999
Norway	–	–

These new peripheral members of the European community formed a second wave of expansion of the EU, following the core Continental group of countries who joined much earlier (with the exception of Austria). The third wave of expansion incorporated the 'accession' countries of Central and Eastern Europe, who began their entry process in 1998. All three of these groups of countries joined the euro. However, it is noticeable that the Nordic countries are much more diverse and arguably strategic in their engagement with Europe. While Denmark entered the EU in 1973, Sweden and Finland did not join until 1995 and Norway has never joined. Of the Nordic countries, only Finland is within the Eurozone currency.

Even as a peripheral European country, Ireland was distinctive in a number of ways. The historical compromise that secured peace on the Continent after the Second World War allowed Continental European countries to coexist for the first time without significant fear of warfare. The grand historical compromise of the post-war era proved of less relevance to specific Irish interests. In this respect, perhaps, Ireland was the first of the EU members to enter the European project from outside this Central European set of concerns and compromises. This in turn meant that Ireland had a different orientation to Europe, which was mediated more narrowly through a socio-economic lens (O'Brennan, 2009).

This meant that sectoral dynamics were highly significant as Ireland sought to 'catch up' in industrial development. Overall, the entry of Ireland was a major challenge for the EU as the first country admitted to the EU with significantly worse structural development and lower national income per capita than elsewhere in the EU (although there were regions within other countries, such as the Mezzogiorno in Italy and the 'Celtic peripheries' of the UK, which were significantly poorer regions hidden within wealthier nation states). Perhaps not surprisingly then, agriculture was one of the major sectoral connections to the EU and the European economy in the initial decade of Ireland's membership. Crucial here was the Common Agricultural Policy (CAP), which significantly subsidised agricultural incomes. Ireland was fortunate that as powerful a country as France had similar concerns about agriculture and was a strong supporter of the CAP. In practice in Ireland, the CAP provided for the relatively orderly management of the decline of agriculture and avoided even more massive outflows of the labour force from agriculture into industry and services or, as was historically often the case in Ireland, into unemployment.

The EU Commission under Jacques Delors extended its policies addressing uneven development significantly beyond the CAP – primarily through the provision of 'structural funds' and indirectly through supports for R&D. Figure 4.3 shows that in the late 1980s, just as Ireland was introducing spending cuts at home, there was a major influx of EU funding. Much of this was related to agriculture, but there were also significant increases in the total non-agricultural funds and in the European social funds that supported training and other measures for labour market inclusion. This increase persisted through the 1990s and only returned to the nominal levels of 1989 in 2007.

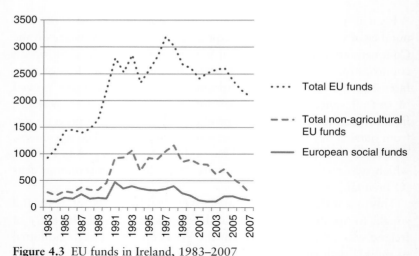

Figure 4.3 EU funds in Ireland, 1983–2007
Source: Department of Finance, *Budget and Economic Statistics*, various years

Figure 4.4 shows the significance of these funds for public capital spending. While in the 1980s, EU capital funding accounted for approximately 6 per cent of Irish public capital spending, this increased rapidly in the late 1980s and from 1991 to 1993 accounted for 20–25 per cent of all Irish public capital spending. Even in the booming late 1990s, EU funds accounted for over 15 per cent of Irish public capital expenditure. It is important to also remember that the vast bulk of productive capital spending in the Irish economy during this period and later came from the public sector (White, 2010). Figure 4.4 also shows the very significant tailing-off of EU capital funds in the 2000s as Ireland became ineligible for structural funds and as the public finances in Ireland improved and capital spending increased further.

Under the EU second and third Framework Programmes for Research and Development in the 1990s, Ireland received the fourth-highest amount of funding per capita and the highest amount per R&D employee of any country in the EU (Peterson and Sharp, 1998: 144). Facilitated by the National Board for Science and Technology – a relatively marginal state agency focused on indigenous innovation – some of the keenest participants in EU projects were the university computer science departments, from which projects leading indigenous software companies of the time emerged (Ó Riain, 2004).

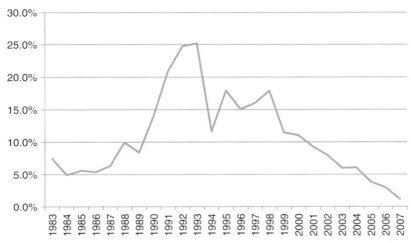

Figure 4.4 EU 'capital' funds as a percentage of Irish public capital spending
Source: Department of Finance, Budget and Economic Statistics, various years

The Structural and R&D Funds were also significant in that they were the means by which a variety of new, sometimes experimental, measures could be taken without having to fight the rest of the state agencies for funding (see O'Donnell (2000) for a broader discussion of the impact of the EU on 'experimentalism' in Ireland). The new development regime could develop alongside the old and did not have to challenge the old development model directly for funds and priority, except in rare cases. Furthermore, the EU funds came with significant requirements in terms of performance and outcome evaluation and accounting. While this sometimes created administrative nightmares, it also helped to foster a climate where regular evaluation of policies became the norm and where clientelism was mitigated. It was not only the financial impact of the EU funds which was crucial, therefore, but the institutional space it facilitated for new initiatives.

As the European crisis shows, the presence of space for strategic action does not necessarily mean that the most beneficial paths will always be followed. Ireland's 'gateway to Europe' strategy was a strategic multi-polar orientation to the world economy, operating at both the sectoral and national levels. However, it was also a strategy that both changed and was challenged over time.

Ireland's relationship with Europe changed significantly in the 2000s. This was linked not only to domestic political shifts, which are examined in the next chapter, but equally to the changing character of the European economic project itself – as public developmentalism within a trading union was supplanted by private financialisation in a monetary union. At the sectoral level, the primary challenges arose from the financialisation of not only the Irish economy but also of the UK, US and European economies to which it was linked. Chapter 3 already examined how this was organised in Ireland and the next section examines the form that financialisation took in the heart of the European project, the core Continental economies of France and especially Germany. In terms of relations between nations, Ireland's multiple interface strategy was challenged by the integration of diverse forms of the coordination of capitalism, both in the relation between Anglo-American and European capitalisms and in the interaction of various worlds of capitalism within the EU. The final section of the chapter examines these tensions in some detail.

Financialising Europe

Papaioannou *et al.* argue that 'financial integration, measured as bilateral bank holdings and transactions, increased by 40% more amongst Eurozone members than countries that stayed out', attributing that growth 'to the euro's introduction eliminating exchange rate risk and coinciding with financial regulatory harmonisation' (2009). What was the character of financialisation in Europe in the 2000s?

The classic case of financialisation is that of the US, driven both by its economic liberalism and the crisis of its industrial strength and economic growth in the 1970s to 'financialise' its economy (Arrighi and Silver, 2000). However, as Krippner (2011) has shown, even the US case is not a simple case of liberalisation. In practice, US policy makers were seeking a degree of discipline on inflationary pressures when they brought in measures that would ultimately liberalise the flow of finance and increase the role of financial markets in the economy. This, as is well known by now, did not provide the desired outcome. The 'liberal' element of the policy was the faith in the market as a system of macro-governance, even if the specific beliefs about what that market governance would provide were in error.

Finance in the UK economy is somewhat different, given its historical importance as a sector or industry rather than necessarily as a structure of macro-governance. The importance of the City of London in the UK's industrial structure has always been significant and dramatically increased during the 1980s, despite a variety of property bubbles and financial crashes including the catastrophic Black Monday in 1987. The promotion of finance as a sector was a critical element in the economic and political strategies of Margaret Thatcher and her Conservative government throughout this era. In particular, the creation of new classes and regions – the professional classes of southeast England, in place of more politically awkward groups such as the manual working classes based in mining and manufacturing – was in many respects an explicit strategy. Once again, finance was as much a political instrument as a natural process of market liberalisation.

As Figure 2.1 showed, financialisation was most developed in the liberal Anglo-American economies – finance in the European economy did not appear to match the Anglo-American model. Nonetheless, the 2000s saw a distinctive mode of financialisation of the European economy that was intimately linked with economic and monetary union, itself linked to a project of broader political and institutional integration. The particular form that this financialisation took, and the process that produced it, had a significant impact on both the creation of the crisis in Europe and the efforts to tackle it – creating new interdependencies between European economies and placing European banks in newly vulnerable positions that threatened the viability of these increasingly interdependent national economies.

The marketisation and Europeanisation of banking

Many observers argue that one of the dimensions of economic liberalisation has been a shift from bank-centred finance to capital markets (Davis, 2011). It is true that capital markets expanded across Europe from the 1990s to the 2000s (see Figure 4.5). A number of smaller European countries had larger capital markets than the US relative to the size of their economy. This was driven in part by asset bubbles but also by a historical reliance on equity credit in countries such as Austria and the Netherlands. The liberal UK had always been heavily reliant on equity finance, in a similar fashion to the US.

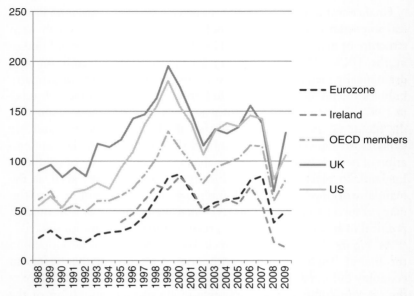

Figure 4.5 Market capitalisation of listed companies (% of GDP)
Source: World Bank

Nonetheless, the EU as a whole was still distinctive in its weak reliance on equity finance and the central importance of bank credit (see Table 4.2). Indeed, equity finance was less significant in the EU than in the US or Japan, although Japan also makes significant use of bank credit. Most strikingly different in the EU is Germany, which saw very modest capital market growth across the two decades. In large part due to this dominance of the core economies in European finance, the EU remains a heavily bank-dominated financial system. The domestic and international credit booms were partly associated with the expansion of equity finance, but were largely organised through bank credit relationships. So, while there are significant shifts towards marketisation and a broader financialisation, the European form of financialisation was still centred on banks and the financial system was more narrowly conceived. Nonetheless, European banks increasingly raised their funds through financial markets and in addition diversified their operations to place additional emphasis on speculative activities and competed with US and UK banks to take advantage of 'innovation' in financial instruments and activities.

Table 4.2 *Relative shares of credit, equity and bond finance, 2005–9 (average of annual data)*

	Bank credit	Equity finance	Private bonds
EU	51	24	25
US	18	38	44
Japan	44	37	19

Source: ECB, 2011: 13

These banks were now operating in a world of the euro and capital market integration in Europe as well as competing with US financial institutions that were making massive profits from more speculative activities – while still bank-centred, the environment for those banks was changing rapidly. Taken together, these changes implied that banks both had greater autonomy and were more exposed to market opportunities and pressures – while the overall financial system remained bank-centred. As Hardie and Howarth (2010) argue:

The varieties of capitalism literature, with its focus on the sources of corporate financing, does not address the question of how banks finance themselves. The (largely implied) conception of banks is that they have stable, unchanging liabilities, able to finance their patient lending. This static view of banks has been challenged in the financialisation literature (e.g., Ertürk and Solari, 2007), in line with the greater emphasis in this literature on processes of institutional change in financial markets. We argue, focusing in particular here on the question of the sources of bank finance, that changes in banking are sufficient for us to question whether a distinction between 'bank-based' and 'market-based' is now useful.

Domestic transformations within Germany are particularly striking and important, as banks departed from their previous close ties to industrial firms, where German banks in particular served as 'Hausbanks' for leading industrial firms, providing long-term 'patient capital'. Beyer and Hopner (2003) argue that the German model of corporate governance underwent very significant changes during the 1990s as a variety of diverse small changes from the mid-1980s onwards coalesced into a significantly transformed overall regime by the late 1990s. These resulted in 'the increasing shareholder orientation of companies; the strategic reorientation of the big banks from the Hausbank paradigm to investment banking that resulted in a loosening or abandoning of ties with industrial companies; the withdrawal of the state from infrastructural sectors via privatisation; and the break of continuity in German company regulation that supported and accelerated shareholder orientation and network dissolution' (Beyer and Hopner, 2003: 180; see also Streeck, 2009: 78–9).

However, Deeg (2007) argues that German banks were not subject to the same degree of financialisation as their US counterparts. Figures 3.1 and 4.5 showed that while equity markets failed to dislodge German banks from their central position in the economy, those same German banks watched US financial institutions' profits race ahead of their own through the 1990s. In response, in the 2000s, European banks involved themselves much more deeply in international financial markets. Between 2001 and 2008, the share of Deutsche Bank's assets that were international increased from 66 per cent to 82 per cent (Annual Reports). It is clear that German banks were less involved in the subprime and related financial markets than the US firms – and often as ill-considered buyers of dubious bond and related products (Deeg, 2007; Lewis, 2010). However, it is not the case that German banks were entirely insulated from this activity. IMF figures show a dramatic increase in German banks' use of securitisation, with issuance in 2006 that was over six times greater than 2004 levels (IMF, 2009: 13). The ability to purchase 'notes' issued by Irish and other peripheral banks, with high credit ratings attached, was attractive to European banks that were seeking assets that could be components in their own securitised financial instruments.

The bubble in German banking may have been shorter and less dramatic than in the liberal economies. It was also concentrated among the commercial banks, with capital adequacy ratios improving in all German banks through the 2000s, except for the commercial banks (IMF, 2009: Appendix, Table 4). Significant elements of the banking system – including the savings and state banks – remained largely outside the bubble and continued to lend to small businesses before and through the crisis (Federation of Small Businesses, 2012: 12). Nonetheless, German financialisation became enormously consequential for countries like Ireland. The triangle of Irish banks, international funders and credit rating agencies connected the Irish social structure of liquidity based on personalised property development lending to the international trade in securitised financial instruments

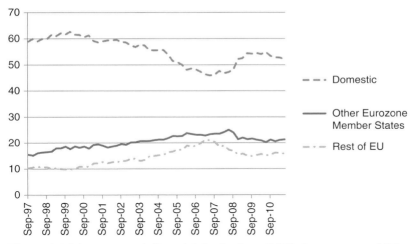

Figure 4.6 Monetary and financial institutions (MFI) loans to non-MFIs: outstanding amounts by residency of the counterpart
Source: ECB statistics

through the standardising effects of credit ratings. In the process, it weakened the ties between financial and industrial capital in both the European periphery and the core. As Hardie and Howarth summarise it: 'The move to market-based assets has had a double effect on bank lending. The first is most relevant potentially with regard to the German LandesBanken: the profitability of trading and securities investment activities encouraged the LandesBanken to turn away from lending to non-financial firms. Second, and most obviously, the securitization of assets has contributed to the financial crisis and a considerable drop of bank lending' (Hardie and Howarth, 2010).

If banks in European countries had become more marketised during the 2000s in particular, they also became more 'European' (Fligstein, 2008). While banking has been partly globalised, the most striking element is its Europeanisation. Figure 4.6 shows that the loans of monetary and financial institutions to non-financial institutions shifted significantly over the 2000s, with the proportion of loans given within the same country decreasing from 62 per cent in 1999 to 47 per cent on the eve of the crisis in 2007. There were significant increases in the proportion of loans going to other Eurozone member states and to

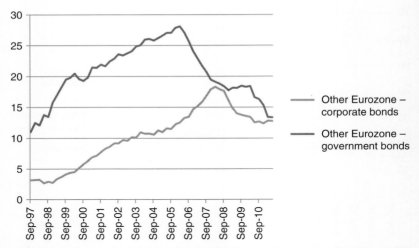

Figure 4.7 Share of MFI cross-border holdings of debt securities issued by Eurozone and EU non-MFIs
Source: ECB statistics

the rest of the EU. These trends were even more significant in the proportion of debt securities issued by Eurozone and EU monetary and financial institutions (Figures 4.6 and 4.7). For both corporate and government bonds, growth in lending to other Eurozone countries greatly outstripped domestic expansion of debt securities over the 2000s, with the increase beginning in earnest after the introduction of the euro.

This Europeanisation also extended to the growing equity markets. Table 4.3 shows that cross-border holdings of equity issued by Eurozone residents increased significantly, diminishing the role of domestic investors. The bulk of this increase in cross-border holdings came from investors within the Eurozone, increasing by 16.5 per cent, with only a 1.6 per cent increase among investors outside the Eurozone.

The politics of European financialisation

But why would European states promote capital liberalisation? In many respects, their success in the post-war years was built on bank-based finance and the steering of capital towards industrial investment. Despite this, Abdelal (2007) argues that financial liberalisation

Table 4.3 *Holdings of equity issued by Eurozone residents*

Year	Intra-Eurozone	Extra-Eurozone
2001	22.1%	5.0%
2002	25.6%	4.8%
2003	26.3%	5.0%
2004	28.1%	5.6%
2005	29.2%	5.5%
2006	31.5%	6.4%
2007	33.1%	6.9%
2008	38.8%	6.7%
2009	38.8%	6.6%

Source: ECB statistics

paradoxically was more advanced in the EU than anywhere else as it was institutionalised as a treaty provision – and that the major promoter of capital liberalisation was France, which was famous for its statism. Abdelal argues that for the French – including Jacques Delors, the leading European diplomat of the era – capital liberalisation in Europe represented an opportunity to project state management of the economy and capital onto the European scale. France was in favour of managed liberalisation in order to promote the place of Europe in the world. The French position was based on creating a centre of power in Europe derived from internal capital liberalisation, but retaining external bargaining power by keeping a degree of state control over flows of capital across that border. It also, arguably, allowed it a place of influence between the more powerful economies of Germany and the US.

Furthermore, more perplexing still, capital liberalisation became a project of the left in France (Abdelal, 2007). This was rooted in the trauma experienced by the Socialist Party in relation to nationalisation in the 1970s and 1980s, when capital flight undermined a determined project of the state. Chastened by the failure of François Mitterand's socialism in one country, brought down by private capital, the Socialist Party now backed the liberalisation of capital in Europe – albeit with a view to being able to steer and discipline capital markets in the long run. Indeed, the European scale of politics has increasingly been seen by left-leaning parties across Europe as the scale at which social democracy could be realised – including by the Social Democratic Party (SPD) in Germany and even, occasionally, the Labour Party in the UK. This took a further twist in the 1990s as social democrats (albeit in centrist clothing) went in search of a new growth model, with Tony Blair and Gerhard Schröder in Europe and Bill Clinton in the US promoting capital liberalisation and the financial sectors as key elements of the (in)famous 'Third Way'.

Perhaps surprisingly, given its strong tradition of patient industrial banking and cultural emphasis on fiscal prudence, Germany was also in favour of financial liberalisation. Indeed, it was sometimes significantly more favourable than France or even the UK, being reluctant, for example, to introduce capital controls during the Bretton Woods era. Furthermore, in debates concerning the EU capital liberalisation directive of 1988, Germany wished to remove the possibility of capital controls even as France and the UK wished to retain this option, for bargaining leverage at least (Abdelal, 2007: 69).

Abdelal places a great deal of emphasis on the role of cultural factors and the fear of inflation and fascism in explaining Germany's support for liberalisation. In this respect, the German support for liberalisation was the mirror image of the French view – where Germany saw liberalisation as facilitating the de-politicisation of money, France saw it as an element in resubjecting capital to political control at the European level.

However, Germany's support can also be understood in more strategic terms, facilitating a variety of political projects even while apparently de-politicising money – in particular through its industrial competitiveness, macroeconomic management and changing banking system. Capital liberalisation could support Germany's industrial competitiveness through laying the foundations for a single currency, ultimately the euro. The euro has been a significant subsidy for German exports, relative to the deutschmark which, had it continued, would have been a much stronger currency and would have made German exports much more expensive. In addition, the banking sector itself became an important export sector in Germany, as was the case in more liberal economies such as the UK and Ireland. While capital liberalisation meant a significant shift away from the bank-centred Hausbank system that had underpinned much of German industrial growth, it could still be seen as a strategy to boost the competitiveness of German exports.

Furthermore, at the macroeconomic level, the liberalisation of finance was seen as reinforcing German 'ordoliberalism'. As noted in Chapter 3, Hans Tietmeyer, the senior German official dealing with the issue, explained the German position as follows:

We saw in full capital liberalisation the possibility for a test of the stability of the ERM – a test by the markets of policy credibility. We wanted a test by world markets, not just European markets. That was why the erga omnes principle was so crucial. Liberalization erga omnes would demonstrate that we had in Europe a stable fixed exchange-rate system with market-proved stability, rather than artificial stability provided by controls. (Quoted in Abdelal, 2007: 70)

German support for capital liberalisation was based on a significantly different rationale from that of the French, who saw it as a strategy for managing the market even while expanding it. European monetary and financial integration would strengthen Europe economically, but it was crucial that this centre of capital in the world economy be exposed to world markets, precisely so that those world financial markets could be a source of 'non-artificial' stability. This external market discipline was a crucial part of the German social compact and was now to be extended to the European level.

As Van der Pijl *et al.* (2011) show, German capital moved to the centre of the Atlantic economy, measured by interlocking directorates among leading global firms. In 1992, German firms formed a national cluster of networks of directors at the margins of a global network dominated by US firms. By 2000, Germany had moved to the centre of an increasingly interconnected European network that was tied somewhat more closely to US firms. By 2005, however, German firms were at the centre of the interlocking directorates of the Atlantic economy. The large Swiss and French firms were largely connected to the global network through their ties to key German firms. Although Van der Pijl *et al.* do not remark upon it, it is also notable that the core companies at the heart of these networks were increasingly in the financial sector – there were both more financial institutions in the network and the key networks ran through Allianz, JPMorgan, Goldman Sachs and a variety of similar firms.

The euro and the project of capital liberalisation in Europe went hand-in-hand. A European financial 'field of action' emerged and was further consolidated through the 2000s. Abdelal's (2007) account of this process is helpful but not completely satisfactory. He emphasises the critical political support for capital liberalisation emerging from the French state. However, while he sees the actions of the French elites as driven by strategic political considerations, he sees the US and UK positions determined by industry interests and sees German support for liberalisation as largely cultural and rooted in an ordoliberalism associated with a focus on exports and fear of inflation. A fuller explanation of European financialisation requires an understanding of the European financial system as part of a broader international financial industry and of each country's approach to capital liberalisation as driven by a combination of the strategic concerns of the state, industry interests and the cultural meaning of finance. Indeed, as will be seen in Chapter 6, the different national constellations of financialisation significantly affected the course of the crisis in Europe itself, not only its emergence.

The German state was just as interested as the French in building Europe as a power in the world, but while France sought to project its statehood onto a global stage through a powerful currency and economic union, Germany sought to secure the conditions that would continue to 'discipline' and promote export industries. Meanwhile, German financial interests were happy to support capital liberalisation, not in the interests of finding new forms of discipline but in search of the massive profits being made by their US counterparts through the 1990s and afterwards. In the construction of the euro, these projects dovetailed relatively easily. However, they remained as underlying tensions that contributed both to the creation of the crisis and to Europe's difficulty in responding to it.

Rather than developing as simply a mirror of the earlier, slower and deeper US process, financialisation in Europe took its own distinctive path. First, it did not proceed on the scale of either the US or the UK. However, it was linked to these more aggressive forms of financialisation through competition in the financial sector itself, driven by European banks responding to US firm profits. Second, it proceeded largely through the banking system rather than through the expansion of alternative lines of consumer credit or markets for corporate governance (although there were also trends in both of these directions). Financialisation in the Anglo-American liberal economies had a knock-on effect on European bank-centred systems by changing the incentives for banks within those systems.

Third, the financialisation of European economies was linked to a broader project of apparently managed economic integration and in particular the monetary union of the 2000s. The financial integration that the euro facilitated was politically significant – the greatest threat to social democratic strategies came less from globalisation in general than from the danger posed by financialisation to the ability of governments to mobilise capital for productive investment (Scharpf, 1991). Fourth, where this financialisation took off most dramatically (i.e., in the European periphery), it was funded through external financial systems. Fifth, this financialisation was built on the expansion of real incomes and living standards in the 1990s rather than on the stagnating real wages in the US and, to a lesser extent, the UK during the 1980s. The growing importance of finance in the European economy in the 2000s was built in part upon the outcomes of the developmentalism of the 1990s. However, as will be discussed later on, this occurred in ways that involved coexistence and interaction with existing economic institutions, providing an additional layer of complexity to the politics of the European crisis.

Governing a financialised Europe

Such changes threw up serious challenges of economic governance – what of the institutions that had emerged to manage them? If finance overwhelmed trade as the organising set of relations within Europe in the 2000s, the second major shift was in the political governance of the region. The critical element here was the project of economic and, particularly, monetary union – the creation of the euro and the associated Stability and Growth Pact. The euro hastened financial integration and it was also the mechanism through which the policy challenges arising out of EMU were to be managed – it provided both the context for economic life and the governance structure through which discipline would be maintained, partly through rules around public debt and deficits and partly through the authority of associated institutions such as the ECB.

The problems of the euro are by now very well known. Indeed, many of its design flaws were well signalled in advance – including in Ireland. At a minimum, such flaws would include the absence of: a centralised authority responsible for the extensive regulation of financial institutions; a mechanism for fiscal transfers to deal with uneven shocks within the Eurozone; macroeconomic and sectoral adjustment mechanisms, such as 'automatic stabilisers' at the Eurozone level and mechanisms for addressing competitive imbalances. There was no lender of last resort for Member States and therefore no 'circuit breaker' to protect against negative feedback loops of spiralling borrowing costs, especially since the ECB was not designed to play this typical central banking role. Member States were highly vulnerable to destabilising credit inflows and outflows, which were facilitated by the financial integration that was promoted by the euro.

Without a banking union, a transfer union or a deep economic union, the project of EMU was highly vulnerable. The difficulties of establishing a monetary union without strong coordination of government fiscal policies has become clear. Equally importantly, the absence of a banking union or even a coherent, effective system of governance of the European banking sector created major problems – all the more so since, as mentioned previously, the financial system itself became increasingly 'European'. In addition to these flaws, which have been widely commented upon, we have already noted the great importance of uneven development within the EU in creating the crisis.

Nonetheless, many of these problems of the euro were anticipated (to some extent at least) and some attempts were made to construct governance mechanisms that could protect against these potential difficulties. Some of these took the form of fiscal rules, while others involved the encouragement of institutional convergence, with the 'open method of coordination' and intergovernmental cooperation promoting institutions such as independent central banks, wage coordination and the liberalisation of labour markets. While part of the logic of integration was that markets would provide crucial discipline within the European economy, policy makers also sought to spread institutions across Europe that they saw as reinforcing that discipline, in the process perhaps revealing a lack of complete faith in these disciplinary powers of marketisation.

Such an approach sought to manage socio-political diversity across the Eurozone and the EU in ways that avoided the exercise of 'political' judgment – or, more accurately, that turned political into technical judgments. It tried to use a universal framework to manage the cyclical dilemmas of the integrated economy, although these internal cyclical tensions were under-estimated due to the bias towards assuming that markets provided a test of stability rather than a source of instability. These universal rules were also to manage the diverse varieties of capitalism within the Eurozone (including both diverse forms of capitalist organisation and uneven development in the core and the periphery) by providing high-level targets that were to provide buffers against shocks to the public finances.

I will examine three dimensions of these governance arrangements within the EU in the 1990s and 2000s. First, I will look at the specific policy changes and rules that accompanied the euro itself – including the harmonisation of currency and monetary policies (especially through shared interest rates and a focus on low inflation), and the debt and deficit rules of the Stability and Growth Pact of the late 1990s that bound all Eurozone members. These have been the focus of recent attention and were the dominant policy instruments of the 2000s, after the introduction of the euro in 1999.

The second dimension is the set of institutional transformations that accompanied these policy measures. Most widely discussed is the establishment of the ECB, and particularly the limited and specific mandate that was given to it to ensure fiscal prudence and guard against inflation, reflecting the stamp of its parent institution, the German Bundesbank. However, there were an earlier set of institutional transformations at the national level in the 1990s. I will examine three of these – the spread of independent central banks, the emergence of neo-corporatist social bargains in the periphery and widespread product market deregulation. It will be argued that, although often seen as moves towards liberalism, these were in many respects closer to the institutions of Christian democratic and other social market economies.

Third, I will examine a neglected dimension of the euro governance structure – the social compacts that anchored the combination of monetary, fiscal and institutional discipline that had been at the heart of the German 'ordoliberal' model and was then largely transplanted to the European level in conjunction with the euro. However, this transplantation was incomplete. In particular, I will show that the new European policy and institutional regime was broadly compatible with the social bargains that were stitched into the 'social market' economies but were at odds with significant elements of the liberal and Mediterranean regimes. The social conditions that had anchored the model in Continental Europe were not present in peripheral and liberal Europe. Nor were they developed at the European level or promoted in the periphery through European policy. These persistent differences in the underlying social compacts were ultimately at the heart of the economic and fiscal imbalances that brought the euro to the edge of extinction.

These three dimensions can be related to the components that Jürgen Habermas has identified as the key building blocks of a political system that need to be put in place to move beyond the European crisis (Habermas, 2012: 22), even if they are much thinner versions of these building blocks than Habermas might have wished. The first component is the 'constitution of a community of legal persons', an approach reflected in the rules constructed as a form of fiscal coordination among governments. The second involves an 'authorization to collective action' which is made concrete in our analysis through the loosely coordinated convergence of governance institutions and forms of collective action in the political economy (including wage coordination, central bank authority and market mechanisms). The third component is 'the shared horizon of a lifeworld in which a collective will can take shape through communication'. In Europe's national societies, this collective will, reflecting both communication and power, was institutionalised in differing social compacts – and the persistent profound differences between these national social compacts emerge as the greatest weakness of the European project, one that helped create the crisis and that has stymied efforts at recovery and post-crisis solidarity.

Policies and rules

The euro was created in part to 'de-politicise' economic management, in part by taking certain policy instruments out of commission (such as exchange rate and monetary policies) and in part by creating limits around other sets of policies (including fiscal policies). This was intended to provide governments with tests of economic stability, but in the process placed a premium on financial regulation (which was greatly emphasised after the crisis, although much less so beforehand) and on fiscal discipline (which was tackled directly in the Stability and Growth Pact rules). The creation of the euro obviously harmonised exchange rate policies. More specifically, the euro policy regime, under the control of the ECB, institutionalised a 'hard currency' policy. In addition, the Eurozone countries shared a common set of interest rates for access to euro funds. The ECB was also mandated to pursue a low inflation policy. The combination of policies favoured growth strategies based on the weakening of currency to support exports rather than a loosening of monetary policy to support domestic demand.

As discussed above, it was largely assumed that 'the market' would be a source of stability within the Eurozone. However, despite this belief in the disciplining power of markets, Continental European governments have always taken a series of non-market measures to ensure this discipline. Faith in the self-regulating disciplinary powers of markets over governments has been accompanied in post-war Europe by strong political governance of markets themselves. Such rules were also central to the monetary union project. It was recognised that business cycle pressures would still exist and that national fiscal problems could undermine the currency, even if these problems were not treated with the urgency they deserved. Nonetheless, these pressures had prompted European policy makers to accompany the single European currency with a set of rules for managing national differences in the public finances – most crucially the rules that government deficits should not exceed 3 per cent and overall government debt should not exceed 60 per cent of GDP.

These rules themselves involve significant institutional shifts, as the management of currency and monetary policy were transferred to the European level and the ECB was given guardianship of this regime, which was focused on low inflation and a hard currency. While other European-level institutions focused on developmental goals (e.g., the European Investment Bank and the structural funds programme), their power was significantly weaker than the central authoritative role of the ECB. As major structural imbalances arose in the European economy through the 2000s, these European developmental policy instruments and institutions played a limited role, while the ECB intervened mainly through the relatively crude instruments of interest rates and monitoring of fiscal rules. When the Irish economy was booming in the early 2000s and needed a more restrictive interest rate regime to cool down the economy, the ECB maintained low interest rates to provide a boost to the large Continental economies that were in the doldrums at the time. It was difficult therefore for a single set of universal monetary and exchange rate policies to accommodate the major structural differences within the European economy without significant counterbalancing measures to address these structural differences and coordinate the real economies of the Eurozone.

More fundamentally still, the mix of policies associated directly with the euro fell unevenly on countries within the Eurozone. Table 4.4 shows how a variety of different economies in Europe fit with the key policy instruments of the euro itself. The indicators focus on the period from 1993 to 1997 as it falls between the currency crisis of 1992–3 and the advent of the euro in 1999. It is a period when the potential euro members were making strenuous efforts to reach the Maastricht criteria for joining the euro, but also when Germany was undertaking the costs and effort of reunification and when the Nordic economies were recovering from their financial crises of 1991–2. The table indicates the average deficit or surplus in the public finances (relating to the deficit rule), government debt as a percentage of GDP (relating to the debt rule), interest rate fluctuations (indicating to what extent variation in interest rates was used as a significant monetary policy), exchange rate fluctuations (related to currency policies as an instrument) and the current account balance as an indicator of structural divergences within the European economy. These 'pre-Euro' indicators provide a sense of which countries' pre-existing economic policy styles and regimes were the best 'fit' for the policy regime associated with the euro.

We can see that many of the European economies ran significant deficits through the mid-1990s, but that these were highest in the Mediterranean economies and that this vulnerability in the public finances extended to the debt level of Italy, Greece and also Belgium. In addition, the Mediterranean economies and Belgium were much more heavily subject to fluctuations in interest rates and in exchange rates. The use of a 'hard currency' policy was by far the most widespread in the Christian democratic Continental core, with the Nordic social democracies following behind, although these countries were more likely to use currency policies for strategic reasons. The UK's relatively soft currency and willingness to run fiscal deficits helps to explain why it remained outside the euro. Mediterranean countries had few if any of the conditions for operating under the euro regime. The Nordic economies are probably closest to the euro policy regime. However, Finland was the only social democratic country to enter the euro – and this was partly as a deliberate strategy to break the cycle of constant booms and devaluations, which were most painfully

Table 4.4 *Macroeconomic policy indicators, 1993–7*

	Deficit/ surplus, 1994–7 (% of GDP)	Debt 1996 (% of GDP)	Interest rate fluctuation, 1993–7	Exchange rate fluctuation, 1993–7 (Hard Currency Index, 1973–93)	Current account balance, 1993–7 (% of GDP)
Christian democratic					
Austria	−4.2	68.1	1.08	1.32 (.52)	−1.98
Belgium	−4.0	127.2	1.73	1.83 (.47)	5.60
Germany	−4.5	58.5	1.24	2.04 (.60)	−0.91
France	−4.6	58.0	1.26	1.23 (.39)	1.37
The Netherlands	−4.0	74.1	1.25	1.38 (.54)	5.51
Social democratic					
Denmark	−2.2	69.4		1.30 (.42)	1.35
Finland	−4.4	57.0	1.39	6.30 (.38)	2.95
Norway	4.4	–		2.24 (.40)	6.10
Sweden	−5.3	73.3		4.06 (.29)	2.65
Liberal					
Ireland	−0.7	72.7	0.33	4.04	2.43
UK	−4.8	51.3	–	6.60 (.15)	−0.93
Mediterranean					
Greece	−7.5	99.4	–	6.07	−1.96
Spain	−6.5	67.4	1.83	3.91	−0.57
Italy	−6.1	120.2	1.66	5.93	2.12
Portugal	−5.0	58.3	2.17	1.61	−2.77

Sources:
Deficit: Average of Annual Balances, General Government Financial Balance, Annex Table 27, OECD Economic Outlook 2011
Debt: Government Consolidated gross debt (Eurostat)
Interest rate fluctuation: Standard deviation of official refinancing rates for Eurozone countries, 1993–7 (Eurostat)
Exchange rate fluctuation: Standard deviation of Effective Exchange Rates, 1993–7 (Eurostat)
Hard Currency Index: Iversen, 2005: 56
Current account balance: average over the period (calculated as total current account over five years/total GDP over five years) (Eurostat)

experienced in the early 1990s (Vartiainen, 2011). The other social democracies retained control of their currency, although maintaining a high level of institutionalised fiscal discipline. It is noteworthy that in many respects Ireland appears to be in a healthy shape in the mid-1990s, with a strong budgetary balance, declining debt levels and a current account surplus. However, it is also clear that it had relatively little policy experience of dealing with hard currency constraints.

This mix of policies associated directly with the euro fell unevenly on the countries within the Eurozone. Of course, this period during the 1990s also saw a process of convergence where the economies entering the euro became more similar to each other than they had been, both in terms of macroeconomic indicators and institutions. Nonetheless, there were issues relating to an excessive uniformity in policy across a diverse regional economy which still contained significant structural and institutional differences. Furthermore, these changes associated with the efforts at institutional convergence can only have been partly embedded within the various societies and therefore it is important to understand how different countries' historical institutional trajectories equipped them for the politics of policy within the euro. Finally, as will be seen, these approaches to economic policy were historically buttressed in the core Continental countries by a set of institutions that could both reinforce these policies and compensate for them. Many of the countries taking on the policy regimes of the euro project did not have such compensating institutions.

The structural divergence within Europe is obvious in the major differences in the current account balance, even during the 1990s. However, the euro rules did not apply to such structural features of the Eurozone economy – as was recognised in the much broader range of rules and macroeconomic indicators developed through the 'fiscal compact' in the years after the crisis. Instead, policy rules focused on maintaining national fiscal balances as a buffer against volatility and uncertainty. Here, too, there were difficulties. France and Germany broke the deficit rules early in the 2000s, creating a legitimacy problem for enforcing the rules more widely. Nonetheless, the 1990s were in many respects dominated by the efforts of potential member countries to reach the budgetary criteria specified for euro membership and the 2000s saw a significant decrease in government deficits across the Eurozone.

However, Table 4.5 shows that significant differences persisted across countries in budget balances – both the actual balance and the

Table 4.5 *Actual and 'potential' budget balances in the 'varieties of capitalism' in Europe, 1999–2007*

	1999–2007 (% actual GDP)	1999–2007 (% potential GDP)	1999–2002 (% potential GDP)	2003–7 (% potential GDP)
Nordics/social democratic	2.5	0.3	0.1	0.5
Continentals/ Christian democratic	−1.5	−1.7	−1.7	−1.6
Mediterranean	−2.9	−4.0	−3.1	−4.7
Liberal (including Ireland)	0.1	−2.5	−0.6	−3.8
Ireland	1.6	−2.7	−0.7	−3.9

Source: actual balances – Eurostat; 'potential' balances – IMF

'potential' balance (calculated by the IMF to take into account the effects of the business cycle). These are contested concepts, but the pattern is clear enough. The Nordic economies did best in terms of 'fiscal discipline', running an actual surplus but also balancing their books, even on the basis of the underlying structural deficit (albeit partly because of the effects of the Norwegian oil boom on Nordic surpluses). While running deficits a little larger than the social democracies, Europe's Christian democracies remained comfortably within the Eurozone criteria. The liberal economies of Ireland and the UK appeared to do better, based on their actual balance, but this masked a significant bubble as their large underlying deficits indicate. In keeping with our analysis to date, this structural deficit emerged in the 2003–7 period. The Mediterranean economies also had significant difficulties with budget deficits, which were already present in the early 2000s.

The project of European integration reached a new high point in the 2000s, with economic and monetary integration, and greatly increased flows of labour and, particularly, capital within the EU. Countries were arguably 'better behaved' during the 1990s when seeking admission to the euro club than they were under the disciplines of the euro itself – although this is also explained by the intensified financialisation of this later period. However, the 'flattening' of the legal and policy space within the Eurozone and the EU masked a deeper process of uneven development and significant financial imbalances. Despite universal fiscal rules, the fiscal policies and outcomes of Member States were diverse – and bore the stamp of the different 'worlds' of European capitalism. Indeed, the social democracies outside the euro stuck more closely to the budgetary criteria than many of the Member States. In the liberal economies, the divergence between actual and underlying deficits was particularly striking, reflecting their exposure to the business cycle and the asset bubble. Although apparently neoliberal, the Eurozone policy rules were much closer to German 'ordoliberalism', linked not only to fiscal conservatism but also, in the Continental core at least, to the broader social compact. In many respects, the most liberal of the EU economies, the UK, deviated the most from these rules and policies. Despite their uniform character, these measures interacted with quite different national worlds of capitalism and their effects within national economic systems were significantly different.

Coordinated institutional convergence in the 1990s

The rules around euro membership are of course widely known and debated. Much less widely recognised is the process of institutional convergence that was promoted throughout the 1990s, largely through the open method of coordination. These institutional convergences took place in a number of different areas and to some extent moved in different directions at the same time. Most obvious is the promotion of market mechanisms through the deregulation of product and labour markets, linked to the 'negative integration of the European economy' (Scharpf, 1999).

Figures 4.8 and 4.9 examine trends in such market-led processes of deregulation. Figure 4.8 refers to the degree of protection afforded to employees across the different clusters of European capitalist economies. There are significant differences between the different types of capitalist economies, with the liberal economies of the UK and Ireland having by far the lowest levels of employment protection. Christian democratic and social democratic countries of the classic European model have substantial levels of employment protection and the highest levels of employment protection are found in the Mediterranean political economies. The 1990s through to the early 2000s was a period of significant liberalisation and deregulation of employment protection, with declining employment protection in

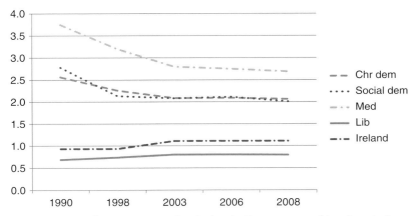

Figure 4.8 Employment Protection Index in European worlds of capitalism, 1990–2008
Source: OECD

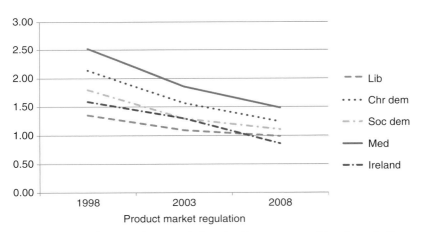

Figure 4.9 Product market regulation in European worlds of capitalism, 1998–2008
Source: OECD

social democracies and Christian democracies, and particularly among Mediterranean countries. Countries converged towards a more liberal model while significant differences between different clusters of countries and types of capitalism remained. Figure 4.9 shows

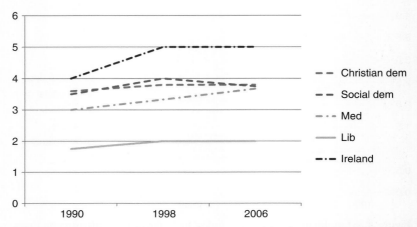

Figure 4.10 Wage coordination in European worlds of capitalism, 1990–2006
Source: Visser, 2012

similar patterns of difference among countries in the degree of product market regulation within those countries. However, it is also clear that there was a strong trend across all clusters of countries towards less regulation of product markets. Therefore, there was significant convergence on a liberal model of employment and product market regulation.

However, not all convergence is liberal. A distinctively European institution – or one that has been most fully developed in Europe – is corporatist bargaining and Figure 4.10 provides a measure of a specific feature of corporatist institutions, the presence of institutions that coordinate wages through negotiation. While I do not assess the effectiveness of these institutions, the claim is that such institutions enable greater control over wage increases and promote wage solidarity (Iversen, 1999). There was a mild increase in wage coordination among European economies through the 1990s and into the 2000s. In particular, the Mediterranean countries and Ireland showed a much stronger trend towards centralised wage bargaining, while Christian democratic and social democratic countries remained stable. The peripheral economies developed a series of 'social pacts', at least partly motivated by the prospect of monetary union and the need to manage cost pressures and enhance competitiveness (Avdagic *et al.*, 2011; Regan, 2012).

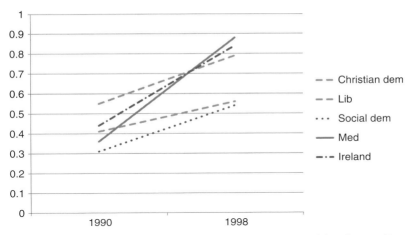

Figure 4.11 Central bank independence in European worlds of capitalism, 1990–8
Source: Polillo and Guillén (2005)

Finally, the 1990s was an era when political economies around the world gave their central banks significantly greater independence from governments (Polillo and Guillén, 2005). Central bank independence provides 'discipline' by creating an institution that is (typically) legally independent and committed to various elements of financial and fiscal discipline – including reducing inflation and maintaining the government financial balance close to surplus. Figure 4.11 shows that during the 1990s there were dramatic trends towards promotion of central bank independence. This was true across all of the worlds of capitalism. However, the most dramatic increases were not in liberal countries but in the Mediterranean and Irish cases, and to a slightly lesser extent the Christian democracies. Furthermore, this is not convergence on a liberal model, as central bank independence is much lower in both the liberal and social democratic countries, but on a Christian democratic model, which had by far the highest level of central bank independence in 1990 and is now clustered in a group with Ireland and the Mediterranean economies.

Formal institutional convergence is therefore a mixed story, with liberal convergence on weakened regulation of product markets and employment, Christian democratic convergence on central bank independence and increasing wage coordination in the periphery in the

1990s (also a strong feature of social democracies). In the EU, these reforms were largely initiated through the Open Method of Coordination, a form of loose coordination across governments and societal actors, rather than through administrative fiat or governmental decision – with the exception of product market deregulation which was put on a legal footing. These measures were intended to remake national institutions – typically in preparation for EMU. They were as representative of the Christian democratic policy mix as of the liberal model. The Mediterranean and Irish economies sought hasty institutional convergence with the 'European model' of institutional management of the economy, arguably without the supporting institutional and normative foundations that were present in the countries where they had been longer established. Furthermore, in some cases they were not the same as the earlier rounds of similar institutions – as the next chapter will explore, corporatist 'social pacts' could take very different forms across countries or over time within the same country. In many respects, alongside Europe's market liberalisation, Europe pursued a project of convergence on a Christian democratic ordoliberal model – through the combination of the creation of the euro, its fiscal rules and the ECB's mandate, alongside the 'open coordination' of trends towards central bank independence and coordinated wage bargaining (particularly in the European periphery).

Social compacts

There were therefore efforts in the 1990s to build institutions that would both promote market liberalisation but also transfer some of the institutions that had been crucial to the Continental and social democratic economies in managing their own export-oriented economies. It is possible to argue that these institutions simply failed to do their jobs as well as they had done in the previous decades in Christian democratic and social democratic economies in Europe. However, this begs the question of why it proved difficult for them to play a similar role in the 2000s. Part of this story is undoubtedly the additional pressures placed upon those institutions by the financialisation of the European economy and the anti-disciplinary effects of financial markets. However, the question goes deeper. Fiscal rules and institutional governance structures are important in their own right, but are rooted in broader and deeper structures of the political economy – the social compact in the society as a whole. Such social compacts link the distributive and productive bargains in the society, both within workplaces and firms and across the whole society. They typically consist of both formal and informal institutional elements that knit together a variety of cross-cutting coalitions and various social ties and solidarities.

I look here at a number of different elements of such social compacts, including measures of the welfare regime, the production regime and the macroeconomic order (Table 4.6). These include the contribution of business to the productive economy through investment in R&D and other forms of industrial upgrading, as well as the organisation of labour in the workplace as measured by the participation of workers in 'learning' organisations. Social spending is included as an indicator of public investment in social reproduction, while public deficits and fiscal balances are included as a summary measure of the balancing of this social spending with available resources. Current account balances for the 2000s are also included to indicate the structural economic position underpinning the social compacts.

This table shows that there are significant differences in the underlying social compacts across the various worlds of capitalism in Europe. In addition to the differences in fiscal policies noted above, it can be seen that there are major differences in the current account balances of the different clusters of countries. The Christian democratic and social democratic countries ran huge current account surpluses from 2003 to 2007, the height of the bubble era. These were reflected in major current account deficits in the liberal and Mediterranean cases. But these differences were themselves rooted in deeper differences in social and business investment and organisation. Social spending was, not surprisingly, higher in the Christian democratic and social democratic countries, but so too was business investment, with business R&D investment running well above the liberal and especially Mediterranean countries right across the period.

Furthermore, the organisation of society and the economy in the workplace was structured differently. Drawing on work by Holm *et al.* (2010), the final column shows what percentage of workers in each country work in a 'learning' system of work, which emphasised worker skills and learning, autonomous decision making and teamwork among other features. Learning systems of work were much more prevalent in Christian democratic and social democratic economies – even than in the putatively innovative liberal economies of the UK and

Table 4.6 *Social compacts in Europe: welfare, production and*
macroeconomic regimes

	Average fiscal balance 1999–2007 (% GDP)	Current account balance, 2003–7 (% of GDP)	Average business R&D investment 1999–2007 (% of GDP)	Social spending, 2002	'Learning' organisation of work, 2000 (Holm *et al.*, 2010)
Christian democratic					
Austria	−1.8	3.98	1.63	34.5	47.5
Belgium	−0.5	6.66	1.35	30.4	38.9
Germany	−2.2	12.54	1.74	33.4	44.3
France	−2.7	−0.32	1.35	36.7	38.0
The Netherlands	−0.5	15.58	1.02	27.4	64.0
Social democratic					
Denmark	2.4	0.62	1.67	38.6	60.0
Finland	3.8	4.99	2.39	33.3	47.8
Norway	12.6	30.25	0.89	32.4	–
Sweden	1.3	4.04	2.73	38.0	52.6
Liberal					
Ireland	1.6	−5.37	0.8	27	24
UK	−1.4	−9.54	1.13	27.9	34.8
Mediterranean					
Greece	−5.3	−5.65	0.18	–	18.7
Spain	0.2	−8.04	0.56	23.7	20.1
Italy	−2.9	−4.42	0.54	28.8	30.0
Portugal	−3.6	−22.90	0.3	27.3	26.1

particularly Ireland. More detailed results in Holm *et al.*'s (2010) study
show that Mediterranean economies had very high levels of traditional
work organisation based on low levels of formalisation of work and
high managerial discretion, while liberal economies tend to emphasise
'lean' systems of work organisation, emphasising worker input and
teamwork, but within a framework of managerial control and hierarchy. The countries with the strongest external economic performance

and the greatest fiscal discipline are also those countries with the greatest social spending, business investment and the strongest emphasis on worker input and participation in the workplace. Fiscal discipline and external competitiveness is not rooted simply in national characteristics or a Continental European conservatism to be contrasted with indiscipline and recklessness in the periphery. Instead, it is rooted in the institutional features of the classic European developmental model and, even more significantly, in an underlying social compact that trades off fiscal discipline against high levels of social spending and protection and that uses both of these to embed a dynamic and inclusive business sector. Even in the decade when financial liberalisation and the design flaws of the euro threatened it most, the European model continued to operate in its Continental core to stabilise the broader economies of the Christian democratic and social democratic countries. The failure to diffuse and generalise this model to the liberal and Mediterranean economies is at the heart of their current fiscal and economic crises.

The long-standing differences between Europe's worlds of capitalism persisted despite the coordinated convergence in policies and institutions. The character of welfare regimes had long been debated in the social sciences, with significant shifts from the analysis of trends and patterns in the level of taxation and spending to a focus on how different welfare regimes are organised in different ways and embody and implement different principles of social provision. Such analyses have identified a range of 'worlds of welfare capitalism' (Esping-Andersen, 1990, 1999). There have of course been lively debates within this literature regarding the membership and the key characteristics that define each of the different welfare regimes. Esping-Andersen himself, for example, focused on the degree of decommodification provided by the welfare state to citizens – that is, the extent to which the welfare state made it possible for citizens to sustain their lives outside the market. However, in many respects, a focus on decommodification does not allow us to understand the particular mix of market and non-market mechanisms within different welfare regimes. It is also important to understand the structure of welfare in order to understand the kinds of social bargains that were likely, or even possible, in the different countries within the EU.

Table 4.7 examines this question by providing comparative statistics for the EU on the particular mixes of social spending, after-tax income and household assets in the total 'welfare' received by citizens in each of those countries. In this case, 'welfare' refers to the total bundle of

Table 4.7 *Social services, income and household assets in citizens'*
average 'welfare bundle'

	Social spending	After-tax income	Household property	Total as % of GDP/ GNP*	Income inequality: 90/10 ratio (2000–2)
Ireland	22.1	39.3	6.7	68.2	4.48
UK	27.9	51.9	3.5	83.2	4.67
Germany	33.4	40.1	3.6	77.1	3.25
France	36.7	47.9	4.0	88.6	3.45
Belgium	30.4	40.1	3.4	73.9	3.31
The Netherlands	27.4	46.0	5.2	78.7	2.78
Austria	34.5	47.8	3.7	86.0	3.15
Denmark	38.6	38.7	3.4	80.8	2.75
Finland	33.3	40.5	3.7	77.6	2.93
Norway	32.4	40.5	3.5	76.5	2.81
Sweden	38	45.5	1.7	85.2	2.96
Spain	23.7	52.1	6.3	82.1	4.69
Italy	28.8	47.0	4.3	80.1	4.50
Portugal	27.3	52.6	5.3	85.2	–

* Ireland data calculated as % of GNP; all others as % of GDP.
Notes and sources:
Government social spending:
Health, education, housing and community amenities, social protection (Eurostat)
Household assets:
Leetmaa *et al.*, 2009
Household capital formation is given in the statistics as a percentage of spending of household disposable income. This is then weighted by the data provided here on after-tax income as a percentage of GDP in order to give an estimate of the percentage of GDP given to household capital formation.
After-tax income: calculated from: (1) labour income share of GDP (OECD Statbank); (2) average income tax burden on employees at average wage (OECD Statbank)

resources received by citizens both through social services and through income – as well as including a measure of investment in household assets (particularly housing). The mix is expressed as a percentage of GDP in order to offer a measure of the total welfare mix for the entire body of citizens. There will of course be significant internal variation and inequalities in this mix, but the focus here is on the structure of welfare available to citizens as a body in each country. The measure of social spending is total government social spending on health, education, housing and community amenities and social protection – capturing most of the key, relatively easily measured social services provided by government. After-tax income is calculated from two different statistical measures – the share of national income going to labour and the average income tax burden on employees at the average wage, which is used to calculate the share of income that is left for labour (employees and the self-employed) after taxes. Finally, household capital formation is calculated from Eurostat figures on households' income, saving and investment. Details of the calculation are in the table notes. All calculations are given as a percentage of GDP, except for Irish calculations, which are provided as a percentage of GNP for the reasons already noted.

The goal of the analysis is to identify, from the perspective of the 'average citizen', the sources of welfare and therefore the degree to which social spending, market income or the build-up of household assets are institutionalised in the different countries. This gives a sense of the degree to which credible commitments were likely to be possible to make in the different countries – for example, whether trade-offs of social spending against increased taxation would be likely to be taken as credible and/or desirable. I place less focus here on the build-up of household assets (which is almost entirely based on property) as these are clearly closely linked to the housing bubbles in the Mediterranean and liberal economies. It should also be noted that the measure of after-tax income refers only to income tax and that a variety of other taxes, including sales tax and social insurance, are either not included or under-estimated.

There are clear differences between the various countries in the mix of social spending and after-tax income available to citizens. Ireland is striking for its low level of social spending, below even the UK and some of the Mediterranean economies. It is perhaps more surprising that Ireland has a relatively low share of after-tax income going to citizens, due to the low share of national income going to labour. Denmark, for example, has a similar level of after-tax income, but citizens are strongly compensated by one of the highest rates of social spending so that the Danish total of national income going to citizens is significantly above the Irish (although this estimate for Denmark may be over-estimated, given that GNP is significantly higher than

GDP in that country). Nonetheless, the basic point applies to other social democracies such as Finland, which has no such statistical complications. It is clear that even from the perspective of citizens' welfare, the mix of social services and income in their welfare is strongly related to their position in the 'worlds of welfare capitalism'. Social democracies, followed closely by Continental Christian democracies, rely most heavily on social spending and much less on after-tax income than the liberal UK and the Mediterranean economies (and the often-exceptional French case). However, to varying degrees, social spending on services and social protection provides compensation for this. There is therefore some degree of trade-off between social spending and after-tax income in citizens' 'bundle of welfare'. Indeed, given that the social democracies in particular rely more heavily on social services than social transfers, this trade-off is likely to be greater than the table indicates. This analysis of course does not take absolute levels of income or social spending into account and this would certainly affect our assessment of the welfare available to citizens of the Mediterranean economies, for example. However, the important feature here is the different mixes of resources available to citizens in different countries, which significantly changes the social and political perspectives within the politics of welfare and the broader social compact.

This analysis suggests that 'social Europe' has proven to be more than a luxury to be added on to the project of market integration, but was in practice a key element underpinning the fiscal discipline and productive upgrading that underpinned the Continental economies. The project of transplanting certain key European institutions from the national to the European level was always incomplete. The rules around fiscal discipline and the national institutions of wage coordination and central bank independence were diffused, but the social compacts that made them sustainable policies did not spread in the same way. Indeed, in many countries, and crucially in Germany, these elements of the social compact were themselves being eroded on the domestic front (Streeck, 2009).

Conclusion

As Senghaas (1985) argued, the post-war history of Europe was centred on the creation of institutions, coalitions and compacts that could manage both the economic relations and social structural changes associated with capitalist development in Europe – and deliver autocentric development. Ireland and the other peripheral countries only partially succeeded (at best) in undertaking this task, even as income converged. In Europe, as in the US (Krippner, 2011), financialisation depoliticised growth and distribution and allowed these cracks in the European economy to be papered over – even as it drove a further wedge between the core and the periphery in Europe. This was reflected in European politics as the euro project further sought to enshrine this depoliticisation in fiscal rules administered in a technocratic manner. This in turn was consistent with the 'permissive consensus' in Europeanisation that created a space for the technocratic and/or intergovernmental advance of the European project (Hooghe and Marks, 2009). However, this came at the cost of a failure to address the very different social compacts, and therefore economic models, that were to be integrated within the European economy.

Fundamentally, the partial policy regime did not stabilise the European economy but turned it inside out. The relationship between the core and the periphery of Europe – and the financial flows between them – was dramatically restructured between the 1990s and the 2000s. The public developmentalism of the structural funds programme was overwhelmed by the capital flows from the core to the periphery associated with financial liberalisation. In the process, a dramatic structural change was produced within the real European economy, which was reflected in significant current account imbalances. Figures 4.12 and 4.13 show the shifting compositions of the core and peripheral economies in Europe as a proportion of the structure of the entire Eurozone economy (for example, the figure relating to German exports indicates what percentage of total exports by all countries within the Eurozone were accounted for by Germany's exports). They show that in the 1990s, Spain, Ireland, Italy, Greece and Portugal saw significant increases in their share of total exports in the Eurozone, increasing from just above 25 per cent in 1995 to approximately 28 per cent in 2001, and that at the same time, these countries' share of domestic demand in Europe increased. Export growth and domestic demand were linked in a reasonably healthy manner, suggesting that the virtuous circle of the European model had begun to embed itself within the European periphery. During the same period, German exports remained stable and Germany's share of domestic demand in Europe declined significantly.

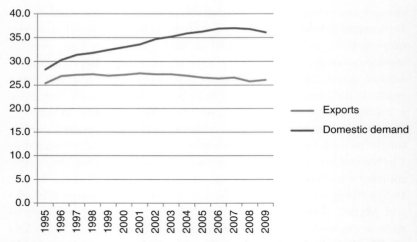

Figure 4.12 Exports and domestic demand in the European periphery, 1995–2009
Note: % is of total exports/demand in the Eurozone (16 countries)
Source: Eurostat

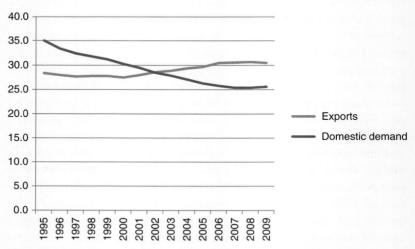

Figure 4.13 Exports and domestic demand in Germany, 1995–2009
Note: % is of total exports/demand in the Eurozone (16 countries)
Source: Eurostat

In the 2000s these patterns shifted. The peripheral share of Eurozone exports decreased once more, although remaining slightly above the 1995 level, while Germany's share of Eurozone exports increased rapidly. However, the peripheral countries' share of domestic demand continued to increase. Just as importantly, Germany's share of domestic demand continued to decline. The 2000s in Germany were a period of increased export competitiveness disconnected from the virtuous circle of increased domestic demand that is crucial to the European model. The virtuous circle of interaction between domestic demand and export competitiveness was broken in both the periphery and in the core, albeit in different ways. This created major structural imbalances within the European economy and suggests that the underlying European model of development was compromised both by the bubble growth in the peripheral economies and by the failure to generalise export growth in the core to the living standards of the broader population. The crucial feature linking both of these processes together was the shift to a deeply financialised relationship between the core and the periphery. We might expect the core economies to be the Keynesian anchors in an economic union while the hungry peripheral economies pursued catch-up through Schumpeterian competitiveness strategies. In practice, Europe was characterised by the opposite – a disastrous combination of a Schumpeterian core and a Keynesian periphery, facilitated by financialisation and core banks.

The challenges of dealing with the European crisis since 2008 have involved not simply the national interests of elites or the level of attachment of individuals to the European project, but have been heavily shaped by different expectations in European countries of what is fair, rational and reasonable to expect of other European nations and citizens. This has been a clash not only of social classes and of national interests but also of institutionalised social compacts. The stabilisation of capitalist economies depends heavily upon the social compacts in the surrounding societies.

Given this approach, it can be seen that the euro and the stability and growth criteria were, in practice, designed to act as just such a framework for integration of multiple social compacts. As is well known, these mechanisms were sorely lacking and Europe was turned inside out, riven by structural divergences and weakened by institutions that were too weak and fragmented to address those fractures.

In the 2000s Europe was left with a set of persistent dilemmas for governing economic life, despite the advent of the euro. How should economies conform to the new economic rules with only recent institutional transformation and a very partial and uneven social compact across the Member States? These questions were all the more pressing because the stability arising out of the 'market test' that German policy elites had expected did not materialise. In practice, the opposite happened as financial 'discipline' disappeared in speculative financial markets and significant imbalances emerged in Europe's economic flows.

The desire of the French left had been to build the social market economy at the European level, having failed to so do at the national level. Ironically, when the institutional shape of the new European economy emerged, it looked more German than French, being accompanied by a distinctly Anglo-American taste for financial speculation. But whether it was the German ordoliberal model advancing through the euro or the French statist model led through the increasingly marginal European Commission, both neglected the foundation of their national models, and the new European model, in deeply institutionalised social compacts. This left significant challenges for national political economies, to which they responded in different ways.

At either end of the spectrum were the Continental countries and the UK. The Christian democratic economies were firmly within the euro and signed up to the policy regime – not surprisingly, given that their economic rules were the basis of the European model (and despite their failure to stick to the rules in the initial years). At the other end sat the UK, outside the euro and with limited or no institutional convergence. It remained 'liberal' and far from this new European terrain. The other cases were less clear-cut. The social democratic economies also had long histories of conforming to similar kinds of policies and building similar institutions – even product market deregulation emerged early in the Nordic economies. However, while they largely followed the economic disciplines of the euro, they almost all stayed out of the euro itself. Because their internal compacts allowed them to follow the disciplines associated with the euro, they were able to forgo the loss of overall control attached to the euro.

Finally, there is the crucial category of the European periphery, including the Mediterranean economies and Ireland. These countries sat in a difficult position. In one way or another, their histories were most closely tied to the liberal model, often mediated through clientelism. The development of the welfare state, and even the administrative state, was at a much lower level than in the Continental economies whose policies and institutions were now spreading into the periphery. They found themselves within the euro, but with only new institutions and weaker social compacts to manage risks and sustain them through crises. This was a difficult politics. However, it is also a common one that will characterise most if not all new entrants into the EU (and potentially other regional economic blocs). Ireland is perhaps the paradigmatic case for examining the dilemmas of such situations as its liberal institutions were long established and its economic and institutional transformation went further and deeper in most respects than in the Mediterranean economies. These were enormous strains for any European country to face, especially those on the wrong side of the structural divide. As will be seen, despite apparently reassuring indicators, Ireland was in fact in a structurally weak position. Furthermore, it dealt particularly poorly with the challenges for economic development and the public finances. Why it did so is the question addressed in the next chapter.

5 | National politics: governing fragmentation, fragmented governance

Introduction: the challenge to national political economies

As the last chapter demonstrated, Ireland was one of a group of countries that faced a very unpromising set of conditions for managing the financial flows, credit booms and economic bubbles that were likely to emerge in the Eurozone. Along with the UK and the Mediterranean countries, Ireland lacked the social compacts that underpinned fiscal discipline in the Continental and Nordic economies. However, this does not mean that the fiscal crisis that emerged rapidly in Ireland in 2008 was inevitable. National politics still played a key role in explaining the pace and extent of the crisis and how it transferred so quickly and dramatically from the financial sector to the public finances. Indeed, national political economies may matter even more in an era of economic and monetary union, given the fairly strict constraints in the areas of monetary policy (Lane, 2011). Weakened in some areas, national politics became ever more crucial in others such as fiscal policy and the shaping of investments towards productive rather than speculative ends.

Ireland therefore faced a significant challenge of managing the process of financialisation in the context of institutions and social bargains that are typically associated with relatively large budget deficits. However, although in the 2000s Ireland ran budget surpluses and its public finances seemed in healthy order, the scale of the collapse of its public finances after 2008 was dramatic. Its budget deficit grew from 0.9 per cent to 15.5 per cent between 2007 and 2011. As will be shown in the next chapter, a significant part of this is due to the public finances bearing the burden of private bank debt. However, even leaving this aside, there was a significant ongoing primary deficit in the government's annual budget. Understanding the conditions that could produce such fiscal fragility is a critical element in understanding the Irish collapse.

This fiscal crisis was reinforced by an economic crisis, beginning with the collapse of construction employment and related local demand, but rooted more deeply in the failure of the Irish economy to build on the industrial development of the 1990s. Many commentators had worried aloud through the 2000s about Ireland's apparent loss of cost competitiveness. However, the issue is much broader. The 2000s brought a stalling of the Irish developmental model, with manufacturing employment declining and overall exports remaining relatively flat. Ireland's development strategy and the institutions that supported it changed significantly in the 2000s and proved a weak counterweight to the growth of financialisation (Ó Riain, 2010)

Ultimately this economic crisis spilled over quickly into major social consequences with a sharp spike in unemployment, rising emigration as the crisis progressed and significant loss of income, household debt difficulties and reductions in public and social services over the course of the crisis years. The social effects of the crisis were amplified very rapidly as Ireland's institutions of social protection were only partly successful in buffering the population from the worst effects of the economic collapse. While Ireland's crisis was fundamentally a crisis of financialisation, this rapidly amplified into a crisis of the whole economy and society. Why did Ireland fail so spectacularly to meet the challenges of economic and monetary union? What were the decisions and processes that made Ireland so vulnerable to the bubble and its collapse? And, even more importantly, what were the conditions in the political economy that made these decisions possible and even likely?

Ireland's failure to meet this challenge initially appears all the more surprising because much research has shown that small open economies in advanced capitalist countries – of which Ireland is one – tend to develop mechanisms which protect them against the vulnerabilities of exposure to the global economy. In Europe, this has mainly taken the form of the development of the welfare state and corporatist political structures to manage the pressures of internationalisation (Katzenstein, 1985). Ireland, however, has barely developed such mechanisms of social compensation for international exposure (Hardiman *et al.*, 2008). Indeed, Ireland is unusual among Europe's small open economies in being the only one of them – with the possible exception of Switzerland and most recently the transition economies – which has a distinctively liberal political economy.

In this chapter I explore the politics, including the political process and the broader political economic conditions, which facilitated this crisis in Ireland. In the next section I review the major ways in which politics in countries such as Ireland has been conceptualised – as clientelist, corporatist or liberal. The following section reviews the political processes that shaped the development of the Irish economy in the periods of economic history that were outlined in Chapter 2. It explores how the historical vicious circle of under-development in Ireland, including its socio-political dimensions, led to a transition to a politics of recovery from crisis in the late 1980s, particularly the emergence of neo-corporatist wage agreements from 1987 onwards. It also examines the politics of how the developmental successes of the 1990s turned in the 2000s to a politics of speculation and the erosion of a sustainable model of development. Having reviewed the political process through which Ireland's development both emerged and was undermined, I go on to examine the broader political conditions that were persistent features of the Irish polity. These persistent features helped to define the set of possible political strategies and coalitions available to political actors in Ireland – in the boom, the bubble and, as will be covered in the next chapter, the crisis. This section explores the fragmentation of economic organisation, the structure of a pay-related welfare state, the dualist nature of the Irish state administration and the oligarchic tendencies of parliamentary and electoral politics. Throughout the chapter, the analysis traces the interaction of clientelist, liberal and corporatist political processes. It argues that where a compromise between liberalism and corporatism had held clientelism at bay in the 1990s to facilitate significant policy initiatives, in the 2000s clientelism and liberalism were reunited to create the bubble economy as deal making trumped developmentalism (Paus, 2012). Ireland's fragile developmental coalition and social compact were further weakened by the conditions of politics in a broadly liberal polity and political economy.

What kind of politics?

The dominant narrative of Irish politics after the crisis of 2008 has been one of deep cynicism, emphasising 'how stupidity and corruption sank the Celtic Tiger' (O'Toole, 2009). This takes many forms and finds many targets, including not only private actors in the financial and property sectors but also public actors such as regulators, public servants and corporatist 'social partners'. There is of course a great deal of truth to many of these criticisms. However, such analyses tell us little about the particular form of politics in Ireland and how we should conceptualise it. Such accounts offer an understanding of Irish politics that emphasises the local, the particular and the specific features of the Irish political system. Its failings are often reduced to the failings of individuals, whether those are failings of greed and opportunism or incompetence. However, it is more helpful to analyse the Irish politics of economic life in the context of comparative cases and concepts rather than in relation to an idealised version of a democratic, liberal market or other ideal. There are three key literatures, each linked to a particular view of the nature of the Irish political economy itself.

A dominant narrative in the analysis of Irish politics has focused on clientelism as its key feature. This is typically linked to the under-developed, traditional or peripheral nature of the Irish political economy. The key comparative cases are the Mediterranean economies, which also appear to suffer from the clientelist disease where politics is reduced to politicians delivering particular benefits to voters in return for political allegiances. Other analysts emphasise the liberal nature of the Irish political economy and typically understand Irish politics as neoliberal in orientation, whether they focus on the dominance of international capital within the Irish economy and in its relations with the Irish state or whether they emphasise relations with Irish corporate elites. Rarely, however, do such analyses investigate the character and process of liberal politics itself or the specific form that it takes in Ireland. Finally, where Ireland had always been seen as an exception to the European pattern of corporatist interest politics, since the 1980s, Irish social partnership agreements have raised the question of what kinds of social pacts these are and how corporatist politics in Ireland should be interpreted. Before undertaking the historical analysis of Ireland's polity, the rest of this section examines how best to understand each of these three forms of politics. In each case the classic theories that emphasised the fixed nature of clientelism, liberalism and corporatism are now giving way to analyses that explore the different forms which each of these can take and how they may interact with other forms of politics within the political field.

Clientelism

The concept of clientelism rests mainly on the idea that social benefits are distributed selectively and in a particularistic way, based on inter-personal ties and one-to-one exchange (Hopkin, 2006). Contemporary analyses of clientelism have moved away from a polarised distinction between the closed, personalised nature of clientelist politics and the open, depersonalised nature of liberal democratic politics. These analyses argue that clientelism can take many different forms and can be present in conjunction with various other forms of political organisation. Clientelism is generally based on ongoing one-to-one ties, but does not necessarily imply corruption. It may devolve into such individual corruption or it may evolve from one-to-one relations into ongoing clientelist ties between political elites and groups or clubs, such as corporate elites, ethnic groups or similar lobby groups (Hopkin, 2006). Whereas Hopkin focuses on selective one-to-one ties that are typically somewhat durable, Piattoni (2001) focuses on the structure of the broader political system and how it creates conditions under which clientelist politics is likely to flourish. In a political system where citizens can gain relatively easy access to political elites and where there is relatively little universal distribution of benefits, clientelism is in practice likely to flourish – whether as one-to-one ties, systems of party patronage or 'machine politics'. In Piattoni's terms, the Irish system of relatively low universal benefits combined with a strong degree of localism in party politics suggests that the conditions are right for extensive clientelist politics. However, it also suggests that these politics can be transformed in a number of different directions – both in the direction of nepotism and corruption, when the political system becomes more closed, and potentially in the direction of corporatism and consociationalism if the distribution of benefits becomes more universalist (Piattoni, 2001). Similarly, Hopkin's (2006) analysis suggests that selective, personalised relationships can evolve into class voting or issue voting as the scope of benefits extends from the selective to the collective level.

The conditions for clientelism in Ireland have been favourable, therefore. However, this more sophisticated understanding of clientelism directs our attention to how these conditions vary across different parts of the political system and across different times, as there can be many different forms of politics in play within the same political system at the same time. Therefore, the new literature on clientelism suggests that attention should be paid to the conditions under which clientelist or brokerage forms of politics can transform or be mobilised into new political patterns, such as corporatism. Many different forms of clientelism can coexist within a political system – including corruption, party patronage, close relations with corporate or lobby groups, and a more generalised set of close ties between political and economic elites that lead to them forming a similar view of what is 'rational'. In the latter case, the analysis of clientelism becomes closely tied to studies of corporate power and elite influence on politics.

In Ireland's case, Komito (1992) provided an early important analysis which suggested that politics in Ireland was characterised primarily not by corrupt interpersonal ties, but by the pervasive importance of 'brokerage', where citizens sought (or were forced to seek) access to the political and state system through a series of brokers, including solicitors, priests and politicians. In Basil Chubb's famous phrase, the task of Irish politicians was 'going around persecuting civil servants' (Chubb, 2006: 272).

Any discussion of these issues in Ireland is typically accompanied by a focus on the importance of Fianna Fáil as the political party which perfected the exercise and maintenance of power through clientelist relationships. However, the distinctiveness of Fianna Fáil is not necessarily to do with extensive corrupt personal relations. Fianna Fáil's strength was based heavily on its insertion into the broader national system of brokerage and its ability to move that system from the local to the national level. Its lengthy period in power from the 1930s to the 1970s only served to consolidate brokerage as the style of national politics.

While clientelist relations between politicians and the public were often simply a form of political communication, brokering and interest aggregation (Komito, 1992), there have also been instances where clientelism became corruption – in the property sector (Cullen, 2002), the beef industry (O'Toole, 1994) and potentially in public procurement and contracting where demands on contractors have been relatively lenient. It may be that clientelism has simply been transposed from the personal to the corporate level, as the Irish economy becomes subject to a 'corporate takeover' (Allen, 2007). Or it may be that the growth strategy increasingly takes the form of a 'growth machine' where political and land-based elites combine to generate profit from changing land uses (Molotch, 1976).

Clientelism can involve corruption or may consist of the legal reconstruction of institutions in favour of the interests of corporations. Both are certainly at work in contemporary Ireland. What is more variable are the developmental rewards derived from different state–corporate relations in different sectors. State support of Shell's drilling operations in Mayo, of Intel's production facility in Kildare and of indigenous high-tech firms around the country yield different developmental rewards (or none) and are embedded in different institutions and even policy regimes.

Liberal politics

Apparently at the opposite end of the political spectrum from clientelism, liberal democratic politics is often taken as the default form of politics in advanced capitalist countries. Unfortunately, this has meant that not enough attention has been paid to the particular forms that politics takes in liberal political economies. It is important to understand how political dynamics intersect with socio-economic processes in order to shed light on the workings of liberalism in the politics of economies such as those in the US, the UK and Ireland.

A good starting point is Monica Prasad's work, which focuses on the dynamics of the political process in different political economies as the foundation of her explanation of why liberalisation advances further and takes different forms in different countries. Prasad compares the UK and the US, where neoliberal politics and policies took hold between the 1970s and the 1990s, and Germany and France, where their influence was much weaker. She argues that the roots of the rise of neoliberalism lie in the political process itself, being facilitated by adversarial politics:

Free market or neoliberal policies did not result from any pragmatic or rational analysis showing that they were the best way to manage the crisis; nor were they the result of globalization, business-group pressure, or national culture. Rather they arose where the political-economic structure was adversarial. States in which the political-economic structure defined labour and capital as adversaries and the middle class and the poor in opposition to one another (the middle class paying for policies that benefit the poor) provided the potential to ally the majority of voters with market-friendly policies, and certain structural changes provided incentives to politicians to mobilise this potential. (Prasad, 2006: 38)

Prasad develops this argument into a number of specific claims. She argues that the US and the UK adopted adversarial policies in the post-war 'Golden Age of capitalism'. These adversarial policies included more progressive tax structures, more egalitarian welfare states and adversarial industrial policies that pitted state control against private enterprise. France and Germany's tax structures were more regressive and their welfare states less redistributive, while their industrial policies were pro-growth and business-friendly. This argument consists of two main claims. First, the famously liberal US and UK had more redistributive tax, welfare and industrial policies. A fuller summary of this first point might be that the US and the UK combined higher levels of income inequality and lower overall tax and spending levels with more clearly and directly redistributive taxes (primarily through income taxes) and with targeted, directly redistributive welfare spending (primarily through means testing and related mechanisms). Kenworthy (2012) provides evidence that the overall redistributive effect is much less once issues like tax credits are taken into account. Nonetheless, the basic point about highly visible redistribution stands. In practice Kenworthy's evidence suggests that liberal political economies combine highly visible redistributive tax and welfare regimes with actual levels of redistribution that are less generous than in social democracies.

Second, Prasad argues that these policies made politics more adversarial. The politics of redistribution is particularly visible and clearly defines categories of persons and patterns of cross-subsidy between them. The underlying much higher income inequality levels are, by contrast, often 'naturalised' as the outcome of apolitical market processes. Even the fuller summary of Prasad's account of redistribution is still consistent with the argument regarding adversarial politics as it is the specific mechanisms of redistribution – direct and visible transfers and targeting of benefits – that generate the adversarial political processes.

Prasad dismisses the 'varieties of capitalism' perspective as she finds little evidence that business group power explains liberalisation in the US and the UK. However, this may lead her to move too quickly on

Table 5.1 *Prasad's varieties of polities*

	Weak labour	Strong labour
Coordinated economies	Technocracy	Integrated labour
Liberal economies	Entrepreneurial politicians	Excluded labour

from the liberal character of the US and the UK themselves. Indeed, the political processes that she outlines are typical of *liberal* political economies. The contribution of her analysis is to direct our attention to how the *form* that progressive politics takes in liberal economies can render those polities vulnerable to more aggressive counter-movements of liberalisation.

This pattern is something that repeats itself in broad measure in Ireland's liberal political economy. However, the matter is not quite as simple as Ireland fitting into the liberal model of the US and the UK. Prasad finds other mediating, primarily institutional factors at work (see Table 5.1). She argues that in the countries with strong labour (Germany and the UK), the integration of labour into the political process was very different. In Germany, the right-wing party partly integrated the working class and labour was a corporatist partner, whereas in the UK, the Conservatives excluded labour and class politics, and incomes policies were highly adversarial. In the weak labour countries, the politics of the state predominated. However, 'in France, the technocracy – state actors constrained by the evolution of economic expertise – restrained the development of neoliberalism, whereas in the US entrepreneurial politicians sought out new issues' (2006: 281).

In short, the liberal economies of the US and the UK combined an underlying adversarial and polarising form of distributive and growth politics with a set of institutions that further encouraged polarisation – either through exclusionary labour politics or through political adventurism. However, Ireland represents a different case. The underlying structure of tax and welfare in Ireland is similar to that in the liberal economies of the US and the UK. However, the technocracy was a significant actor in the Celtic Tiger years (particularly in the 1990s) and labour was incorporated through neo-corporatist structures from 1987. Indeed, neo-corporatism was in part a creation of a conservative party, Fianna Fáil, itself a mass catch-all party with strong historical working-class appeal and strong network ties throughout the society. On these particular institutional measures, Ireland has been closer for large portions of the past twenty-five years to France and Germany than to the US or the UK. Ireland's case straddles the categories of Prasad's table, with all the contradictions and potentials that this implies.

Indeed, it may well be that the liberal family of political economies divides into two groups – the US, the UK and Canada, where institutional dynamics of state and labour politics aggravate the adversarial politics of the political economy (and therefore potentially make it more vulnerable to further liberalisation), and Ireland, Australia and New Zealand, where the institutional importance (at varying stages in history) of labour and the technocracy act as countervailing forces.

Corporatist politics

Indeed, Ireland had from 1987 to 2008 one of the longest historical unbroken series of corporatist national social pacts. A history of clientelism and liberal economic policies meant that the conditions for corporatist politics were poor – and a series of relatively unsuccessful experiments with national wage agreements in the 1970s seemed to confirm this (Hardiman, 1988). Despite the relative weakness of the centralised peak associations that typically were associated with corporatism in Europe and the patchy history of national wage agreements in the 1960s and 1970s, a series of centralised pay deals began in 1987 that continue today (Hardiman, 1992, 1998). Unlikely as Ireland seemed as a location for corporatist pacts, the agreements that were signed rested upon a hard core of 'compensatory exchange' (Roche, 2007). Unions delivered wage restraint and industrial peace to employers, while employers delivered guaranteed (modest) wage increases and the prospect of growth to workers. Government was central. Employers were to receive the fiscal discipline that they desperately wanted, while unions were guaranteed the safeguarding of the real value of social benefits, a limit to the severity of cuts in public services, steady public employment levels and, crucially, decreases in income tax that would compensate for the wage restraint they had offered employers.

Ornston (2012) has recently compared Irish corporatism unfavourably with corporatism in Finland and Denmark. He argues that corporatism in all of these countries came under severe pressure in the

1980s and 1990s. In keeping with other analyses of Nordic economies in the 1990s and 2000s, he argues that corporatism was reinvented in Denmark and Finland in order to support industrial transition, redesign welfare state supports, and adapt systems of social protection and wage bargaining and industrial policy supports to an era of globalisation and structural change. He argues that:

If a crisis forces stakeholders to jettison conservative corporatist bargains, stakeholders can use existing patterns of cooperation to achieve more complex and sophisticated objectives. More specifically, they can convert neo-corporatist institutions to invest in new, supply-side resources such as risk capital, skill formation, research and development. This pattern of 'creative' corporatism has very different implications for economic adjustment. In contrast to conservative corporatism, investments explicitly target new enterprises, occupations and industries. In contrast to competitive corporatism, high-quality inputs support more knowledge-intensive activities such as research and design. (Ornston, 2012: 11)

In this way economic progress and social equality were reconciled in the face of challenging circumstances. In our terms, the classic European model was retooled for a new era as corporatism in Denmark and Finland took on a new 'creative' character. Ornston argues that in Ireland, while significant advances were made, corporatism remained at the level of 'competitive corporatism'. Rather than emphasising upgrading and dynamic adjustment, this form of corporatism emphasised labour market flexibility, wage restraint and the cost competitiveness of Ireland as a location for foreign investment and of indigenous companies. The structural basis of Irish development remained unchanged in this approach:

Yet Ireland has struggled to identify and invest in new supply-side resources. As a result, multinational and indigenous enterprises alike occupy a comparatively low-end position within new, high-technology markets. For example, Irish high-technology exports plummeted after the dot-com crash. Subsequent gains in income and employment were based on unsustainable growth in non-tradable industries such as residential construction. Irish stakeholders are aware of these problems and promoted investment in new, supply-side resources. These investments have played a constructive role in promoting research and indigenous entrepreneurship. Yet creative corporatist bargains remained limited relative to Denmark and Finland, because stakeholders could not exploit the same tradition of cooperation among firms, trade unions, financial intermediaries and state agencies. As a result, Ireland continues to struggle, both in the availability of new, supply-side resources and within more knowledge-intensive, high value-added activities. (Ornston, 2012: 187)

Rather than building corporatism on the classic organisational and political conditions for social pacts in Europe, Irish corporatism began from social pacts and sought to build new governance capabilities around and through these pacts. The corporatist agreements in Ireland, emerging in response to a crisis, sought to build the conditions for their own existence as they developed. But elites, no more than Marx's men, do not make history under circumstances of their own choosing. Ireland's corporatism was associated with the building of innovative governance capabilities (Sabel, 1996; O'Donnell, 2000). It is perhaps best to understand Irish corporatism, at least in the 1990s, as the product of competing tendencies towards competitive and creative corporatism. The politics of corporatism in Ireland was also character-ised by a number of tensions. These included conflicts within corpor-atism itself about the nature of the economy and the polity that was being built. They also included tensions between clientelist, liberal and corporatist political dynamics. How did these tensions play themselves out across the recent history of Ireland's political economy?

The politics of vicious and virtuous circles

Ireland's economy has been characterised, as was seen in Chapter 2, by a variety of crises. Nonetheless, it also appeared in the 1990s to have undergone a transition from structural under-development into advanced capitalist economy status. What have been the political dynamics that have underpinned these vicious and virtuous cycles of the Irish political economy? How did the virtuous circle of development in the 1990s emerge from the vicious circles of under-development in previous decades? In this section I explore this question. The following section examines how these gains were eroded and a virtuous circle was transformed once more as development was undermined.

The vicious circle

When Ireland received its independence from Great Britain in 1922, it was left with a legacy of institutions and political economic structures that in many respects reflected those of its coloniser. The system of public administration not surprisingly mirrored the Whitehall model, while the absence of a parliament was soon rectified with the establishment of a system that in many important respects borrowed from the UK Westminster model. In addition, even at this early stage, Ireland's welfare state was significantly under-developed compared to other welfare states (Cusack *et al.*, 2007). Other institutions too were borrowed from the UK, including a pluralist system of industrial relations where many of the unions themselves (especially craft unions) were English-based unions. Nonetheless, it can be argued that the state institutions based on the UK model that were inherited from the colonial era helped to stabilise Ireland in the 1920s and 1930s, when Ireland might easily have experienced a period of military rule or even dictatorship, as was the case in a number of the Mediterranean societies. In the decade after independence, Ireland only reinforced its liberal character, with the conservative Cumann na nGaedhael party pursuing policies of free trade and relative continuity with the British era.

In 1932 Fianna Fáil came to power, just less than a decade after losing the civil war of 1922–3. Fianna Fáil was to spend most of the next forty years as the majority government, coming to be one of the most spectacular success stories in comparative politics. It managed to build a mass membership base and an appeal as a 'catch-all' party. In Stein Rokkan's terms (1970), Fianna Fáil came to be the national 'founding party', despite spending the first ten years of the state in the political wilderness. During the 1930s, Fianna Fáil cemented its position in large part through building a 'red–green alliance'. Always the party of the small farmers, from the 1930s Fianna Fáil consolidated its base among the relatively small urban working class, in part through a programme of social housing that provided both employment and accommodation. Unlike in the Nordic countries, where the red–green alliance became the foundation of the social democratic and labour parties which sometimes forged alliances with the much smaller agrarian parties, in Ireland this red–green alliance was flipped on its head. Fianna Fáil, a party closer to the Nordic agrarian parties than to the social democrats, benefited from the Irish red–green alliance. A much smaller and politically marginalised Labour Party was left to attempt, largely unsuccessfully, to build its support among workers and later the professional middle classes.

As noted above, the decades of Fianna Fáil rule were decades in which the brokerage form of politics was consolidated. Indeed, being a party of 'permanent government' enabled Fianna Fáil to operate much more effectively in this brokerage role. Ireland had deviated significantly from the UK political model in establishing an electoral system based on proportional representation. Typically, such systems favour parties of the left (Cusack *et al.*, 2007). However, Fianna Fáil's ability to use the brokerage system to build a national presence and to establish itself as the 'natural party of government' meant that Ireland proved to be an outlier once more as a society with a highly developed proportional representation electoral system and a very weak party of the left.

The turn to foreign investment during the 1960s added a second wave of liberalisation to the Irish political economy, with a renewed focus on free trade and the attraction of FDI as the building block of an export-oriented economy. This was also, however, linked to the expansion of the state itself and the growth of 'modern' institutions such as the welfare state, even if that growth was more limited than elsewhere. Ireland's political development until the 1980s was largely a matter of the interplay of liberal and brokerage politics, with Fianna Fáil acting as a key institution in knitting these styles of politics and institutional ties together. By the 1970s, Fianna Fáil had enjoyed four decades of hegemony, albeit in the context of comparatively poor economic development and weak institutional capacity. In 1973 the party was firmly dislodged from government by a coalition composed of Fine Gael and the Labour Party. This represented the most serious challenge to Fianna Fáil's political power since it had entered into constitutional politics in the late 1920s. It reacted to this political challenge with political vigour, but in a way that proved to be economically disastrous. For the 1977 election, it provided a plan for economic growth based on rapid fiscal expansion, providing a belated and sudden dose of apparently Keynesian policy. This was brokerage on a grand scale with the provision of selective benefits to a very large number of people in the society. Unfortunately, this policy offensive combined with significant structural economic under-development so that most of the benefits of this expansion flowed straight out of the country through the purchase of imports. In addition, the expansion coincided with the emerging international debt crisis in the late 1970s and early 1980s. Just as Mexico and other countries were finding themselves in the midst of a dramatic debt crisis in 1982, Ireland ended up saddled with massive public debt and deficits in the same period. The liberal political economy and the politics of brokerage had interacted disastrously. After a period of political instability from 1981, a new Fine Gael–Labour coalition sought from 1983 to 1987 to rein in the public debt, with only limited success. By the mid-1980s, Ireland's unemployment and emigration had soared, and the Irish economy and indeed Irish society faced an exceptionally severe crisis.

1987 and all that

However, in 1987 the first of a twenty-one-year series of social pacts was signed. In retrospect, this has been marked as the beginning of Ireland's recovery, but the economic history, as already discussed, is more complex, with painful economic and fiscal retrenchment in the late 1980s, an international recession and significant high-profile factory closures in 1991, and jobless growth through the early 1990s. In the long term, however, these social pacts proved significant in Ireland's recovery. While not arriving completely out of the blue, they were significantly more extensive, long term and stable than the wage agreements concluded on a more fleeting basis in the 1970s. The conditions for corporatist pacts in Ireland still appeared to be missing as union and employer organisation remained fragmented.

The core of the social partnership deals was a political exchange among unions, employers and the state. This exchange remained a crucial element in Ireland's social pacts from the early agreements, which contained very little other than these core elements, to the later agreements, which by the 2000s came to contain almost the entire programme for government (even if this programme had not itself been developed within the partnership process). The core of this exchange was the provision of industrial peace and wage restraint by unions. The role of the state here was crucial, as the quid pro quo for these concessions by unions was the provision of tax cuts by the government in order to improve living standards while improving wage competitiveness and controlling inflation. The danger here was the worsening of the fiscal crisis through reducing the tax intake, especially as the state was already saddled with massive debt. The pact therefore relied heavily on economic growth to fill the gap in public finances, which was to be the employers' contribution (Teague and Donaghey, 2009). However, in the early pacts and through the 1990s, cuts in public spending (or later spending restraints) were also a significant part of the package.

While my analysis does not attempt to explain the origins of partnership in Ireland, it is worth noting a number of key features. First is the key role of the state, in common with a variety of other countries in Europe during this time and a key distinguishing feature from the Continental European corporatism of the 1970s which was primarily organised between employers and unions. Second, the social pacts were made more likely by the process of European economic integration (Regan, 2012). The demands of market integration on wage and other forms of competitiveness and later of monetary integration on fiscal discipline were a strong motivating force for states to mobilise the consent of unions and employers through social pacts. Furthermore, these social pacts in Ireland and other European countries were promoted through the EU itself, albeit through the loosely defined 'open method of co-ordination' (O'Donnell and Moss, 2005). Third, unions too had reason to participate in these new social pacts, despite particular elements being difficult for them to swallow. In Ireland in particular, the spectre of Thatcherism and the attack on the unions in the UK was a significant motivating force (Hardiman, 1992). For union leaders, faced with Thatcher- and Reagan-inspired attacks on unions in the UK and the US and without a strong electoral left to provide domestic protection, new social pacts offered the most realistic pathway to a more European social democratic form of economic governance.

But such strategic considerations, important as they are, bring their own risks. A focus on strategic action can under-estimate both the degree of 'muddling through' by actors involved in the evolution of such agreements and the genuine innovation in relationships and governance associated with these pacts. Nor does the understanding of actors' more abstract motivations for participating in itself explain how and why the pacts could be achieved. As already noted, a comparative perspective rightly points to the weaknesses of the Irish situation for building deeper social compacts. However, these considerations are peripheral for the actors involved in domestic politics as they must deal directly with the limits and potentials of these conditions. The Irish social pacts were remarkable primarily because they were both a set of particular agreements and political exchanges and a project of institution building which was building the very institutions and conditions necessary for these agreements and exchanges to persist and grow. As one of the key participants has put it, the 'ship' of social partnership (the institutions that allowed the actors to participate) was built at sea as partnership negotiations were well underway (O'Donnell, 2008).

This was all the more challenging because there were many liberal aspects to the early pacts, including fiscal retrenchment, the entry into an integrating European market and the continuing reliance on FDI. If liberalism left its stamp, then so too did the politics of brokerage. Most observers agree that Fianna Fáil's role in developing these pacts was crucial, precisely because of its extensive capabilities in brokering across class relations with the state. Nonetheless, these relatively stable features of partnership proved to be compatible with a changing set of governance relations within partnership itself over the next two decades.

The first social pacts in 1987 and 1990 were brokered primarily among the elites of the trade union federation, the employers' association, the farming associations and the most senior civil servants and politicians. These elites developed relatively close and trusting relations which enabled them to make credible commitments to one another. They also appear to have been able to engage in a degree of genuine dialogue and open exchange of views, and to explore new political economic strategies and negotiate some of the difficulties of the 1987–94 period. This suggests that there is some truth in the view that new social pacts incorporated a degree of dialogue between organised interests and political experimentalism (O'Donnell, 2000), but that this was largely contained within relations among a relatively close elite group, who then of course needed to gain their members' acceptance for these agreements. This period from 1987 to 1994 was therefore one in which governmental and class elites negotiated an often painful process of stabilising the macroeconomy.

The 1990s: deepening and extending

Whereas the period of the early 1990s had been based on close cooperation between a relatively narrow group of elites, the late 1990s 'Celtic Tiger' period included significant new institutional innovations with a variety of efforts to extend and deepen 'partnership governance'. After a series of early legitimacy problems, the social partnership institutions were extended in the mid-1990s to partly incorporate organisations of the community and voluntary sector, and the National Economic and

Social Forum was founded (Larragy, 2006). Local-level partnerships were established that sought to deal with social exclusion and became key actors in local community development (Varley and Curtin, 2002). There were also some institutional innovations in the social welfare and education system during this period, including, for example, the transformation of some welfare inspectors into liaison officers. Similarly, we have already seen how a little-recognised but highly significant industrial policy alliance between science and technology-oriented state agencies, technical professionals and university constituencies emerged which supported the deepening of technical capabilities and collective learning across the Irish economy.

Rather than a grand alliance or an agreement negotiated by a small group of elites, these institutional innovations emerged through a variety of different new constituencies and groups that acted as 'institutional entrepreneurs'. Most of the institutional innovation was driven by actors outside the party political system, including business groups, civic and social groups, and agencies within the state. These innovations therefore emerged in spaces outside or in the gaps between the dominant political institutions in Ireland. In some cases, such as industrial policy, the crisis of the 1980s did not dislodge the dominant institutions, but gave other agencies concerned with the development of Irish-owned industries the additional organisational space and legitimacy to build their own policy agenda (Ó Riain, 2004).

The party political context was favourable at the time. The 'rainbow coalition' of Fine Gael and Labour from 1994 to 1997 provided greater freedom for the 'democratic experimentalism' of partnership institutions (Sabel, 1996) and promoted the role of Combat Poverty and the National Economic and Social Forum in national policy making (Larragy, 2006). However, the primary impetus for the institutional innovations of the era came from alliances of state bureaucrats and actors in civil society and business – and the party political system was largely content to give them the space to develop these initiatives. As previously noted, the availability of EU structural funds provided not only organisational resources but also institutional spaces within which new programmes could emerge without having first to fully dislodge the existing dominant policy system.

By the end of the 1990s, Ireland appeared to have 'made it' and to have 'converged' on European standards of living and even exceeded them. As was demonstrated in Chapter 2, this convergence was very partial. Nonetheless, there were a series of significant institutional projects underway in the political economy that promised to be building blocks for continued development to go alongside improved living standards. These included institutions of a developmental network state to support industrial upgrading and a network of new programmes in community development and labour market support, both operating within an overall context of improved investment and stable macroeconomic management. Significant tensions were also building, with increasing wage pressure as well as increasing stresses on infrastructure due to increased economic activity and a rapidly increasing population. The following section explores how the financialisation of the 2000s was both facilitated by certain political conditions and came to be internalised within the social compacts and political institutions that had underpinned the development of the 1990s.

Refusing the future: eroding the gains of the Celtic Tiger era

In the early years of the millennium the Irish economy showed significant signs of overheating, with a surge in inflation linked to the euro as well as to growing demand in the Irish economy. The period from 2000 to 2003 saw the growth of serious tensions within the social partnership process itself. Public sector workers sought increases to 'keep pace' with rising wages elsewhere in the economy, these efforts including a teachers' and nurses' strike in 1999. The inflation of these years put increased pressure on wages across the economy and on the partnership process itself to the point that, while all previous partnership agreements had been signed for a three- to four-year period, the private pay provisions of the deal signed in 2003 only extended for eighteen months. It appeared that Ireland's political economy faced a turning point, or at least a set of issues the response to which would define the future shape of the Irish political economy.

In the subsequent years leading up to the crisis of 2008, Ireland experienced a weakening of the core agreement at the heart of social partnership deals, a significant erosion of the state's public finances and a weakening of the political capacity to manage the process of development and growth. How these developments emerged is the topic of this section, while the underlying conditions that allowed this form of political erosion to take place are explored in the remaining parts of the chapter.

Weakening of creative corporatism

For some, the corporatism of the 1990s was simply another form of brokerage politics, now writ large at the national level in the form of brokering between various 'insiders' which over time increasingly favoured particular sections of the workforce, particularly the public sector. From the left of the spectrum, corporatism was simply a cover for liberalism, with social partnership agreements delivering consent to free market policies and increasing the power of markets and corporations much more effectively than the free market itself could (Kirby, 2002; Allen, 2003). Both sides can point to some evidence for their claims. Public sector wages increased more quickly than those in the private sector for most workers through the 2000s, but at the same time, the share of national income going to workers fell in Ireland and across Europe from the early 1980s until the early 2000s (Flaherty and Ó Riain, 2013). Precisely because of the apparent contradictions in the record of Irish corporatism, it requires a more nuanced treatment in order to understand its contributions, its potentials and its weaknesses.

As discussed above, Ornston (2012) compares corporatism in Ireland unfavourably to the forms of corporatism in Denmark and Finland. He argues that there are three main kinds of corporatism: a 'conservative' version, which sought to manage employment relations in a stable economy (and which was the primary form analysed in the literature on 'old' social pacts); a 'competitive' version, which controlled inflation, managed public spending and delivered wage restraint in order to make industry competitive; and a more dynamic, innovative, 'creative' form in countries such as Denmark and Finland, where corporatist agreements allowed for institutional innovation and the negotiation of often-profound adjustment to economic change. In the creative model of corporatism, politics was able to both promote and shape the direction of dynamic change within the economy and society.

Ornston identifies the provision of risk capital, the provision of supports for training and other forms of labour market adjustment, and the provision of supports for R&D to facilitate industrial adjustment and upgrading as key policy measures in creative corporatist systems. While acknowledging that Ireland made efforts in all of these areas, Ornston ultimately classifies Ireland as a competitive corporatist economy. However, a closer look suggests a more complex pattern. Table 5.2 provides a comparative look at 'competitive' Ireland,

Table 5.2 Key indicators of types of corporatism in selected European economies in the late 1990s and mid-2000s

		Ireland		Denmark/ Finland		Austria/ Belgium		UK	
		Late 1990s	Mid-2000s	Late 1990s	Mid-2000s	Late 1990s	Mid-2000s	Late 1990s	Mid-2000s
Risk capital									
Business	Early stage venture capital (% of GDP)	5.2	2.0	6.7	4.5	4.4	1.2	4.7	8.7
Public	Sectoral aid (% of GDP)	.69	.19	.81	.55	.37	.13	.18	.08
Active labour market supports									
Business	% of labour costs spent on training	2.4	2.2	2.7	2.1	1.5	1.5	3.6	1.3
Public	Spending on active labour market policies (% of GDP)	0.95	0.53	1.35	1.04	0.67	0.67	0.09	0.05

R&D

Business	Business-funded R&D	.82	.70	1.48	1.93	1.31	1.72	.86	.74
Public	Government-funded R&D	.29	.38	.78	.79	.79	.84	.55	.56

Dates:

Venture capital, 1998–2001 and 2003–6

Training, 1999 and 2005

Active labour market policy, sectoral aid, R&D: 1996–9 and 2003–6

Sources: EVCA, 2010; Cedefop, 2010; Eurostat

Notes: the Eurostat data on sectoral aid offer the advantage of comparison, although they only cover aid scrutinised by the EU. Irish data on grants and subsidies to enterprise (CSO, 2012) do not track this series directly, but offer the same basic picture – with the CSO figures indicating that state aid consisted of 0.81 per cent of GDP from 1998 to 1999 and 0.52 per cent from 2003 to 2006. Note that these figures are almost identical to the Eurostat figures for Denmark and Finland.

Figures given in percentage of GDP understate Ireland's spending effort, given the gap between GDP and GNP. An added 15 per cent on to the existing figure for Ireland gives a truer measure of Ireland's share of national resources devoted to particular goals.

'creative' Denmark and Finland, 'conservative' Austria and Belgium, and the liberal UK for each of these three key policy areas for both the private business and public sectors. The analysis provides indicators for both the late 1990s and mid-2000s, with the specific periods indicated in the table notes. Most of the indicators are offered as a percentage of GDP and it should be noted that this generally under-estimates Ireland's efforts in these areas because of the significant gap between GDP and GNP noted in Chapter 2.

Looking first at the late 1990s, there are a number of important aspects to Ireland's comparative position. First, it is strikingly different from the UK, especially in the area of public supports for business, which are much higher in Ireland, and in public spending on active labour market policies, which is almost non-existent in the UK but was very significant in Ireland in the late 1990s. This is particularly important given that these spending figures relate only to active labour market policies and not to 'passive' spending such as unemployment assistance. Therefore, Ireland differs significantly from the liberal UK in the activism of its public agencies in support of business and labour activity. Comparisons with other small open economies in Europe are also instructive. Except for R&D investments, where Ireland has his-torically been particularly weak, Ireland's efforts to develop business through risk capital and public aid and to activate labour were signifi-cantly higher in the late 1990s than in the classically 'conservative corporatist' countries of Austria and Belgium.

In the 1990s Ireland was comparable to Denmark and Finland in its levels of risk capital provision, driven by the state, and of supports for training. As an aside, it is also worth noting that there are differences between Finland and Denmark. Both are high in terms of R&D levels, but Finland provides higher levels of risk capital, both through private venture capital and public state aid, and Denmark's training effort is higher in both the private and public spheres. Nonetheless, it is striking that in this period of the late 1990s, Ireland appears closest to the 'creative corporatist' economies in its provision of risk capital and training and active labour market supports.

The 2000s present a different picture. The profiles provided at the height of the financial bubble in Europe show that in most countries and in many different categories, levels of support for economic adjust-ment declined. While this process varied across the different types of countries and different types of supports, the shift in Europe as a whole from developmentalism to financialisation is clear in the figures. In the UK, for example, business spending on training declined while venture capital increased. Denmark and Finland weakened their efforts in all areas of promotion of risk capital and labour adjustment. Ireland's fall was particularly dramatic, except in the area of R&D, where the state concentrated its resources during this period. Despite remaining at a very low level of R&D as a percentage of GDP, Ireland had one of the highest growth rates in R&D spending and personnel across the OECD. This was particularly the case in the public system. However, in the areas of risk capital and labour market policy, the Irish public effort declined very significantly, such that it fell well behind Denmark and Finland and, in the case of active labour market policy, even behind Austria and Belgium. Nor is it the case that Ireland simply did not need venture capital or active labour market policy in the 2000s. Indeed, Ireland continued through the height of the boom to have the highest rate of jobless households in the EU (Whelan *et al.*, 2012). In addition, the challenges facing export industries based in Ireland in the 2000s were widely recognised and the need for significant additional support for the development of Irish-owned companies, for example, through the promotion of venture capital, was widely discussed.

Ornston's analysis fails to distinguish clearly enough between the Irish economy of the late 1990s and that of the 2000s. Ireland was more 'creative' than Ornston recognises in the 1990s and the drop-off in this creative effort in the 2000s was even more dramatic than he noted. There is a significant broader point here. If Ireland's form of corporatism changed so dramatically from the 1990s to the 2000s, this cannot be due to constant structural features of the economy or polity. Instead, the story of Irish corporatism is one of surprising if hidden progress in the 1990s, but a progress whose promise was never fulfilled and indeed was undermined in the 2000s.

Table 5.3 explores the challenges of industrial adjustments in the late 1990s and through the 2000s in more detail. It provides details of the main manufacturing export sectors as well as the computer software and R&D services sectors. Based on EU-wide data, it provides a snapshot for each sector's employment in Ireland in 2007, how employment changed in each sector in the late 1990s and during the 2000s, and which European countries gained the most employment in each of these sectors across this ten-year period from 1997 to 2007.

Table 5.3 *Employment in export sectors, 1997–2007*

Sector	Total Irish employment 2007	Change in Irish employment 1997–2001	Change in Irish employment 2001–7	Leading countries gaining employment 1997–2007 (indicative)
Office machinery and computers	12,175	4,440	−7,603	Poland
Electrical machinery	7,657	−654	−5,516	Czech Republic Poland Spain Slovakia Romania
Communication equipment	7,782	−758	−4,999	Czech Republic Slovakia Finland
Other machinery	12,715	−1,103	−1,262	Spain Austria
Recorded media	15,274	1,195	−3,559	Spain Poland
Chemicals	23,999	3,305	231	Spain Belgium
Rubber and plastics	9,671	−451	135	Czech Republic Poland Spain France
Non-metallic minerals	11,821	1,007	1,184	Spain
Fabricated metal	14,242	1,229	1,289	Spain Poland
Medical devices	25,846	5,294	5,914	Spain Italy Misc. others
Computer software and services	33,546	10,238	14,370	Germany France Italy UK Misc. others
R&D	3,181	543	2,380	France UK

This provides a picture not only of the trends in Irish export industry employment but also of the major competitor locations for foreign investment and the other growth economies in each sector across Europe. The high-profile ICT manufacturing sectors grew in the late 1990s, but declined dramatically in the 2000s. This applies to both computing and communications equipment and to the manufacturing of software ('recorded media'). Related areas declined more slowly or saw relatively slow growth, including general machinery manufacturing and supply industries such as rubber and plastic. Nonetheless, some manufacturing sub-sectors did reasonably well. In particular, medical devices replaced ICT as the lead manufacturing sector in Ireland. While the output of the chemicals and pharmaceuticals sector increased enormously, this did not translate into major employment growth in the 2000s. Export service sectors also saw rapid growth in employment, with software a particularly dynamic sector (Ó Riain, 2004). Indeed, the number of jobs added in computer software per annum was roughly the same in the mid-2000s as in the late 1990s and the level of employment would have been significantly higher had it not been for the dot-com bubble of 2001–3.

The overall stability of the Irish export sector from 1997 to 2007 masks a number of different trends. First, there were important changes over time. The late 1990s saw significant growth in almost all areas. This was slowed dramatically by the dot-com bubble of 2001–3, which coincided with the inflation and wage push in the general macroeconomy. While sectors such as software recovered from the dot-com fiasco, others such as computers and communications equipment never did and went into significant decline. Second, over time, Ireland lost employment in the labour-intensive low- or medium-tech sectors. Irish wages rose rapidly in the 2000s, as did productivity (although the meaning of productivity in Ireland comes with a health warning, given transfer pricing and other accounting arrangements in transnational corporations). Nonetheless, compared to competitor countries in Eastern Europe, Ireland's wages were significantly higher. In these sectors the main competition came from Eastern Europe, although Spain also made gains in many of these sectors in the late 1990s. In a similar fashion to Ireland, Spain saw a boom in export manufacturing employment in the late 1990s which was sidelined by a property and credit bubble in the 2000s.

Third, the sectors where employment expanded significantly also expanded in the major core economies of Europe. Wage competition was significantly less important in these areas. Ireland lost out in the lower-wage, more labour-intensive sectors and a failure to control cost competitiveness hastened the loss of those jobs. However, it made greater progress in sectors where it was competing with other high-wage economies to develop more sophisticated industries including medical devices and software.

Given the inevitability of some increasing costs during and after Ireland's economic boom, a movement into higher-wage, more sophisticated sectors was an inevitable challenge to be managed by the Irish political system. However, while this management was relatively effective in the late 1990s, it was much less so in the 2000s. Failing to manage cost competitiveness resulted in dramatic declines in certain sectors where Ireland was already exposed. At the same time – and arguably more importantly – the expanded industrial supports for the kind of transition to more sophisticated sectors that could have ensured continued job growth were not forthcoming. Indeed, as has been noted already, the 'creative corporatism' that would support such a transition was at its high point in the late 1990s and was sidelined and eroded significantly in the 2000s when it was arguably needed even more.

In conjunction with the decline in developmental effort in the 2000s, the Irish state expanded its use of tax incentives (or 'tax expenditures') across the 2000s (Collins and Walsh, 2010). In property, these were extensive and are well documented.

Irish property developer Simon Kelly (2010) notes in his account of the property bubble and crash that he was told in the early 2000s by the then Minister of Finance that a certain tax incentive was introduced instead of a policy regulation because the government did not want to interfere in the market. Kelly remarks wryly that the Minister seemed unaware that the incentive constituted a very direct and significant market intervention. This is clearly state intervention – but of what kind? The cross-national evidence shows that extensive use of tax incentives as a policy instrument is strongly associated with liberal political economies. Table 5.4 draws on OECD (2008) research across seven countries and the work of Collins and Walsh (2010) on tax incentives in Ireland. It gives a summary overview of the extent of tax expenditures in each country and of the importance of the

Table 5.4 *Tax expenditures in eight countries, mid-2000s*

	Developmental state	Christian democratic		Mediterranean	Liberal			
	Korea, 2006	The Netherlands, 2006	Germany, 2006	Spain, 2008	Ireland, 2006	UK, 2006–7	US, 2008	Canada, 2004
All tax expenditures as % of total tax revenues	14.3	5.1	8.5	12.5	20.2	35.2	33.7	44.4
All tax expenditures as % of GDP	1.75	1.06	0.26	1.41	6.48	4.90	5.21	5.16
Retirement and health	0.31	0.06	0.00	0.17	1.96*	2.32	2.07	1.95
Business/R&D/ employment	1.04	0.79	0.04	0.60	1.85**	1.07	0.80	1.09
Housing and property	0.05	0.05	0.18	0.41	2.08***	1.20	1.05	0.20

Sources: OECD, 2008; Collins and Walsh, 2010

Note: categories of countries based on Esping-Andersen, 1999

* Pension relief plus health in Collins and Walsh, 2010: Tables 2 and 3

** Enterprise and employment in Collins and Walsh, 2010: Table 2

*** Mortgage interest tax relief and property incentives (ongoing costs) in Collins and Walsh, 2010: Table 2 categories of incentives of most interest for this analysis. Care should be taken in interpreting the Irish figures as it has not been possible to harmonise them as the OECD research was able to do for the other countries. Nonetheless, the Irish case can be compared in terms of the orders of magnitude involved, which are often significant.

The OECD study shows that the three liberal economies studied (the US, the UK and Canada) were much more likely to use tax expenditures than the four non-liberal countries (Germany, Korea, the Netherlands and Spain). Ireland fits firmly within this liberal group. Property and housing incentives (including tax relief on mortgage payments) were also much more significant in liberal political economies. However, tax incentives for housing in Spain were higher as a percentage of GDP and the four countries with the largest housing bubbles had the highest rates of property-based tax expenditures. The only area of tax expenditure where the non-liberal economies were close to and even exceeded the levels in liberal countries was in business incentives, where the UK, the US, the Netherlands and Korea led the way in the OECD study. Germany barely used tax expenditures as a policy instrument.

Ireland made extensive use of tax expenditures in all areas – although care must be taken with the specific comparisons with other countries, it fits firmly with the liberal countries and particularly with those that added to their property bubbles through tax expenditures. Tax expenditures are clearly a 'liberal' form of 'state intervention'.

Ireland's corporatism cannot be reduced to a 'competitive' form. Significant creative corporatist elements were present in the 1990s and they were relatively successful in promoting industrial adjustment. Moreover, these 'creative' Irish policy efforts were comparable to, if not quite at the level of, the more dynamic European economies. This potential was not built upon and the 2000s saw a significant erosion of creative, developmental efforts by the Irish policy system and the growing dominance of 'liberal' forms of state intervention, such as the use of tax incentives.

Fiscal hollowing out

In the 2000s, therefore, an emerging 'creative corporatism' was sidelined by the financialisation and liberalisation that was examined in some detail in Chapter 3. However, the difficulties being stored up for

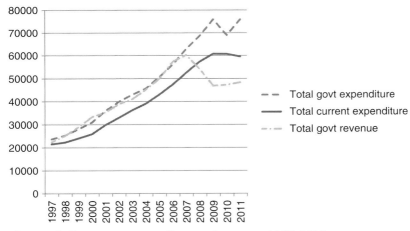

Figure 5.1 Government expenditure and revenue, 1997–2011
Source: Department of Public Expenditure and Reform Database

the state and the public sector in the 2000s went further than this. One of the particularly difficult features of Ireland's crisis has been the large deficit in the public finances. This has been partly due to the state taking on the burden of banking debt, but has also been caused by a very large deficit in the primary budget balance of the state. Figure 5.1 shows the trend in government expenditure and revenue from 1997 to 2011. It shows a steady and rapid rate of increase in both current expenditure and total expenditure from 1997 to 2007. However, it also shows that until 2007, Ireland's expenditure closely matched its revenue and Ireland maintained public finances that were in balance while still being able to increase public spending and make significant capital investments.

Yet, after 2007, this happy situation turned rapidly to crisis. Government revenue dropped by over €10 billion within two years, while expenditures continued to rise until 2009 due to continuing commitments, but also increasingly to social protection payments and bank debt and debt interest payments. By 2009, the gap between spending and revenue had widened to over €20 billion per annum from a position of balance in 2007. Some problems in the public finances were inevitable given the collapse of the banking sector, the cost to the public purse of that collapse and the decline in economic activity

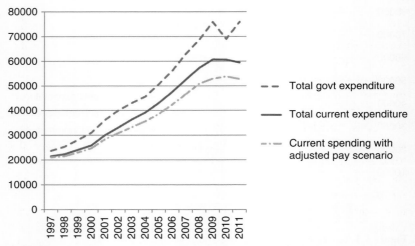

Figure 5.2 Government expenditure and pay, 1997–2011
Source: Department of Public Expenditure and Reform Database

during these years. However, the scale of the crisis in the public finances was also due to the underlying structure of state revenues.

Figure 5.2 examines the expenditure side of these difficulties in more detail. Government spending certainly increased rapidly over the ten years to 2007. However, this spending was hardly disproportionate as a proportion of national income. Total government spending was at 37 per cent of GDP in 1997 and 2007, a year when the average for the EU-27 countries was at 46 per cent of GDP (Ireland's expenditure as a percentage of GNP would in fact fall just under this figure). The figure also shows that capital spending was a significant development of public spending, particularly through the 2000s. However, the focus of political debate in the course of the crisis has been on the public pay bill. The figure provides a projection of current spending by the government if the public pay bill had expanded only in line with increasing public sector numbers and inflation rates. There are a number of assumptions built into this very conservative projection, which involves no increases in monetary living standards. First, despite much commentary on rising staffing levels in the 'bloated' public sector and a policy focus on reducing public sector numbers, the numbers in the public service in Ireland are lower than in most similar countries. The OECD report on the Irish public service (OECD, 2008) noted that Ireland had a relatively small public service and the analysis in Chapter 2 suggested that significant expansion in the public sector would be required for Ireland to achieve a sectoral employment profile similar to most small open European economies. Second, public wages could of course be a factor that increases inflation. However, the increase in inflation in the early 2000s was driven primarily by other factors (including the euro) and pre-dated the major increases in public pay levels. Third, there are other issues which would suggest that this is a conservative estimate. These include the presence of a much wider 'discrimination effect' in the gap between men's and women's pay in the private sector than in the public sector (Russell *et al.*, 2005). The pay gap between public and private sector is also much wider at the lower rates of pay (McGuinness *et al.*, 2010). Furthermore, the trend takes no account of the increasing professionalisation and rising education levels within both the public and private sectors and the heavily professional character of public sector employment, especially in health and education. Fourth, the inflation figures used in this analysis take no account of rising house prices, which were a significant source of wage pressure across the period. Nonetheless, it is clear that for a variety of reasons, public pay rates increased significantly in the 2000s and that current expenditure would be significantly lower without that expansion in pay. This growth was concentrated in the bubble years, with the gap between actual current expenditure and current spending under the adjusted pay scenario being relatively small until 2003–4. The following five years or so saw this gap expand relatively rapidly.

Figure 5.3 examines the structure of government revenues over this period where the collapse in government resources was particularly disastrous after 2007. The chart shows that this collapse was rooted in the structure of government revenues and not simply in reduced economic activity. It shows total government revenue but also revenue under two different scenarios. The first is total government revenue without capital gains or acquisition taxes, corporation tax or stamp duty taxes (stamp duty was a real estate sales tax which was charged on the buyer as a percentage of the price paid for each property transaction). These areas of taxation were closely linked to the credit and property bubble of the 2000s, and the gap between this line and total revenue shows the increasing reliance of public finances on these 'bubble taxes' (Ó Riain, 2010).

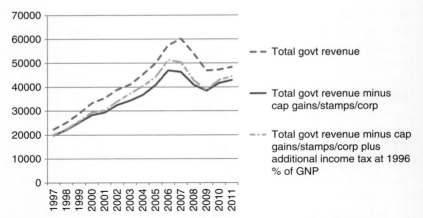

Figure 5.3 Government revenues and taxation structure, 1997–2011
Source: Revenue Commissioners, *Annual Reports*, various years

Each of these taxation areas had seen huge increases in the state's tax revenues. These increases were based on expanded activity as each of the areas of taxation was set at a relatively low level or was vulnerable to structural changes in the economy. While corporation tax had increased from 10 per cent to 12.5 per cent in 2003, this was a very low level by European standards. In addition, the real rate of corporation tax paid was significantly lower than this (as is true of many other European countries). Capital gains tax had been cut from 40 per cent to 20 per cent in 1998, helping to fuel the property bubble. Stamp duty had emerged as a major source of revenue due to the property bubble, despite being introduced in part to attempt to damp down property activity.

All of this was combined with a set of significant income tax cuts during the Fianna Fáil/Progressive Democrat government from 1998 to 2002. In 1997 a new government had come to power formed by Fianna Fáil and its minority partners, the Progressive Democrats, the closest Ireland had to an ideologically liberal party, combining economic policies based on low taxation, low spending and deregulation with a set of social policies that were broadly liberal. Even as the Celtic Tiger economy boomed in the late 1990s, the Fianna Fáil/Progressive Democrat government was making policy changes and decisions that would have serious effects long after that period.

Table 5.5 *Income tax rates, 1996–2002*

	Tax rate at lower band	Tax rate at upper band
1996–7	27	48
1997–8	26	48
1998–9	24	46
1999–2000	24	46
2000–1	22	44
2001	20	42
2002	20	42

Table 5.5 shows the steady cuts in income tax rates from 1996 to 2002 with the 'Rainbow' government of Fine Gael, Labour and the Democratic Left making making minor cuts at the lower rate, but the Fianna Fáil/Progressive Democrat government cutting the lower rate significantly over a five-year period and reducing the upper rate from 48 per cent to 42 per cent. In addition, the tax base shrank both in terms of the types of tax and in terms of the proportion of workers within the tax net. As a country with very high rates of wage inequality, one of the mechanisms negotiated for securing the living standards of lower-paid workers was the setting of the tax net so that it only applied to workers receiving more than the minimum wage. Figure 5.3 also shows that even maintaining the income tax take at the proportion of GNP at which it was set in 1997 would not have erased the gap in government revenues, although it certainly would have made a difference. It can be seen in the case of government revenues that the gap between non-bubble taxes, tax revenue and total government revenue widened significantly from around 1999 to 2003, a period when pay dynamics remained relatively sustainable. The structural weakening of the tax base was even more rapid during the bubble years of 2003 to 2007. While revenue in Ireland was dangerously dependent on growth in general, this dependence was heightened to disastrous levels by the reliance on these 'bubble taxes'. From the early 2000s onwards, the tax position became increasingly unsustainable. Overall, even as creative corporatism was eroded in the 2000s, so too was the prudent fiscal management of the late 1990s. While much of the damage was done in the bubble years from 2003 onwards, the foundation for these difficulties was laid in the period

from 1998 to 2002, particularly on the revenue and taxation side. Ireland signally failed to manage rapid growth in the 2000s.

Conditions of the looming crisis

The dramatic growth rates and historical developmental leap taken by Ireland in the 1990s inevitably led to some very significant inflationary pressures. This was a significant challenge to the institutions and strategies that had underpinned growth and development in the 1990s. It would no doubt have taken very strong institutions to avoid all fiscal difficulties during this time. However, the arrival of the Fianna Fáil/Progressive Democrat government, combining a commitment to tax cuts with a 'growth machine' economic policy, put paid to any possibility of this. While apparently maintaining a prudent fiscal balance, Ireland's public finances, and increasingly its development model, had been hollowed out. The rest of this chapter explores the conditions that made this hollowing out possible – and even likely.

Fragmented economy

The bubble in the Irish economy was rooted in a failure of economic coordination. The financial system, the structure of the macroeconomy and the foundations of public finances all suffered from failures of balancing institutions and sustainability. This was due to a deeply fragmented political economy. While sectoral differences are significant in all advanced economies, the fragmentation of the Irish economy went deeper still. Critics had long noted the 'disarticulated' character of the Irish economy, with a dynamic exports sector driven by foreign firms which were largely disconnected from the Irish-owned production sectors and the broader domestic economy. This can be extended by identifying four distinct 'projects' in the Irish political economy, each of which grew from the mid-1990s to 2007 and each of which was grounded in different business models, different social coalitions, different industrial relations and different forms of public support. Table 5.6 outlines the key features of these four projects.

The first 'project' was based around the export economy, in both manufacturing and business services, and accounted for 28 per cent of employment in 2006. The other three sectors were based more firmly in the domestic economy. The public sector, dominated by social service

Table 5.6 *Four projects in the Irish political economy*

	Export economy – manufacturing and services	Public sector – social services	Construction and allied activities	Personal service economy
Share of jobs 2006	28%	22%	13%	26%
Jobs added 1997–2006	102,000	154,000	130,000	130,000
Value added	Yes, high productivity	Social investment	Yes, low productivity	Low productivity
Link to taxation system	Corporate tax		Capital gains and stamp duty	VAT and social insurance
Primary social class	Professional/technical	Professional	Craft	Sales and service
Gender profile 2006	Male (varies by sector)	Female (36% of all female workers)	Male (21% of all male workers)	Male and female (33% of all female, 25% of all male)
Union membership	Low	High	Low	Low
Work organisation	From 'Taylorist' to 'lean' production	'Learning' production	Traditional work organisation	Traditional work organisation
Industrial relations	Non-union human resource management	Union; partnership	Direct managerial and craft control	Direct managerial control
Dominant state project	Developmental network statism	Social partnership	Growth machine	Regulatory state

employment in education, health and social protection, accounted for 22 per cent of jobs. A total of 13 per cent of all employment was in construction and allied activities, while personal market services accounted for 26 per cent. These broad sectors each added significant numbers of jobs in the decade up to 2006 and were roughly equally important to employment growth.

The social foundations of each sector were distinctive and it is these different features that form them into 'socio-political projects' (Peillon, 1982). The exporting economy and the public sector were dominated by the professional classes. Manufacturing and computer services were dominated by men, while the public sector had an increasingly female workforce – to the extent that 36 per cent of all female workers in 2006 worked in the public sector. Construction was dominated by largely male craft workers, with 21 per cent of all male workers working in construction in 2006. The personal service economy was dominated by sales and service occupations, with relatively low levels of formal education and skill, but accounting for a very large proportion of all employees, including about one in four men and one in three women.

These different workers worked under quite different conditions. Union density decreased in all sectors except the public sector, even though union membership increased in absolute numbers over the period. Each sector was associated with a quite different model of industrial relations, which became increasingly fragmented from the 1990s onwards (Roche, 1998). While arbitrary managerial control and highly mobile labour markets were the norm in construction and the service economy, the management of private and public sector professionals was quite different. In the public sector, unionisation remained relatively high, but indicators such as teamwork, opportunities for learning and employee autonomy suggest that a 'learning' model of work was well advanced in the public services. In the private sector in Ireland, such team-based methods were increasingly widely used, but typically within a context of greater managerial control (Holm *et al.*, 2010; O'Connell and Byrne, 2012). These were therefore not simply different sectors with different techno-economic characteristics, but were 'carriers' of different social coalitions and ways of organising work and employment relations.

Overall, then, each of these sectors was rooted in a quite different model of political economy. The personal service economy was relatively lightly regulated, including, for example, deregulation of product competition and already low levels of employment protection. A 'developmental network state' (Ó Riain, 2004) promoted the export economy while a 'growth machine' (Molotch, 1976) supported the rapid growth of construction. The expansion of the public sector has been largely linked with the institutions of social partnership. However, public sector expansion was as much a project of party politics, and the social partnership process had a wider reach across the public and private sectors. Each of these four projects was therefore in some sense 'socially embedded' in a different set of non-market institutions.

Each, however, was also 'liberal'. The expansion of private market services resulted in a lightly regulated sector providing relatively less skilled employment. The growth machine in construction was associated strongly with the large credit bubble driven by financial and property interests. Developmental network statism promoted the expansion of trade and international investments, even as state agencies used their industrial supports to attract foreign firms and to shape the activities of domestic companies. Social partnership too, while expanding public spending and employment significantly over the period, also produced a public system based in the high-growth years on comparatively low rates of taxation and spending.

Inter-sectoral links are crucial to the organisation of different worlds of capitalism. For example, the linking together of the fates of these high-productivity and low-productivity sectors is a key component of the Nordic model as wage restraint and shared welfare services control costs in the export sectors, while employers in the service sector are forced to improve productivity due to the relatively good conditions under which their employees work (Streeck, 1997; Pontusson, 2011). How then were these disparate projects in Ireland, with their different institutional and socio-political logics and different techno-economic characteristics, coordinated?

These sectors had remained broadly in alignment through the rapid growth of the 1990s, reinforcing each other's growth in a process of 'autocentric development' (see Chapter 2). However, as has been mentioned earlier, the 2000s saw significant imbalances within the domestic as well as the external economy – between the export and domestic sectors, between cost competitiveness and living standards, between spending and the tax structure, and between the property sector and the rest of the economy. The institutions that were to govern this increasingly complex economy themselves became more fragmented and failed to manage this task of internal coordination.

The fragmentation in governance at this time operated along a number of dimensions. O'Donnell *et al.* (2010) argue that a 'double segmentation' of partnership developed with a delinking of macroeconomic policy and industrial relations and a separation between public and private sectors within industrial relations itself, making the goals of social and economic policy transformation very difficult to attain. Uneven union density across sectors meant that the ability of unions to promote coherent and balanced development across sectors was limited. Similarly, industrial and innovation policy was separated from policies around upgrading of the workplace, with the former located in industrial development agencies while the latter was organised primarily through the social partnership institutions. There was no clear institutional mechanism for bringing macroeconomic concerns to bear on discussions of developments in welfare state, industrial and innovation policy or industrial relations, unlike in a number of European countries, where a central agency of some kind provides ongoing macroeconomic analysis and where there are institutional mechanisms to bring that analysis into various other spheres (Regan, 2012).

Furthermore, there was also a significant degree of fragmentation within each of these key policy areas. In the area of industrial and innovation policy, the promotion of Irish-owned firms had improved significantly in the 1990s, in part through the institutional separation of the state agencies responsible for foreign investment and domestic industry (Ó Riain, 2004). Ironically, this meant that the major expansion of science and technology funding in the late 1990s was defined largely by the needs of the foreign-owned firms, as Forfás and IDA Ireland shaped this policy process. Regan (2011) argues that industrial relations came to be characterised by a 'voluntarist' and 'exclusive' form of collective bargaining with no formal extension of negotiated wage agreements to non-union employees. Some significant advances were made in social policy in the period, including increases in pensions and belatedly in social welfare rates, as well as some innovations in healthcare (for example, the promotion of primary healthcare centres) which were apparently driven by social partnership processes in the face of civil service resistance (Regan, 2012).

However, such developments were overwhelmed by the broader credit and property bubble that was the dominant force shaping relations between sectors in the 2000s. In the 2000s, macro-level coordination was increasingly organised through markets, including markets for land, the expanding international market for labour through migration and in particular capital markets and the investment allocation decisions of banks and other financial institutions. The most serious implications were in the area of taxation. In each project of the Irish political economy, taxation policy was a significant mechanism of intervention (in keeping with the tendency towards reliance on tax incentives in more liberal economies – see Table 5.4). Corporate taxes were kept low to attract foreign firms, while Pay Related Social Insurance (PRSI) and the broader 'tax wedge' were reduced in order to promote small service employers. Crucially, of course, the property sector was promoted by low rates of capital gains taxes. Even the initial attempt to cool down the property sector through the use of real estate transaction taxes (stamp duty) ended up making the public finances dangerously dependent on the property bubble. While 'rational' in terms of the promotion of each project in the political economy, the overall structure of taxation was to prove disastrous. The problems with Ireland's taxation system related not only to its low levels of taxation but also to the structural fragility of that system.

Each of these sectoral projects was institutionally coordinated in ways that helped to promote their growth. However, the global coordination across these sectors and the management of the economic and socio-political tensions among them was either disjointed (in the case of public institutions) or speculative (in the case of governance through private capital and land and labour markets). These were then in turn heavily influenced by both electoral and party politics and the investment allocation decisions of banks and capital markets. The macro-level coordination that had been provided through dense elite networks in a less complex economy in the late 1980s and early 1990s was no longer equal to the challenge of coordination. A more ambitious set of partnership institutions had been developed in the 1990s and, as will be discussed later on, the number of public agencies expanded rapidly during this time. However, the mechanisms of network governance at the macro-level remained weak.

These weaknesses in governance were overcome in the 2000s through rapid growth and the boost it provided to the public finances, helping to hold the tensions between the four projects of the political economy. Teague and Donaghy (2009) have emphasised that the reason that social partnership persisted in Ireland was simply that it was able to deliver growth. Such a view, like many others, glides over the significant changes from the late 1990s to the 2000s and fails to explain how partnership delivered that growth. Nonetheless, it does point to a crucial element of the strategies for managing the economy in the 2000s. While the basis of Ireland's growth in those years was unsustainable, this growth allowed for the depoliticisation of investment and distributional politics. Ireland's public finances became 'addicted to growth' (Ó Riain, 2010). The Irish 'social bargain' increasingly came to consist of a loose network of diverse, more localised 'bargains' in distinct production regimes, lubricated by growth and the increasing revenues available to government. This fragmented and/or speculative governance ultimately underpinned the bubble economy, the disarticulated growth in the real economy and the erosion of the public finances. While there were significant elements of local coordination, overall the governance system suffered a significant collective action failure.

The politics of the wage-earner welfare state

In addition to production regimes, the 'welfare regime' forms the other key element of capitalist political economies (Ebbinghaus and Manow, 2001). While state spending increased significantly in the 2000s, Chapter 4 showed that the Irish welfare regime was comparatively focused on providing households with more after-tax income rather than significantly expanding the social services available to citizens. The structure of the Irish welfare state itself, in common with other liberal and Mediterranean welfare states, relied more heavily on transfer payments than on services. Indeed, the major policy report on the welfare state in the 2000s – the National Economic and Social Council (NESC) report on the 'developmental welfare state' – argued for both a rebalancing of income transfers, social services and active measures, and for a more flexible system of supports across the life course (NESC, 2005).

Ireland is typically classified as a liberal welfare regime based on its relatively low levels of taxation and spending, and on the significant use of means testing and other qualification mechanisms for benefits. However, there are a variety of aspects to the welfare state in Ireland which distinguish it from the pure ideal type of the 'liberal welfare regime'. Ireland's welfare state is better understood as a 'pay-related' welfare state (Ó Riain and O'Connell, 2000) or what Castles (1985) has called a 'wage earner welfare state', referring to the 'antipodean' welfare states of Australia and New Zealand. In this model, a basic, relatively low level of universal payments and benefits is provided with significant opportunities for topping up those benefits through occupational or contribution-based schemes. In the Australian and New Zealand cases this is focused more heavily on benefits linked to occupation and worker status, while in Ireland it operates primarily through the use of contribution-based schemes or the ability to use market income to gain access to public supports or to enhance them. This contrasts with other liberal welfare states such as those in Canada and the UK, with weaker wage earner elements, but where some of the major expansions in welfare were related to historical moments that allowed the building of national public institutions – for example, the National Health Service in the UK. While there are some welfare and wage-earner elements in the US system, it conforms much more closely to the classic liberal ideal type of an exceptionally low safety net.

Evaluated as an overall model of welfare spending, this was clearly a version of the liberal model. However, from the perspective of those citizens who can afford to top up the state-provided benefits, privately provided social supports were heavily subsidised by the public purse. In practice, the growing middle classes of the 1990s received extensive public subsidies for their pensions, healthcare, housing and education. For the middle classes that were growing through the private sector, these subsidies came largely in the form of tax incentives and reliefs. For the growing public sector, many of these supports were directly linked to their public employment (Ó Riain and O'Connell, 2000). Supports for the growing professional classes went beyond education to health, housing, pensions and other crucial factors shaping an internationally competitive labour force (see Table 5.7). Even as personal taxes were lowered, the Irish middle classes benefited from public subsidies and tax breaks – and so, by extension, did their employers. In short, the welfare state was in some respects strengthened for the middle classes even as it remained a minimalist support for the most excluded. The state did not withdraw – it provided crucial supports, but on an unequal basis. The professional classes in the high-tech and related sectors benefited from this two-tier system, as did their

Table 5.7 *Elements of the wage-earner welfare state in Ireland*

Policy area	Universal elements	Wage-earner welfare (occupational or pay-related)
Social protection	Unemployment assistance and other benefits	Unemployment benefit
Education	Public education, primary to tertiary	Subsidised private schools Occasional schemes allowing tax relief on educational fees
Childcare	Child benefit payments Pre-school payment	Maternity leave – statutory minimum with higher public sector rates
Health	Public access to hospital care system Means-tested medical card access to doctor care Drug subsidies (with means-tested element)	Private insurance allows priority access to public and publicly subsidised private providers National treatment purchase fund as market for private providers
Housing	Limited provision of social housing	Mortgage interest tax relief
Pensions	State pension	Public employee pensions Tax relief on private pension contributions Contributory old-age pension

employers (Ó Riain and O'Connell, 2000). Not all policy develop-ments are in the same direction, of course, with some dilution of the 'wage-earner' aspect of social security through abolition of pension and job-seeker pay-related benefit in 1984 and through the gradual erosion of entitlement to pensions and working-age wage-earner entitlements (Murphy, 2013).

Both the low level of social spending in the welfare mix of citizens and the pay-related nature of Ireland's welfare state militated against an expansion of universal social services as a key component of the Irish social compact. While the NESC (2005) project of the 'devel-opmental welfare state' attracted much policy discussion, the shift towards services and activation from income support was very limited.

How did this institutional context of welfare translate into particular attitudes to aspects of the welfare state? Table 5.8 provides a comparison of attitudes to welfare across the various worlds of welfare capitalism in 2008, based on a special module of the European social survey. Unfortunately, similar questions are not available for the earlier periods around the early 2000s.

Table 5.8 reports on the percentage agreeing or strongly agreeing that welfare and social benefits have particular effects, including on poverty, equality, personal behaviour, and degree of care about yourself, the family and others. Social democratic societies are clearly the most positive towards the welfare state, assessing welfare and social benefits as preventing poverty, promoting equality and making it easier to balance work and family life, while having very few negative behavioural effects. The clear fault line in the social democratic societies is the politics of immigration, where worries about immigrants being attracted by welfare are at least as high as if not higher than in most other European countries. However, the Nordic economies are also much less likely to see a risk to business and the economy from the welfare state. While the Nordic social democratic compromise may be fracturing (Kvist and Greve, 2011), it has not yet broken.

The Christian democratic societies are somewhat less cohesive, with greater concern for the cost on business and the economy as well as for the behavioural consequences of social benefits. France and particularly Germany are also distinctive in that they are much less likely to see the welfare state as promoting equality, and they are more likely to worry that welfare will attract immigrants. Given that worries about the effects on the economy are relatively mild in Germany, the politics of welfare appears to be shaped as much by social as by economic concerns.

Ireland and the UK tend to be among the societies that have the greatest worries about the behavioural consequences of welfare and social benefits, as well as the attraction of immigrants. In particular, about two-thirds of Irish and UK respondents thought that welfare and social benefits make people lazy, well above any other European countries. Ireland and the UK are also much less likely to say that welfare and social benefits make for a more equal society, although Ireland in particular approaches Continental and Nordic levels of support for the idea that welfare and social benefits make it easier to balance work and family life and in particular to prevent poverty.

Table 5.8 *Percentage agreeing or strongly agreeing that welfare and social benefits have certain effects*

	Prevents poverty	Makes more equal society	Easier to balance work and family	Makes people lazy	Makes people not care about others	Makes people not care about selves or family	Attracts immigrants	Too much strain on economy	Too much cost to business
Liberal									
Ireland	71	53	61	63	40	40	79	60	58
UK	57	41	58	66	49	50	76	52	51
Continental Christian democracies									
Belgium	70	69	70	42	42	39	59	39	56
France	66	59	65	47	49	53	71	52	58
Germany	67	45	59	40	43	35	82	39	45
The Netherlands	75	65	65	41	46	29	57	25	43
Nordic social democracies									
Denmark	72	60	62	29	39	29	67	26	25
Finland	62	67	67	34	37	23	64	20	33
Norway	65	67	71	43	39	22	71	25	34
Sweden	67	64	74	37	27	25	57	26	36
Mediterranean*									
Greece	57	60	56	18	21	17	50	36	32
Portugal	57	53	55	44	36	33	41	46	47
Spain	53	57	59	41	34	21	70	41	49
Eastern European									
Hungary	22	14	18	47	43	39	24	53	70
Poland	46	37	46	47	44	46	25	29	41

* Italy not in survey

Indeed, the picture of Irish welfare attitudes that emerges is not a uniformly negative one. Instead, Irish respondents tended to agree that welfare and social benefits would prevent poverty and make it easier to balance work and family life, and to a lesser extent promote equality. However, this was counterbalanced by particularly high levels of belief that welfare and social benefits make people lazy, attract immigrants and place a significant strain on business and the economy (although the latter is likely to have been heavily influenced by the growing economic crisis during the time that the survey was undertaken in late 2009). Ireland therefore shows both high percentages of people providing positive assessments and high levels of people providing negative assessments.

Table 5.9 looks a little more closely at this combination of relatively positive and negative assessments. It shows that it is not simply that opinion in Ireland is more polarised, but that many citizens hold both positive and negative beliefs at the same time. Such combinations of positive and negative views held by the same person are much more widespread in Ireland than elsewhere. This is particularly the case on questions of poverty, where 44 per cent of Irish respondents agreed or strongly agreed that welfare and social benefits *both* prevent poverty *and* make people lazy – two statements which in most other countries were seen as largely contradictory. To a lesser extent, the same pattern holds in terms of family dimensions of welfare, with one in four believing that welfare and social benefits both help to balance work and family life and make people not take care of themselves and their family, although the Irish results are less distinctive on this dimension. Interestingly, Ireland showed similar patterns in relation to attitudes to immigration, where high levels of belief that welfare and social benefits attract immigrants (generally thought to be a negative belief) combine with Ireland's second-highest level of responses in the EU that 'immigrants are good for the country's economy'. Rather than simply being hostile to welfare and social benefits, Irish citizens are deeply conflicted about the consequences of welfare and social benefits spending and the degree to which they are willing to make the necessary economic and social commitments to support them.

In the case of such ambiguity in attitudes, political and institutional factors would seem to be crucial in determining how attitudes are turned into specific policies and practices. There is therefore some space for political and administrative creativity. Table 5.10 explores

Table 5.9 Combining negative and positive assessments of welfare in a variety of countries

	% who agree/strongly agree that welfare BOTH prevents poverty AND makes people lazy	% who disagree/strongly disagree that welfare BOTH prevents poverty AND makes people lazy	% who agree/strongly agree that welfare BOTH helps to balance work and family life AND makes people not take care of themselves and their family	% who disagree/strongly disagree that welfare BOTH helps to balance work and family life AND makes people not take care of themselves and their family
Liberal				
Ireland	44	4	26	7
UK	36	4	29	5
Continental Christian democracies				
Belgium	30	5	28	4
France	31	6	35	3
Germany	26	5	22	6
The Netherlands	30	4	20	7
Nordic social democracies				
Denmark	20	7	19	7
Finland	19	6	16	3
Norway	27	4	16	4
Sweden	23	4	18	2
Mediterranean*				
Greece	10	13	8	11
Portugal	25	7	21	9
Spain	21	10	13	13
Eastern Europe				
Hungary	11	15	8	18
Poland	22	12	22	10

* Italy not in survey

Table 5.10 *Attitudes to welfare and to institutions in Ireland, 2006*

	Healthcare efficient?	Tax authorities efficient?	Healthcare fair?	Tax authorities fair?	Trust in country's parliament	Trust in politicians	Trust in the European Parliament
Welfare ambiguous/ positive	4.46	4.98	6.09	5.06	3.74	3.09	4.70
Welfare ambiguous/ negative	3.59	4.52	6.02	4.74	3.00	2.34	4.12
Welfare supporters	4.58	5.51	6.44	4.98	4.19	3.53	5.03
Welfare sceptics	3.98	4.89	6.22	4.51	3.34	2.76	4.49

Welfare ambiguous/positive: people who agree/strongly agree that welfare BOTH prevents poverty AND makes people lazy

Welfare ambiguous/negative: people who disagree/strongly disagree that welfare BOTH prevents poverty AND makes people lazy

Welfare supporters: people who agree/strongly agree that welfare prevents poverty AND disagree/strongly disagree that welfare makes people lazy

Welfare sceptics: people who disagree/strongly disagree that welfare prevents poverty AND agree/strongly agree that welfare makes people lazy the Irish public's attitudes to the institutions that might deliver this creative policy making and development. It compares three different groups of citizens – welfare supporters, welfare sceptics and those who are ambiguous about welfare and social benefits in terms of their effect on poverty prevention and laziness. It examines each of these groups and their basic attitudes towards the efficiency and fairness of both the public administration in healthcare and tax, and how much trust citizens can have in politicians and the institutions of Parliament in Ireland and Europe. Responses to the questions about institutions were ranked on a scale from zero to ten, with a higher score indicating a more positive attitude towards the institution.

The table shows clearly that across all groups, assessments of the public administration, even the beleaguered healthcare and taxation authorities, are more positive than the assessment of national politicians. The pattern of attitudes to public administration across the three groups of citizens is very mixed, with no clear relationship between general attitudes to welfare and attitudes to the various public institutions. Those who are ambiguous about welfare and social benefits are more likely to think that healthcare is efficient, but less likely to think that it is fair, whereas they are more sceptical that tax authorities are efficient, but more likely than the other groups to believe that they are fair. However, the link between trust in the political system and assessments of the benefits of welfare and social benefits is much clearer here across all spheres. Welfare supporters are the most positive towards politicians, welfare sceptics the least and those with ambiguous attitudes fall clearly between the other two. In addition, trust in national politicians runs behind trust in the national Parliament, which in turn runs behind trust in the European Parliament for all groups.

Even as politicians and parliamentary politics took clearer control of the direction of policy in Ireland in the 2000s, they lacked the trust of the citizens. Meanwhile, as noted in the initial discussion of Prasad's analysis of liberalism, belief in the fairness and efficiency of public administration was significantly higher. Added to the weak institutionalisation of social spending as part of the 'welfare bundle' for citizens and the wage-earner structure of many welfare benefits, these attitudes made the construction of a social compact based on expanded and widely available social services even more challenging. Without significant trust in the politicians that would have to deliver it and with relatively weak histories of universal social benefits, the obstacles to providing a credible commitment that wage restraint could be traded for enhanced welfare through social services was always going to be a difficult sell.

In such circumstances, the temptation was always that the cash nexus would become the focus of political exchange. As the bargains struck through social partnership and partisan politics expanded in terms of their scale during the 2000s, they relied most heavily on the return of after-tax income to citizens across the income distribution. While inequality persisted and significant weaknesses in labour market participation continued, households saw significant real increases in wages and, as the decade went on, social benefits. International Social Survey Programme data (not reported) show that the willingness of Irish citizens to give the government responsibility for expanding social services increased significantly between 2001 and 2006. However, this was too little too late. The structural flaws in private financialisation and of the public finances were already in place, and the international financial crisis was well advanced on its route towards the Irish economy. With fragmented production regimes, weakening structures of network governance, speculative private finance and a welfare regime that favoured cash rewards over social services, the underlying political economic conditions for managing Ireland's boom were not particularly promising.

Dualist state

Entering the 2000s, the possibility existed to build on the gains of the 1990s to deepen both the production and welfare regimes and put the macroeconomy on an even more sustainable footing. However, in practice, this period laid the foundation for the crisis that emerged in 2008. A wide range of the factors that shaped this crisis have been discussed and the characteristics of the production and welfare regimes in Ireland that made these policy failings all the more likely have just been reviewed. In the face of these structural challenges, the political tensions in the early 2000s and the availability of credit-fuelled growth, avoiding a bubble economy would have required a significant degree not only of political creativity but also of quite resilient institutions that could resist the temptations offered in this context. What were the institutions that policy makers and elites operated within?

It has already been noted that corporatist and developmentalist institutions emerged to play an important role through the 1990s, but lost much of their capacity in the 2000s. However, these institutional shifts were part of a broader system of governance. This system of governance was built upon a system that was largely inherited from the UK and the colonial era, including the Whitehall system of public administration and the Westminster system of parliamentary democracy. I have argued that the 1990s was an era in which public agencies were provided with a space in which they could exercise significant influence in a number of areas, in part because the focus of partisan politics was elsewhere. This space extended into the late 1990s, even as the new Fianna Fáil/Progressive Democrat government was making a number of policy decisions which were to have major long-term consequences. In the 2000s, partisan politics and in particular the politics of the electoral cycle came to dominate the political landscape once more. In the rest of this chapter I will examine the foundations of the Irish executive and representative public organisations, based on the Whitehall and Westminster models. I first examine how the wave of formation of public agencies in the 1990s led to the creation of a dualist state system, built upon the foundations of the Whitehall civil service model. In the following section I explore how a parliamentary system based on the Westminster model, but with a strong electoral system of proportional representation results in a highly centralised, almost oligarchic system of party government.

The Irish civil service was established largely along the lines of the 'Whitehall model'. This was a system of departmental hierarchies governed primarily through a permanent civil service under the direction of a government minister, with most civil servants being trained as generalists and pursuing their entire careers within the civil service. Relatively few of the civil service personnel were trained as experts in the field and in many cases upward mobility within the system was largely through movement across different departments. Internally within departments, the structure was typically hierarchical and close to a classic Weberian bureaucracy. In many respects, in a society based heavily on brokerage, this bureaucratic state system – at least in the national government – proved an important bulwark against corruption and clientelism. Nonetheless, there were significant problems of lack of expertise and the relatively under-developed size and resources of the civil service. As Breen *et al.* (1990) characterised it, the Irish state and its public administration had relatively high levels of autonomy from societal interests, but relatively little capacity to implement its programmes.

In the 1990s in particular, the number of state agencies formed on an independent or quasi-independent basis outside the civil service expanded rapidly. It is possible to examine this expansion in more detail and in historical context due to the availability of the Irish State Administration Database (Hardiman *et al.*, 2008). This database tracks the formation, closure and key areas of functions of each state agency formed outside each of the government departments and commercial semi-state organisations since the foundation of the state in 1922. The expansion of the 1990s came on the heels of two earlier, much less extensive rounds of expansion – each ended by an economic crisis. In the first phase, the new agencies largely added a developmental and sectoral management capacity to the colonial state. In the 1920s government agencies largely brought over, and somewhat added to, the institutions of colonialism. The 1930s saw the addition of a range of agencies relating to agriculture and to the development of enterprise, and this modest expansion of the colonial institutions came to an end with the economic crisis of the 1950s.

The 1960s saw a second phase of state expansion, the building of a modern state apparatus that proceeded alongside the growth in education, welfare, industrial development promotion and the general reach of the state during this period (Breen *et al.*, 1990). A number of additional agencies in areas such as health and safety, legal infrastructure and public order were added in the 1970s, but the crisis of the 1980s put an end to this period of the consolidation of the modern Irish state. However, by far the largest expansion in the number of state agencies was in the third phase of growth in the 1990s and 2000s.

Table 5.11 shows the major components of this growth. The table is organised primarily based on the function of the agencies that were added, of which four dominated: adjudication, advisory, regulation and delivery. Under each of these functions, the main policy domains involved are also listed. Taken together in each of the periods of the 1990s and 2000s, the detailed sub-categories listed in the table account for just under two-thirds of all added agencies. The table therefore gives us a sense of the key components of the expansion of the number of state agencies through these two decades. It is important to note that the figures refer to the number of agencies rather than their overall

Table 5.11 *Net state agencies added, 1990–2007*

	1990–2000	2000–7	Indicative examples of agencies
Net agencies added – all types	81	59	
Adjudication *of which:*	11	13	
Public order	3	4	Criminal Assets Bureau (1996), Personal Injuries Assessment Board (2004)
General public services	3	2	Information Commissioner (1997), Irish Financial Services Appeal Tribunal (2004)
Social protection	2	4	Equality Tribunal (1999), Disability Appeals Officer (2007)
Advisory *of which:*	15	14	
Social protection	1	6	Crisis Pregnancy Agency (2001), Health and Social Care Professionals Council (2007)
Education	6	2	Advisory Council for Science Technology and Innovation (2001), National Council for Special Education (2003)
Regulation *of which:*	18	27	
Health	5	4	Irish Medicines Board (1996), Health Information and Quality Authority (2007)
Enterprise	4	1	Competition Authority (1991), Irish Financial Services Regulatory Authority (2004)
Transport	1	4	Commission for Aviation Regulation (2001), Road Safety Authority (2006)
General public services	2	4	Irish National Accreditation Board (1993), Commission for Public Service Appointments (2004)
Education	1	6	National Council for Curriculum and Assessment (1999), State Examinations Commission (2003)

Table 5.11 (*cont.*)

	1990–2000	2000–7	Indicative examples of agencies
Delivery	41	6	
of which:			
Enterprise	15	1	Ports Companies (1997), Enterprise Ireland (1998), Digital Hub Development Agency (2003)
Education	4	−1	National Centre for Technology in Education (1998), Skillnets (1998)
Recreation	5	3	Irish Museum of Modern Art (1991), Horse Racing Ireland (2001)

Note: because of the double-classification of agencies, it is difficult to provide an assessment of exactly what proportion of agencies are covered by the detailed sub-categories above, but I estimate that it is approximately half of all agencies formed during the period.

budget or numbers of employees, which could vary significantly across agencies and policy domains and functions.

In addition to the data noted in the table, it is worth noting that the state withdrew significantly from actively trading in the market through a series of privatisations. There were sixteen fewer state trading agencies in 2007 than in 1990. This trend operates in parallel with the expansion of the number of regulatory agencies, which increased by forty-five over the two decades. One significant element in the expansion of state agencies has therefore been the marketisation of the economy and the shift of the state from direct producer and/or active competitor in the market to a regulatory role. A second clear trend is the increasing importance of non-judicial bodies that are involved in adjudicating disputes (for example, the Equality Authority). This driver of agency expansion relates to the expansion of the liberal rule of law into new areas of everyday and commercial life. Taken together, the regulatory agencies and those engaged in adjudication are driven largely by 'liberal' demands on the state. They account for almost one-third of the agencies added in the 1990s and an estimated two-thirds of the agencies added in the first seven years of the 2000s.

The agencies most closely related to a more 'activist' role for state agencies in directly delivering services and/or providing policy direction are those agencies classified as engaged in delivery or providing advisory capacity. For these two groups of agencies, the ratio is reversed, with the 1990s being the greatest period of expansion, when advisory and delivery agencies accounted for approximately two-thirds of new agencies, with this dropping to about one-third in the 2000s. In itself, these trends provide an indication of the changing focus of state activity across the two decades, although the building of delivery and advisory agencies in the 1990s presumably left limited room for further expansion in the 2000s.

What drove the expansion of advisory and delivery agencies through the 1990s and 2000s? The OECD report on employment in the public service identifies a number of key characteristics of Irish agencies: 'Irish agencies would [have]... governing boards, separate legal identities from that of the State, and with few civil servants as employees. Agencification in Ireland is primarily motivated by policy independence, the separation of policy and implementation functions, and the provision of representative boards, with only implicit objectives of improving performance and increasing flexibility' (OECD, 2008: 302). The OECD report appears to be correct in arguing that the goal of most agencies was not to reshape the core activities of the civil service itself (in the OECD's terms, 'improving performance and increasing flexibility'). Instead, agencies were largely formed to provide new capacity that was not otherwise available within the civil service. In the enterprise sector in particular, the influence of the model of the IDA was crucial in legitimating the idea of the quasi-independent agency. Indeed, one of the major clusters of agencies that formed related to such developmental concerns, including agencies across enterprise, science and education.

There are many debates regarding these agencies. Critics have questioned the sheer scale of the expansion and the growth in managerial or executive positions within the agencies. The OECD (2008) queried the impact of the agencies on improving public service operational efficiency. McGauran *et al.* (2005) argued that the expansion of these agencies consisted in a weakening of democracy as many of the agencies effectively made and implemented policy, but from a position outside the parliamentary process and through elites appointed unilaterally by the government. These are important issues that require more detailed examination. The example of enterprise suggests that such agencies were effective in certain cases (Ó Riain, 2004). However, they were subject to a variety of pressures, both of over-centralisation and weakening accountability and oversight, as McGauran *et al.* had feared, and of fragmentation between agencies and of policy effort, as well as being too weak to resist or shape the speculative actions of the financial system (Ó Riain, 2009).

However, for our purposes, the most important question is the impact of the expansion of these agencies on the overall structure of the Irish state. These state agencies in the 'public service' became the primary vehicle for the development of state capacity through the 1990s and 2000s, while public administration through the 'civil service' of government departments remained relatively stable. Here too, the classic case had been an enterprise agency, where the IDA had begun within the Department of Industry and Commerce, but had become such a successful vehicle for the administration of industrial development that, over time, policy formulation moved from within the government department to public service agencies. This arrangement was further formalised in 1994 with the formation of a new set of agencies, including an over-arching policy and strategy agency called Forfás. Public service agencies became a vehicle then for many new policy initiatives and the formation of such agencies entered the repertoire of action for politicians and policy makers seeking to respond to political demands. At the same time, such agencies became the vehicles for much of the innovation within public administration over this period. However, they operated largely at arm's length from the existing government departments, sometimes combining a reporting relationship to the department with an almost lobby group-like pressure upon the department. This could be dangerous territory and a series of agencies that had been set up to tackle poverty and inequality were abolished in the years just before the crisis hit for largely political rather than fiscal reasons.

The overall effect of this was to produce a new dualism within the public administration of the state itself. While the civil service departments took care of most of the standardised delivery of public services, much of the policy development and organisational innovation was officially located in agencies that were at arm's length from departments. In practice, agencies and departments were often largely autonomous and the innovation in agencies failed to spur innovation in departments, even as coordination across agencies was often difficult and partial. Much of this coordination was heavily based on individual network ties among the key executives in agencies and departments. While 'joined-up government' was one of the catch-phrases of the era, in practice, the joining-up of agencies and depart-ments was quite hit and miss, often depending on the structure of personal ties. This also produced a structure where, even with greatly expanded spending, the state layered a series of new policy initiatives and programmes on top of a relatively unchanged basic system of administration and social services. The formation of new, semi-autonomous agencies had seemed like an effective way to produce innovation without having to face the substantial reform of civil service departments. However, it ended up producing a dualism between what remained a comparatively under-resourced system of social services (in international terms) and a growing set of agencies that could quite effectively undertake particular projects without substantially reforming the structure of the overall system. In effect, this new state structure reproduced the kind of dualism that was seen in the fragmen-tation of the political economy and the pay-related welfare regime. While there are examples of both innovation and waste in this agency sector, it was also clear that these agencies had only limited power in setting the overall direction of policies.

Hierarchical electoral politics

While state agencies had expanded rapidly in number, their ability to affect the direction of the overall policy system would seem to be somewhat less than observers have thought. Electoral politics, which had appeared weaker for some time, came to the fore again in the 2000s. As noted earlier, Fianna Fáil enjoyed a remarkable period of electoral dominance from 1932 to 1973. However, Irish electoral politics was much more unstable in the following quarter of a century, with a series of alternating Fianna Fáil and Fine Gael/Labour govern-ments. There were also a number of periods of highly unstable govern-mental arrangements (1981–2) and even a Fianna Fáil/Labour coalition from 1992 to 1994.

Figures 5.4 and 5.5 show the underlying electoral dynamics behind this shift away from Fianna Fáil's hegemony. Figure 5.4 indicates Fianna Fáil's share of total seats from 1961 onwards. Until the early 1980s, Fianna Fáil was typically able to secure a slim overall majority of seats and form a majority government. However, between 1981 and

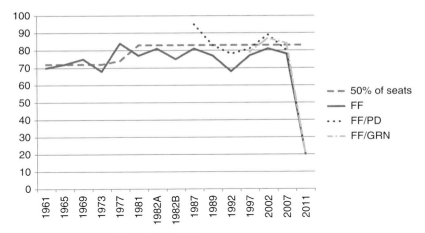

Figure 5.4 Fianna Fáil's electoral history

1992, its share of seats fell below 50 per cent, so that it was forced to form governments based on support from independent Members of Parliament. Where Fianna Fáil's seats fell too far below the majority, the opportunity presented itself for Fine Gael and Labour to form a coalition. However, Fianna Fáil's ability to re-invent itself is also striking, once more as a party of permanent government but this time in a series of coalitions with junior partners. The Progressive Democrats, a free market liberal party formed in a bitter split from Fianna Fáil in 1985, became its coalition partner a mere four years later. When the Progressive Democrats fell on hard times, Fianna Fáil replaced them in 2007 with the Green Party. In one of the apparent laws of Irish politics, each party that has seen through full-term coalition governments with Fianna Fáil has ultimately faced electoral destruction, with both the Progressive Democrats and the Greens currently having no parliamentary representation. Irish electoral politics has therefore gone through three main arcs: first, a period of Fianna Fáil dominance as a majority 'permanent government'; second, a period where Fianna Fáil struggled to respond to a more socially liberal Ireland, allowing for a variety of governmental arrangements; and finally Fianna Fáil's re-invention of itself as once more the party of permanent government, but now in a series of coalitions.

Figure 5.5 shows why it was possible for Fianna Fáil to re-invent itself in this way, outlining the electoral fortunes of three potential

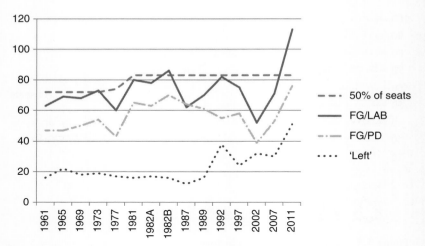

Figure 5.5 Fine Gael and Labour coalition possibilities

alternatives to Fianna Fáil-led governments. Electoral support for 'left' parties (Labour, Sinn Féin, the Workers' Party, the Democratic Left and a series of smaller parties now linked in the United Left Alliance) has historically been very low, although it has been increasing since the late 1980s. A coalition of 'liberal' parties, Fine Gael and the Progressive Democrats, was more viable electorally, but never reached a level of support that would have allowed them to form a government. While neither of these liberal or left coalitions was ever actually on offer to the electorate, neither of them was in any case close to the level of electoral support required to provide a viable alternative government. In practice, then, the uneasy alliance of Fine Gael and Labour has been the only viable electoral alternative to Fianna Fáil, with the peaks of electoral support in Figure 5.5 coinciding with the formation of coalition governments. An intriguing alternative is a 'populist left' government of Fianna Fáil and Labour, which formed in 1992 and lasted two years. Perhaps the greatest obstacle to this has been Labour's fear of electoral decimation in the wake of coalition with Fianna Fáil, a fear which does not seem irrational when the fate of the Progressive Democrats and the Greens is recalled.

The arrival of the Fianna Fáil/Progressive Democrat government in 1997 was not therefore simply a one-off electoral event, but was the product of a broader set of shifts in Irish electoral dynamics. It represented the reformulation of the historical project of Fianna Fáil hegemony, but in a new form, including the possibility of coalition. This was Fianna Fáil's strategic response to the modernisation and liberalisation of Irish society, and it proved a remarkably effective political strategy from 1997 to the first post-crisis election of 2011, when support for Fianna Fáil was decimated and the Progressive Democrats disbanded.

This electoral re-alignment is all the more interesting for how it connected to the politics of social class and the different projects of the political economy that have been covered earlier in this chapter. While it is difficult to find reliable data on party voting connected to both occupation and sector, given the large scale of the survey required to provide reliable estimates, Table 5.12 provides some information on the percentage of all workers and of managers and senior officials

Table 5.12 *Percentage who say they would vote for Fianna Fáil in an election, 1994*

	All occupations	Managers and senior officials (number of cases)
Agriculture, forestry, fishing	43.6%	
Mining and quarrying	35.4%	
Manufacturing	35.7%	39.1% (69)
Electricity, gas and water supply	24.2%	
Construction	40.5%	57.7% (52)
Wholesale, retail, repair	34.6%	45% (131)
Hotels and restaurants	31.9%	
Transports, storage and communication	30.7%	
Financial intermediation	35.8%	
Real estate, renting and business activities	27.6%	
Public administration and defence	38.7%	
Education	31.9%	
Health and social work	37.4%	
Other services	25.9%	
Total	35.2%	41.8%

Source: Living In Ireland survey, individual dataset, 1994

in various economic sectors who said that they would vote for Fianna Fáil in an election. The data are from 1994, at the start of the boom years and three years before what proved to be a decisive election in shaping the road to the crisis of 2008. They show that while 35 per cent of people in all occupations said they would vote for Fianna Fáil, that share of the vote was significantly higher in agriculture and construction. The relatively low vote for Fianna Fáil in real estate, renting and business activities shows they were relatively weak among workers and elites in business services and computer software (where many managers at the time voted for the Progressive Democrats). There are fewer sectors for which there are enough managers in the survey to provide a reliable estimate. However, it can be seen that Fianna Fáil support among managers was higher than in the overall population at 42 per cent. The small employer sector of wholesale and retail gave them slightly more support than the national average, while Fianna Fáil support among manufacturing sector managers fell just below the national average. What is perhaps most striking is that 58 per cent of managers in construction said that they would vote for Fianna Fáil in an election. The bulk of the remaining manufacturing managers reported that they would most likely vote for the Progressive Democrats in an election. Therefore, the electoral alliance of Fianna Fáil and the Progressive Democrats also represented a class and inter-sectoral alliance between the export-oriented managers and the construction growth machine.

These small differences in electoral fortunes are greatly amplified in Irish politics by the dominance of government within the parliamentary system. Table 5.13 summarises two measures of centralisation of the parliamentary process in European democracies provided by Döring (2001). Based on these data, the scores for the two measures are combined into an average 'score' for the centralisation of parliamentary procedural power in government in each of these countries, organised by the worlds of welfare capitalism. There is a clear link between the parliamentary process and the form of capitalism in the broader political economy. Ireland and the UK, rooted in the Westminster model and liberal market economies, have exceptionally high levels of concentration of procedural power in government. Government dominates parliamentary procedures and controls the timetable of legislative committees. Indeed, in Ireland, the role of committees and other processes outside the parliamentary chamber in government

Table 5.13 *Centralisation and decentralisation of parliamentary institutions*

	Government dominance of parliamentary procedures	Control of the timetable in legislative committees	Average 'score'
Liberal market economies			**1**
Ireland	I	I	1
UK	I	I	1
Mediterranean economies			**2.7**
Italy	VI	II	4
Greece	II	II	2
Portugal	III	II	2.5
Continental social market economies			**3.4**
Austria	IV	II	3
Belgium	IV	III	3.5
Germany	IV	III	3.5
The Netherlands	VII	IV	5.5
Switzerland	III	III	3
France	II	II	2
Nordic social market economies			**3.75**
Denmark	V	IV	4.5
Finland	V	I	3
Norway	IV	II	3
Sweden	V	IV	4.5

Source: Döring, 2001

Note: average scores calculated as an average, where I =1, II = 2 and so on

has been historically particularly weak. It is in the Continental and Nordic social market economies that we find the greatest decentralisation of power in parliamentary procedures, allowing opposition parties to take a bigger role in shaping policy even when not in government. In this group it is only France, the icon of 'statism', that even begins to approach the Irish and UK levels of concentration of power in government. In the Irish system, government has almost complete control over parliamentary procedure and the development of policy priorities and content. Indeed, even within government, backbenchers are largely reduced to the role of localised interests of representation and policy development is highly concentrated in the cabinet of 15 government ministers, appointed directly by the Prime Minister.

This tendency towards hierarchy and concentration of power within government was particularly evident in the Fianna Fáil/Progressive Democrat governments from 1997 to 2011. Table 5.14 shows the distribution of department ministries across the six individuals who spent more than ten of the fourteen years across this period as a minister. In addition, Charlie McCreevy is included as he spent the first seven years of the period as Minister for Finance before leaving to take up a position as EU Commissioner. This was the core group of key figures of the period, with a small number of others figuring in prominent ministries from time to time – perhaps most importantly Michael McDowell of the Progressive Democrats, who served as Minister for Justice for five years before leaving politics. There is a remarkable concentration of ministerial power among a small group. The group of seven accounted for all of the cabinet years as Taoiseach and Minister for Health, and about 80 per cent of the cabinet years as Ministers for Finance, Enterprise and Foreign Affairs. Control over these ministries was particularly heavily concentrated in the inner core of Taoiseach Bertie Ahern, Micheál Martin, Brian Cowen and Mary Harney. When we extend that core to include Noel Dempsey and Dermot Ahern, this also extends the reach of this group into a series of other departments where about one-third of the cabinet years are attached to this group. There are a number of other individuals, such as John O'Donoghue and Mary Coughlan, who could be included with Dempsey and Dermot Ahern in this 'outer core'. The key positions in Irish politics for a period of fourteen years were held by an inner core of four or five individuals supplemented by an outer core of another four or five. The rest of the cabinet posts were more dispersed and were often allocated based on regional and other electoral considerations. The Westminster model of liberal governmentalism combined with the structure of Irish politics to produce an oligarchy within Irish democracy from 1997 to 2011.

Table 5.14 *The distribution of ministers and ministries, 1997–2011*

	Ahern, B	McCreevy	Cowen	Martin	Harney (PD)	Dempsey	Ahern, D	% of years held by core
Taoiseach	11		3					100%
Finance		7	4					79%
Enterprise				4	7			79%
Foreign affairs			4	4			4	80%
Health			3	4	7			100%
Education				3		2		36%
Environment						5		36%
Justice							3	21%
Social							5	36%
Marine/communications						3	2	36%
Tourism/transport						4		27%
Agriculture								0%
Arts/Gaeltacht								0%
Defence								0%
Public enterprise								0%

Conclusion

Ireland's apparent exit from the vicious circle of under-development in the 1990s did involve genuine economic and social progress, but also significant institutional innovations within the political economy. In particular, industrial development was driven forward both by multi-national capital and by an emerging 'developmental network state'. Macroeconomic stability was provided through neo-corporatist social partnership agreements from 1987 onwards. Taken together, these provided a form of what Darius Ornston has called 'creative corporatism' (Ornston, 2012). While many authors, including Ornston, have described Ireland as a case of competitive corporatism, this chapter has argued that this label poorly describes the Irish experience. While Ireland shares certain features of the competitive corporatism model – including an emphasis on cost competitiveness and relatively low public spending – the label obscures key features of both the 1990s and the 2000s. In the 1990s, Ireland delivered supports for active labour market policy, risk capital and (to a lesser extent) R&D that approached the levels provided in the European social market economies. Irish corporatism in the 1990s was therefore more creative than the competitive corporatism description allows. On the other hand, there was very little that was competitive about the Irish economy in the 2000s when in many respects Irish corporatism devolved into a form of 'corporate pluralism' (Regan, 2012). Nonetheless, there were important institutional innovations in the 1990s that held the potential for a significant transformation of the Irish political economy in the 2000s.

However, at the start of the 2000s, there were significant challenges for the Irish political economy. In attempting to sustain its competitiveness as a peripheral location, Ireland faced significant cost pressures from economic growth and rising living standards. At the same time, such inevitable cost pressures made the need for industrial upgrading and the deepening of development ever more urgent. There was a significant twin challenge here – to manage the upgrading of the Irish economy while simultaneously managing increasing costs within Ireland. Both of these challenges were amplified by external forces. The advent of the euro provided a nasty inflation shock, while the bursting of the dot-com bubble in 2001–3 rattled the manufacturing and high-tech service sectors, just as the Irish economy faced its first serious bout of macroeconomic overheating. The politics of responding to these challenges was also made more difficult by the availability of a growth model based around a property bubble and supported by a domestic 'growth machine'. This challenge too was amplified by external forces – in this case, the availability of cheap credit as interest rates in the Eurozone were kept low to reflate the German economy.

Therefore, the political challenge was substantial for Ireland in the early 2000s, despite the significant successes of the late 1990s. Nonetheless, the degree to which the policy system and the society failed to manage these challenges was dramatic. Costs and development were poorly managed while public finances became dangerously unsustainable. In understanding why Ireland's development in the 2000s took the path it did, it is important to look beyond the failings of personalities or particular individuals to the structure of institutions and the context in which these individuals operated. These problems in the Irish political economy are ultimately rooted in the interplay between liberal, clientelist and corporatist politics. Ireland's historical under-development was underpinned, on the one hand, by liberal post-colonial institutions that did not prove up to the task of promoting development and, on the other hand, by clientelist or brokerage politics which reproduced the dominance of Fianna Fáil for a number of decades and more generally exerted a deeply conservative influence on the society as a whole. In the 1990s, corporatism appeared to offer a way out of this vicious cycle, a new pathway that was distinctive as much in its institutional innovations as in its economics. This chapter has argued that the institutional innovation of that decade was genuine and significant changes occurred which contained potential for further development. These institutions still had their own difficulties and significant critiques regarding questions of democracy and accountability are well taken. However, the 2000s saw the resurgence of the combination of liberalism and clientelism in a new form. The property and banking 'growth machine' drove many of the key economic decisions of the decade while corporatism was hollowed out in part to become a more narrow form of political exchange in an increasingly speculative economy.

I examined this process along four different dimensions. These included the production and welfare regimes in the political economy and the dynamics of state administration and parliamentary and electoral politics in the political system itself. Ireland's production regime was characterised by four major projects within the political economy. Each of these was promoted by a distinct set of domestic institutions, which played a significant role – for better and for worse – in their growth and development. However, political fragmentation and an emphasis on pluralism and market coordination led to a major collective action failure at the macro- or systems level. While each project was growing, coordination across projects of the macroeconomy was left to increasingly speculative markets in labour, and particularly land and money. The welfare regime was historically characterised by a low level of taxation and spending, which was characteristic of liberal welfare states. The 1990s and the 2000s saw a significant expansion in the numbers working in the public sector, although Ireland remained significantly below European levels of public sector employment (OECD, 2008). However, the distributional projects of the welfare state centred primarily on income transfers rather than the expansion of services. This was reinforced by the 'pay-related' or 'wage-earner' structure of the Irish welfare regime. Negotiations about social welfare, in the broadest sense, focused primarily on the cash nexus rather than on shared public services and social investment.

On the political side, a state administration that had historically been poorly resourced and based on the Whitehall model expanded its policy capacity in the 1990s primarily through the formation of public agencies outside the system of government departments. The net effect of this development was to create a dualism within the state, with much of the innovation in policy development and delivery located in agencies that were relatively far from the day-to-day operation of the core systems of state administration and services. This dualism weakened the capacity of the state to provide overall coordination and/or a counterbalance to the destructive effects of the financial markets. This fragmentation in the system of state administration created the conditions under which party politics became dominant once more in the 2000s. The Irish parliamentary system is based heavily on the liberal Westminster model, which in practice concentrates power very strongly in the government of the day. In Ireland, this took a particularly extreme form, with a small group of ministers dominating Irish politics for a decade and forming what in essence proved to be an oligarchic system of government.

The economic failures that led to Ireland's crisis of 2008 were deeply rooted in the institutional structure of the political economy and in particular in the interaction between liberal and clientelist politics. The final chapter examines how these institutions responded after 2008 in the face of the crisis that they had helped to create by their inability to resist the temptations of the bubble economy and the pressures, both domestic and international, to inflate that bubble further.

6 | *Crisis: the difficult politics of development and liberalism*

The sudden arrival of Ireland's hidden crisis

Over the summer of 2008, talk continued in Ireland of a possible slowing of growth, with much talk of a 'soft landing', which would result in a painful but temporary adjustment in the Irish economy. Such talk came to an abrupt end in September of that year as the full extent of the crisis in the Irish banks became evident and the Irish state guaranteed the bulk of their liabilities. The guarantee extended to a total potential amount of two to three times GDP at the time. Over the previous years, a number of commentators had warned of the unsustainability of the Irish bubble economy. Some warned of declining competitiveness, others focused on the broader weaknesses of a liberal economic model, while others warned specifically of crises in the housing market – with fewer warning of problems in the banking system (Kelly, 2007). Many of the key elements of Ireland's crisis had been flagged by a variety of observers. In many cases these observers were pilloried by both the media and leading politicians. Nonetheless, when Ireland's crash came in the late summer of 2008, the severity of the banking crisis and the extent of its reach across a variety of interlocking areas came as a shock to almost all observers and policy elites.

Ireland's crisis began in the financial sector, but spread rapidly into the fiscal, economic, social, reputational and political realms (NESC, 2009; Kirby and Murphy, 2011). Each of these crises evolved out of an underlying structural weakness which, in all cases, was masked by an apparently positive overall trend in the 2000s (see Table 6.1).

The financial crisis of 2008 came at the end of a period when the banking system had provided the Irish economy with a steady stream of credit, arguably for the first time in its history. However, underneath this improved lending performance, the financial system

236

Table 6.1 *Ireland's crises and their 'hidden' origins*

Crisis	Trend	Underlying weakness
Financial	Increased lending	Favouring assets over productive investment
Economic	GDP and employment growth	Reliance on construction and associated local demand
		Declining 'competitiveness' and weak investment
Fiscal	Budget surplus	Increased dependency on asset-based taxes
		Increased public sector spending without sustainable financing
Social	Declining income inequality	Structural inequality in the labour market
Reputational (political)	FF/PD government re-elected 2002, 2007	Structural 'addiction to growth'
	External economic agencies' approval	Financialisation of politics, political exchange focused on payments rather than services

had promoted asset speculation over productive investment, with the banks accumulating massive portfolios of bad loans linked almost entirely to property. This should not have been as surprising as it proved to be – the Central Bank of Ireland itself warned in 2007 about the dangerous concentration of banking loans in property, an excessive focus on commercial property and how such a lending profile was linked to economic bubbles (Woods, 2007). Ireland's fiscal crisis emerged rapidly in an economy which had run a primary budget surplus since the late 1990s and had reduced its debt to GDP ratio to 25 per cent over the previous twenty years. However, structural weaknesses in the public finances had also been widely identified, even if commentators disagreed as to their specific characteristics. The combination of low tax and spending always rendered Ireland's fiscal model vulnerable (Ó Riain, 2004, 2006), while many economists worried aloud about increased public spending through the 2000s and in particular increases in public sector wages (Boyle *et al.*, 2004). Yet, the factor that turned these structural pressures into an acute crisis was the increased dependency of the state on the 'bubble taxes' from capital gains and real estate sales. The financial and fiscal crises were tightly linked together through the property bubble, the core of the bank's business model and the source of the state's surging but vulnerable tax revenue.

Where Ireland had seen rapid economic and employment growth in the 2000s, it experienced an equally dramatic collapse in both, starting in 2007 but accelerating rapidly after the financial crisis in 2008. Many commentators had warned of the dangers of a shift from an export-oriented economy to one based on local demand and 'privatised Keynesianism' (Lane, 2003; Ó Riain, 2006; Crouch, 2009). While some authors emphasised declining competitiveness, others focused on the decline in investment effort and a weakening impulse towards developmental strategies in the global economy (Lane, 2003; Ó Riain, 2006, 2010). These structural weaknesses came together in the dramatic decline in the construction industry (starting in 2007 but collapsing in 2008) and then in employment related to domestic consumer demand. The debt problems associated with Ireland's financial crisis and rising unemployment due to economic decline combined to create a widespread social crisis. This social crisis was all the more traumatic as it came at the end of a period of unprecedented growth in employment and labour force participation, with tight labour market conditions reducing income inequality and increasing living standards in even the lower half of the income distribution. The bubble economy produced higher levels of home-ownership, even as house prices increased rapidly.

However, this growth masked serious structural weaknesses and inequalities in the labour market. At the end of the 1990s, despite employment growth, Ireland had faced serious problems with high unemployment rates among particular groups of the population, particularly those with relatively low educational qualifications. The construction boom provided employment on a grand scale for many of these workers, especially young men. Indeed, in some respects it reinforced this structural weakness as it appears that some young men left school early to take up work in construction and other industries. When the property bubble burst, this structural weakness was translated very rapidly into a crisis of unemployment and, following soon in its wake, huge difficulties in repayment of mortgages and other household debts.

Throughout the 2000s, Ireland received a variety of relatively positive assessments by external economic agencies – despite some concerns over wage competitiveness and related issues (O'Leary, 2010). Within the Eurozone, Ireland comfortably met the Stability and Growth Pact criteria for government budgetary balances and overall government debt. However, once again, behind these positive leading indicators were a series of major structural problems, indicated most clearly in the increasingly large current account deficits in Ireland and the rest of the European periphery. Disputes with German and French authorities over Ireland's corporate tax rate served mainly as irritants through the 2000s, but were an indicator of deeper political tensions. When the financial bubble burst, these tensions could not be avoided as Ireland's ability to adjust was more intertwined than ever with the decisions of other countries through their joint membership of the Eurozone. In this context, underlying political tensions translated very rapidly into a significant reputational crisis. Domestically, by 2008, the Fianna Fáil/Progressive Democrat coalition had been in power for eleven years and had been re-elected twice, most recently in 2007 (albeit with the Greens replacing the Progressive Democrats). It apparently had very high levels of public legitimacy. However, underlying this electoral success was an eroding social and political contract where the revenues from the financial bubble had enabled the papering over of political cracks and the avoidance of decisions about Ireland's future that had loomed large at the end of the 1990s. This structural weakness was magnified by electoral cycles and manifested itself in a lack of political capacity to respond effectively to the crisis, at least in its early months.

These six crises of the Irish political economy and society emerged from structural weaknesses that turned into acute, disastrous problems – despite having been masked by positive trends through the 2000s. The rest of this final chapter explores how these crises unfolded in Ireland, what responses were formulated in Ireland and Europe, and what made it so difficult for both the Irish and the European systems to develop an effective response. In analysing these questions, I first briefly outline the unusual severity of the crisis in Ireland and the distinctiveness of the Irish response, focused almost exclusively on fiscal consolidation. I then go on to explore the course of the crisis around three major dimensions: first, the intertwined financial and fiscal crises; second, the interaction of the economic and social crises; and, third, the interlinked reputational and political crises. The following section examines how these crises of government finances, growth and legitimation formed a 'trilemma', making both austerity and stimulus strategies very challenging. Nonetheless, I argue that Ireland's response was distinctive for its narrow focus on fiscal consolidation and lack of development of alternative, or even complementary, policy measures. The rest of the chapter then explores the social and political conditions that made it difficult to generate such responses within Ireland and, perhaps more tellingly, within Europe as a whole.

The Irish crisis in comparative perspective

Ireland's crisis was exceptionally severe. In an IMF paper comparing recent banking crises to other historical crises, Laeven and Valencia (2012) find that Ireland's banking crisis was among the most severe in world economic history. They assess the impact of banking crises in terms of the fiscal costs of the banking crisis (or how much governments spent to resolve the crisis in the financial system) and increases in public debt and lost output (as measured in the decline in GDP from its trajectory of growth). Ireland's crisis of 2008 was the only historical crisis to merit a place in the top ten on each of these different dimensions. Disentangling the costs of the financial bubble to both private investors and the public purse is complex. Laeven and Valencia (2012) estimate the fiscal cost of Ireland's banking crisis at $40 billion while the NESC estimates that it is closer to €64 billion once all costs are included (NESC, 2012). There are also opportunity costs attached to the state taking on the cost of the financial crisis, particularly in the weakening of the state's ability to undertake a more activist fiscal policy or engage in stimulus or investment strategies. Regardless of how specific elements of financing are accounted for, both Ireland's banking crisis in itself and its effect on the public finances were exceptionally severe, and the degree of entanglement between financial and fiscal problems was exceptionally high.

In the real economy, Ireland's crisis was no less severe. The construction sector had inflated to such a degree that its decline in employment which began in 2007 turned into a full-blown collapse in 2008. The knock-on effects in terms of local demand and public spending only added to the crisis in the real economy (see Table 6.2). In addition, unemployment rose sharply to 14.6 per cent in 2011. By any measure, the economic and social crises in Ireland were among the most severe in Europe.

Table 6.2 *Growth and employment, 2008–11*

	2008	2009	2010	2011
GDP – value	178,882	161,275	156,487	158,993
GNP – value	153,565	132,911	130,202	127,016
Unemployment rate	5.7%	12.2%	13.9%	14.6%
Employment rate	60.1%	54.8%	52.6%	51.7%

Source: CSO

Ireland undertook a policy response to the crisis that was distinctive for the degree to which it focused on fiscal consolidation or 'austerity'. It is also distinctive in that, as a member of the euro, it has not been in a position to devalue its currency in order to boost international competitiveness. Table 6.3 compares a number of the worst-hit economies in the crisis based on a number of key policy indicators. The left-hand columns provide a picture of the fiscal policy response in Ireland, Spain, the UK, Iceland and Denmark. This shows that Ireland's fiscal response was to focus on fiscal consolidation, as was the response of Iceland. The other economies in these early years of the crisis pursued some degree of discretionary fiscal stimulus, alongside most of the other OECD countries (Cameron, 2012). The underlying weakness of the public finances in Ireland is evident from the other two columns on this side of Table 6.3. Ireland entered the crisis with a weak structural balance in the public finances in 2007. In addition, it took on a far greater proportion of the costs of the banking crisis between 2007 and 2009, where it outstripped even Iceland in the cost to the state of financial system debts. While the UK also had a structural deficit entering the crisis, its financial crisis was less tightly linked to the public finances, both in terms of the bailing-out of banks and the tax structure itself, while Iceland had somewhat healthier public finances even as it took on a major proportion of the costs of the banking collapse. While Denmark had a significant crisis in its private banking system, the public finances were largely insulated from the worst effects of this crisis and had in any case entered the crisis period in a fairly healthy state.

The other side of this response related to currency policy. As members of the euro, Ireland and Spain did not have this available to them as a policy instrument – nor did Denmark, which, despite having

Table 6.3 *Comparative policy contexts and responses to crisis*

	Structural balance 2007	Direct fiscal costs of financial crisis 2007–9 (% of GDP in 2009)	Discretionary fiscal measures 2008–10 (% of 2008 GDP)	Euro member	Currency vs euro	Currency vs dollar (January 2008– December 2009)
Ireland	−2.4%	49.0%	−4.4%	Yes	n/a	−2%
Spain	0.2%	1.8%	3.5%	Yes	n/a	−2%
UK	−4.1%	8.7%	1.4%	No	−17%	−19%
Iceland	3.3%	20.3%	−9.4%	No	−42%	−44%
Denmark	2.9%	3.1%	2.5%	No	n/a	−2%

Sources: Laeven and Valencia, 2012; OECD, 2012

its own currency, tracks the euro. However, devaluation of currency was a significant aspect of economic policy in the UK and, in particular, Iceland. The Spanish case is interesting in that it was able to pursue a degree of fiscal stimulus in the early years of the crisis that contrasted sharply with Ireland's approach (Dellepiane and Hardiman, 2012). Yet, the structural weakness of the economy and emerging problems in the banking system undermined many of the effects of this stimulus and the election of a conservative government in 2011 consolidated a shift towards austerity. None of these countries, with the possible exception of Denmark, which was in a much stronger position to begin with, provides an ideal response to the crisis and each continues to suffer. However, it is clear that Ireland's predicament was particularly difficult. Underlying public finances were weak, the state took on a dramatically higher proportion of the cost of the financial crisis and euro membership meant that devaluation and/or monetary loosening were not national policy options.

Therefore, Ireland represents one of the limiting cases of an economy where fiscal consolidation and the protection of the financial system have been the key elements of policy during the crisis. This has occurred in an economy that has escaped some of the structural weaknesses of the Mediterranean political economies. The impact of the bursting of the property bubble had of course very significant effects on national income and employment as the construction sector collapsed. However, much of the economy that was built through the developmental years of the Celtic Tiger era remains in place, if neglected and somewhat bruised. This chapter explores the course of the crisis in this Irish context of a particularly severe shock combined with unpromising conditions for policy responses.

The course of the crisis

Ireland's crisis is in its fifth year at the time of writing in mid-2013, with each of the dimensions of the crisis still exerting negative pressures on the economy and society. This section examines the course of the crisis through three pairs of interlinked dimensions – the financial and fiscal crises of debt, the economic and social crises in the real economy, and the reputational and domestic political crises of legitimacy and democracy.

Debt: financial and fiscal crises

How did the financial and fiscal crises become entangled in practice in Ireland? The main events relating to the financial crisis, and in particular its link to state finances, are outlined in Table 6.4. While broadly outlined in chronological order, the table also organises the events in terms of a number of key processes that shaped the course of the financial and fiscal crisis in Ireland.

The importance of the international environment should not of course be under-estimated, even recognising the domestic failures discussed in Chapter 3. While there had been a number of warnings of the coming disaster, these key early moments included the crisis of Northern Rock in the UK, representing the nightmare scenario of extensive bank runs, and the admission by BNP Paribas that it was unable to value the subprime mortgage-based assets in three of its funds. The chill associated with these events went well beyond their specific impacts as both suggested that the financial bubble of the 2000s was built on sand. The year 2008 brought the bursting of the financial bubble into the heart of the US financial system, which was one of the primary motors that had driven its expansion. With major institutions being bought out (Bear Stearns), bailed out (Freddie Mac and Fannie Mae) and filing for bankruptcy (Lehman Brothers), the financial crisis had hit the heart of the international financial system. Of course, it should be remembered that a number of German banks had also gone bankrupt in the

Table 6.4 *Key events in the Irish financial crisis*

Date	Event
The evolution of the international financial crisis	
August 2007	BNP Paribas freezes three funds as it cannot value the subprime-based collateralised debt obligations (CDOs) within them
September 2007	Northern Rock crisis in the UK
March 2008	Bear Stearns bought by JPMorgan
7 September 2008	Federal Reserve bails out Fannie Mae and Freddie Mac (holders of significant numbers of subprime mortgages)
15 September 2008	Lehman Brothers files for bankruptcy
October 2008	Three Icelandic banks collapse
	Bailing out of British banks (including Lloyds, RBS and HBOS)
	Troubled Assets Relief Program in the US
Ireland's early commitment to finance Irish banks	
30 September 2008	Bank guarantee in Ireland
December 2008– February 2009	Government plans to inject funds into the three key banks, totalling around €12 billion
	Central Bank of Ireland emergency liquidity assistance made available to banks from early 2009
	Anglo Irish Bank 'hidden loans' controversy in December
	Anglo Irish Bank nationalised in January
The state takes on banks' 'bad loans'	
April 2009	National Assets Management Agency (NAMA) announced
October 2009	NAMA established
	By 2011, NAMA is estimated to take on €90 billion of loans (in nominal value) at a 'haircut' of approximately 58%
Cost of banking crisis grows	
February–June 2010	Government takes direct stakes in Bank of Ireland and AIB, rising to 36% and 18% respectively at this time; ongoing cash injections and increasing stakes in these three and smaller financial institutions
	Capital tier 1 ratios improving

Table 6.4 (*cont.*)

Date	Event
July 2010	Bank of Ireland and AIB pass European banking stress tests, but these tests are widely seen as too soft
August 2010	Standard & Poor's increases estimate of total cost of banking bailout to around €50 billion
September 2010	Government increases assessment of the cost of the Anglo Irish Bank bailout to Irish state, rising from €22 billion to €34 billion and increasing Irish borrowing costs
November–December 2010	Government seeks to impose losses on junior bond holders Apparent efforts to impose 'haircut' on bond holders meets international resistance, apparently including US Treasury Secretary Timothy Geithner
December 2010	AIB effectively nationalised as government takes 93% stake
November 2010	Irish state enters €85 billion bailout programme of EU/ECB/IMF (and including Irish reserve funds)
March 2011	Stress tests on Irish banks published, revealing a further €24 billion needed

mid-2000s, including a number with operations in the Irish Financial Services Centre. However, 2007–8 brought a cluster of such events as the widespread nature of the problems in the financial system became evident to investors in that market. Three major Icelandic banks collapsed in October 2008 as the financial crisis came to Europe, with the bailing-out of a number of major British banks. As the events of the year between BNP Paribas freezing its funds and Lehman Brothers filing for bankruptcy unfolded, it became evident that the crisis in the financial system was not one of liquidity (or insufficient flows of funds), but of solvency (or the underlying value of assets and the stability of financial institutions).

As these events unfolded internationally over the summer of 2008, the underlying weakness in Irish banks became obvious. This culminated in the government guaranteeing the assets and liabilities of the major Irish banks on 30 September 2008. The pressure for the controversial guarantee came primarily from the demand to save Irish banks, justified at the time due to their 'systemic importance'. However, while

AIB and Bank of Ireland may have been systemically important, it seemed clear that the role of Anglo Irish Bank within the Irish economy, while crucial to the property sector, had little broader systemic weight. The more significant issue, it seems, was the potential knock-on effects both within the Irish and, particularly, the European financial systems. The Minister for Finance in 2008, Brian Lenihan, told the Irish media of a phone message that he received from ECB President Jean-Claude Trichet just before the guarantee in September 2008 telling him to 'save your banks at all costs'. While never confirmed or denied, this story suggests that there were significant fears within the ECB of contagion effects across the European financial system, both in terms of investor confidence and also of direct losses of asset values and defaults on loans.

Furthermore, the Irish bank guarantee was remarkably generous in the degree of coverage that it provided. The economic rationale for providing a guarantee was compelling for depositors and smaller businesses, but much less so for institutional investors and bond holders. Since senior bond holders had much the same legal rights as depositors, it would have been difficult to impose full losses on these large institutional investors. Nonetheless, a variety of other bond holders were also covered by the guarantee and escaped relatively unscathed. While the Irish government had some success at a later date in imposing losses on junior bond holders, the guarantee left the Irish state on the hook for the vast majority of the costs of the banking crisis. Once the guarantee was in place, the government began to inject funds into the three key banks in late 2008 and early 2009. In addition, during this period, more and more details began to emerge about questionable practices within the banks. Most spectacular among these, though hardly unique, were the efforts by Anglo Irish Bank to mask its own financial position and prop up its share prices by providing loans to their largest customers to buy shares in the bank.

The events of this period were crucial as they represented an early, sweeping and legally binding commitment by the Irish state to the most troublesome financial institutions within the Irish economy. It also provided a signal of future fault lines within the Eurozone reaction to the financial crisis, as the ECB's Jean-Claude Trichet's phone call in the interest of saving the banks – therefore implicitly supporting a sweeping guarantee – was in contrast to protests from finance ministers across the Eurozone when the guarantee was introduced.

Having guaranteed the banks' liabilities, the question arose of what to do with the 'non-performing' loans within the Irish banking system, almost all of which were linked to property investments. As well as direct recapitalisation of the banks, the state now undertook to take on large tranches of these loans, albeit at a reduced value. In April 2009 the National Assets Management Agency (NAMA) was announced and established in October of that year. By 2011, NAMA was estimated to have taken on €90 billion of loans in nominal value at a 'haircut' of approximately 58 per cent. While NAMA was to trade these assets at a later date, it was unclear whether these assets could be traded at a value that would cover the costs to the public finances, with most commentators forecasting that it would ultimately make a loss (Whelan, 2010). Overall, the Irish state took on the problems of the Irish financial system through the bank guarantee, the direct injection of funds (including the provision of emergency liquidity assistance from early 2009) and the taking on of the bad loans of the banking system. While much public comment regarding NAMA focused on the apparent 'bailing out' of developers, in practice NAMA was a mechanism for underpinning the financial system by saving banks from most of the cost of these non-performing loans. This twin strategy was designed to place a firewall around the problems of the financial sector, containing them within the public finances and minimising the knock-on effects and uncertainties within the financial system in Ireland and Europe.

The course of events over the following months and years revealed some of the effects of this strategy. As will be seen later on, they had implications for the economic, social and reputational crises. But there were a number of additional effects within the nexus of private and public finance itself. In taking on the recapitalisation of the banks, the Irish state was inevitably put in the position of becoming a major shareholder within them. Indeed, a number of economists argued in 2009 that the Irish state should move to nationalise the key pillar banks quickly with a view to restructuring and reselling them. While this course of action was resisted, the state gradually slid into ownership of the banks as the full extent of the internal weakness of the banks and the external funds required became clear. While Anglo Irish Bank had been nationalised early in 2009, AIB was almost fully owned by the state by 2011. Bank of Ireland was 36 per cent state-owned at this point. However, this form of nationalisation by drift had its

disadvantages. In particular, the extent of restructuring of bank operations was minimal. Whether banks were to be resold or not, the
period of majority state ownership offered the opportunity to remake
the organisational culture and capabilities of each of the 'pillar banks'
(Ó Riain, 2009). However, this opportunity was largely neglected,
although some successes were achieved in the later years of the crisis
(NESC, 2012).

The uncertainty about the degree to which the state would need to
pay for the financial crisis, and the full extent of the cost that would be
involved, had other damaging effects. In particular, through 2010 a
series of re-estimates appeared, each of which increased the size of the
hole estimated to exist in the banks' accounts – and by extension the
impact on the public finances. It was not simply the scale of the fiscal
costs of the financial crisis that weakened Ireland's creditworthiness on
international markets in 2010 but the ongoing uncertainty around
those costs. It appears likely that the ECB again played an important
role, fearing the scale of Irish commitment to supporting banks in the
face of this uncertainty as well as fearing the extent to which its own
support would have to be extended to the Irish banking system.

The scale of the asset value crisis in the Irish banks was enormous.
However, some key features of how this crisis was dealt with made its
impact more damaging than it might have been. The cost of the
financial crisis was largely transferred into the public finances. In the
process, a firewall was created within the financial system limiting
the knock-on effects of the Irish banking difficulties within the international financial system, but amplifying them within the domestic
public finances. The nationalisation of banks, which occurred by drift
even though it was largely inevitable, was a missed opportunity for
restructuring the banks as organisations that could support the real
economy. The uncertainty associated with this policy of 'kicking the
can down the road' at both the Irish and the European levels was a
significant contributory factor in increasing Ireland's borrowing costs
and ultimately making the external bailout of November 2010
inevitable.

Through all these events, the role played by international constraints
is also important. Trichet's phone call of 2008 appears as the first of a
number of international interventions that set the parameters of the
Irish response, even if not determining all of its features. Similarly, in
another unconfirmed but never-denied report, US Treasury Secretary

Timothy Geithner is said to have blocked an Irish plan in December 2010 for imposing additional losses on Anglo Irish Bank bond holders. In 2013, the ECB allowed Ireland to undertake a restructuring of the 'promissory notes' which the Central Bank of Ireland had used to finance the debts of Anglo Irish Bank from early on in the crisis. This restructuring was significant in reducing the impact of this financing on the public finances in the decade to follow. However, the Rubicon of debt default was not to be crossed – and the possibility that these arrangements crossed the line into governmental 'monetary financing' was the subject of much controversy at the European level. The episode was significant in managing the impact of fiscal adjustment, but it also politically and symbolically reinforced the firewalling of the financial sector and the prohibition on monetary policy.

However, the direct costs of the financial crisis only account for a portion of Ireland's overall government debt. Coffey (2013) calculates that in 2012, 22 per cent of Ireland's debt was accounted for by the costs to the state of the banking crisis, 25 per cent of the debt was pre-existing in 2008 and 40 per cent had accumulated due to the ongoing annual budget deficit. The remainder was due to changes in cash balances. Assessing the composition of Irish debt in terms of these volumes of costs tends to over-estimate the effect of ongoing deficits because it counts the cost of financial bailouts simply in terms of their direct financing, without taking into account how these costs are amplified over time within the overall debt dynamics. Indeed, the IMF issued a paper in 2013 that examined debt reduction during a period of fiscal consolidation (Eyraud and Weber, 2013) and calculated that the Irish debt to GDP ratios would only have grown to 68.1 per cent in 2011 compared to the actual level of 106.5 per cent if non-fiscal policy factors (primarily the cost of bank recapitalisation and related policies) were excluded. The total increase in debt to GDP ratios in Ireland in these four years was 81.5 per cent. These IMF simulations suggest that just over half of this (53.1 per cent) was due to the ongoing fiscal deficit, while 47 per cent of the increase in the debt to GDP ratio was due to other factors, primarily the cost of bank bailouts. This is a significantly larger estimate than analyses which focus on the 'static' costs of banking debt.

Nonetheless, a significant portion of the government debt is accounted for by the ongoing primary budget deficit. Chapter 5 showed the collapse of government revenues, in particular from

Table 6.5 *Fiscal adjustment in Ireland, 2009–13 (% of GDP)*

	Change 2009–13	Further adjustment required
Adjustment to stabilise debt	9.2	4.6
Adjustment to reduce debt	9.2	6.9

sources linked directly to the property bubble, in the wake of the crisis and analysed the components of increased spending during the 2000s. Table 6.5 shows the extent of Irish fiscal adjustment between 2009 and 2013, along with the outstanding amounts of required adjustment (based on IMF figures). The adjustment undertaken, and planned, is one of the largest in the history of advanced capitalist economies (Whelan, 2010).

Ireland's fiscal consolidation has been dramatic and driven by both ongoing budgetary challenges and by the cost of the banking crisis to the state. The Irish response to closing the deficit has involved using a mix of revenue and expenditure changes, with relatively little focus on boosting growth as a mechanism for deficit production. The adjustments have been concentrated as a matter of policy two to one in favour of cutting expenditure rather than increasing revenue. The IMF Fiscal Monitor estimated that from 2009 to 2012 in Ireland, measures designed to increase revenues accounted for an adjustment of 2 per cent of GDP, primarily through direct taxes. However, much the greater part of the adjustment was borne through expenditure cuts, with cuts in benefits, capital spending and public pay accounting for an adjustment of just over 6 per cent.

On the revenue side, changes have involved increases in taxation, including social security taxes, property taxes and some increases in sales taxes, along with new levies on public sector workers. While a number of changes in taxation have hit the population as a whole, some have focused specifically on the public sector. Most controversial among these was the 'pension levy' of 2009, which involved deductions of up to 9 per cent on public sector salaries and effectively operated as a tax as it did not affect the value of the pension. A smaller levy was applied to private pension funds in 2010.

Changes in expenditure have involved a reduction of employment in the public sector, an internal rationalisation of public spending, direct cuts to public sector wages, a reduction in capital expenditure and the rationalisation of benefits through changing eligibility rules and entitlements.

Meanwhile, in most cases, programme spending declined, as did funding of the community and voluntary organisations that provide many of the state's services: 'nearly all of these "social" sub-headings have had funding reduced, with many of these reductions higher than the overall reduction in State expenditure of 11 per cent between 2008 and 2012. Conversely though, there has been an increase in the funding provided in some areas, which are mainly demand-led. For example, there has been a 44 per cent increase in funding to medical card services' (NESC, 2013: 91). Automatic stabilisers have increased significantly in Ireland due to the depth of the crisis and the focus on income transfers within the welfare state (Cameron, 2012). While overall public spending remained relatively stable in the early years of the crisis, 'there have been cuts in a range of public services accessed particularly by the less-advantaged, while there have been increases in demand-led income transfers, such as Jobseeker's Allowance' (NESC, 2012: 92)

After initial cuts in public sector pay, the Fine Gael/Labour government of 2011 set itself an 'iron triangle' of commitments. These included no additional income taxes, no changes in the rate of social transfer payments and no further cuts to salaries during the period of the 'Croke Park Agreement' between public sector unions and the state. These commitments were honoured, in name at least, between 2011 and 2013, although there were significant changes to entitlement to benefits, the marginal tax rate had been increased significantly by the universal social charge and pension levy, and the Croke Park Agreement was controversially renegotiated a year early.

Callan *et al.* (2012) find that government budget changes from 2008 to 2011 were largely progressive in terms of income. The 2012 budget was more regressive, as has also been suggested for the 2013 budget. Nonetheless, overall the response to the crisis has reinforced the existing, problematic welfare state structure. The focus has been on protecting transfers of income rather than universal services. While there have been efforts at organisational reform, the capacity of the public sector in terms of its already comparatively low numbers of staff has been further reduced. The focus on cuts in numbers and services has reinforced the Irish model of a low level of general welfare state provision, strong on transfers but particularly weak in terms of services (albeit combined with some targeted interventions).

The real economy: economic and social crises

In almost all financial and fiscal crises, a revival in economic growth is crucial to escaping the debt burden upon the state, businesses and households. However, economic growth in Ireland has been largely non-existent since 2008. Despite increases in GDP, GNP collapsed between 2008 and 2010 and continued to decline slightly subsequently. Although exports and the activities of multinational corporations experienced a resurgence, this did not translate into increased activity in the domestic economy or into improvements in employment until mid-2013, when some signs of possible small improvements emerged. Five years into the crisis, the key factors generating the social crisis remained in place. What was the troubled course of the 'real economy' in the intertwined economic and social crises?

The growth and employment crises consisted of a number of linked but conceptually separate economic processes. Figures 6.1–6.4 show the trend in key components of GDP and in the main sectors of employment in the Irish economy (taking quarter three in 2007, the peak of GDP and employment, as equal to 100). The collapse of capital investment had already begun before the financial crisis, but increased rapidly from late 2008, when capital investments in Ireland fell dramatically and construction employment followed their decline remarkably closely (Figure 6.1). Although difficult to disentangle from more general weakening of domestic spending, there were also declines in employment in related professional areas, including legal services, engineering and architectural services.

Shortly after the initial impact of the crisis, the domestic economy experienced a sharp contraction, driven both by rapid increases in unemployment and by new taxes and budget cuts introduced in 2008 and 2009 (Figure 6.2). As personal consumption declined, so too did employment in industries that were dependent upon consumer spending, including retail, accommodation and food and other personal services. Professional and administrative services declined even more, most likely due to their link to the construction sector. However, employment in the FIRE sector remained relatively stable up to 2010, reflecting its relative autonomy from the losses being taken by the banks. The Irish economy appeared to undergo a rebalancing of sorts

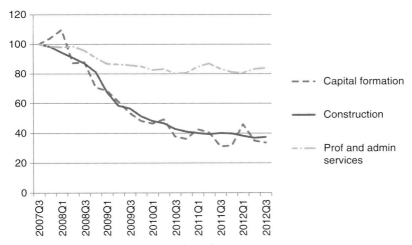

Figure 6.1 Capital investment and employment
Source: CSO, *National Accounts* and *Quarterly National Household Survey*

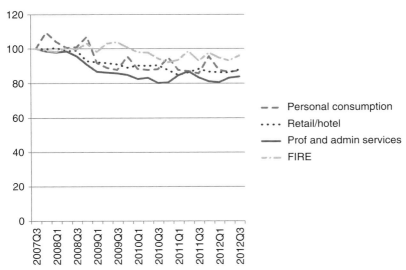

Figure 6.2 Private consumption and employment
Source: CSO, *National Accounts and Quarterly National Household Survey*

during these years as exports, and the overall trade balance, surged impressively from late 2008 onwards (Figure 6.3). However, only a small number of sectors significantly increased employment over this time. These included pharmaceuticals, rubber and plastics

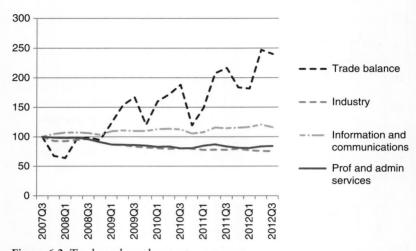

Figure 6.3 Trade and employment
Source: CSO, *National Accounts and Quarterly National Household Survey*

manufacturing and ICT, with the ICT sector accounting for the bulk of the improvement in employment in export-oriented sectors. Despite its welcome impact on the accounting of the debt to GDP ratio, the employment effects of this export boom in the real economy were relatively weak.

Finally, Figure 6.4 shows the decline in public spending associated with the policy of fiscal consolidation (which also contributed to the decline in capital investment in Figure 6.1). Public spending declined quite significantly from late 2009, reflecting a series of measures reviewed in the previous section. Indeed, the decline in spending on public employees was greater than the figure indicates, as government spending includes significant increases in social transfers. These data suggest a puzzle as quarterly national household survey data show both education and healthcare increasing employment during this period, even in the face of cuts. However, official figures show a significant and growing decline in public employment, with an even greater decline in government spending from 2010 onwards. This suggests that employment in private educational and healthcare industries has expanded, although it is not clear to what extent this is linked to increased state contracting for services or to expanded private spending.

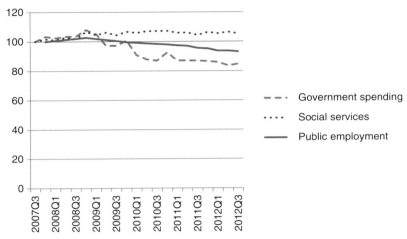

Figure 6.4 Public spending, public administration and social services employment
Source: CSO, *National Accounts* and *Quarterly National Household Survey*
Public employment from Department of Public Expenditure and Reform Databank

Taken together, these trends add up to a major increase in unemployment in the early years of the crisis which was not halted until the second half of 2012 (CSO, 2013). Growth in ICT, professional services (e.g., legal and other services) and high-tech manufacturing (e.g., pharmaceuticals) added to full-time employment during these years. However, many other sectors saw decline in full-time employment with some expansion of part-time positions, with male part-time employment increasing particularly rapidly during these years. Moreover, there was significant evidence of various forms of exit from the labour market, including emigration, an increase in the numbers of inactive workers and a suggestion in 2012 that some unemployed workers were returning to small-scale farming.

Figures 6.5 and 6.6 show how these trends in different sectors intersected with the structural inequalities in the labour market, linked to class, gender and education. These tables track the experience of two cohorts of workers between 2001 and 2011, showing how workers aged between 25 and 34 and between 35 and 44 in 2001 were faring ten years later. Most striking is the effect of education as the probability of remaining in employment ten years later is strongly related to the

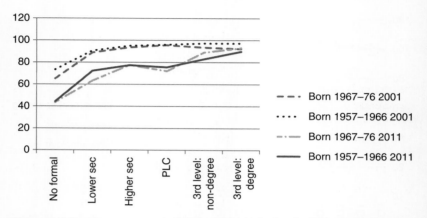

Figure 6.5 Employment rate in 2001 and 2011 by level of education for men born between 1957 and 1966 and 1967 and 1976
Source: Quarterly National Household Survey Microdata, Central Statistics Office

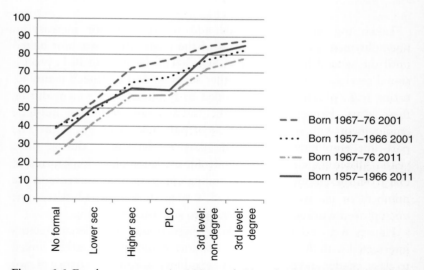

Figure 6.6 Employment rate in 2001 and 2011 by level of education for women born between 1957 and 1966 and 1967 and 1976
Source: Quarterly National Household Survey Microdata, Central Statistics Office

educational level. While there is almost no difference in the employment rate of workers with a third-level education ten years later, there is a 15–20 per cent gap between the employment rates in 2001 and in 2011 of those with low levels of education. For women, this effect is particularly pronounced among the younger cohort. Significant gender differences in the participation rate are obvious and the crisis appears to have intensified this gap when we look at the experience of men and women in the younger cohort. The effect of the crisis on employment was dramatic but also dramatically uneven. In addition, these trends would only be reinforced by the nature of the employment growth in 2012, which was largely in areas that employed those with higher levels of education. The major effect on the employment of those with third-level education was in the new cohorts entering the job market.

These patterns of labour market activity inevitably shape the distribution of income and the relative degree of financial pain suffered by different groups within the society during the crisis. Data on the distribution of income across the years of the crisis show that the Gini coefficient, a widely used measure of income inequality, decreased between 2007 and 2009, only to rise once again in 2010 and 2011. At the top of the income distribution, workers with higher educational levels have largely weathered the worst of the unemployment crisis, although losing significantly in terms of income. At the very bottom of the income distribution, incomes are being supported more than ever through transfer payments from the state. Ireland ranks very highly in Europe in the degree to which social transfer payments boost low incomes and alleviate poverty, although this should be tempered by the fact that part of the reason that transfers are effective is because underlying rates of inequality and poverty are comparatively high in Ireland relative to the rest of Europe, with a particularly high proportion of 'jobless households' (Whelan *et al.*, 2012). Nonetheless, rates of consistent and relative poverty rose steadily in Ireland during the crisis (CSO, 2013).

We have seen that the impact of the unemployment crisis fell most heavily on those with lower levels of education, particularly among those with post-leaving certificate or similar qualifications (reflecting in large part the employment decline in both construction and market services). Income losses are also relatively higher among this group, which includes many craft workers (CSO, 2012). This translated in many cases into serious difficulties with maintaining payments on often large mortgage debts.

**Table 6.6 *Mortgaged private households in permanent housing units,*
*2006 and 2011***

	2006	2011	Change
All persons	593,513	583,148	−10,365
Persons at work	495,216	459,805	−35,411
All unemployed persons	14,757	50,792	36,035
Not in labour force	83,540	72,551	−10,989

Table 6.6 shows the changes in numbers of households with mortgages between 2006 and 2011, using census data on household
ownership and employment status. The total number of households
with mortgaged private accommodation decreased by just over
10,000, matching the number who exited the labour force. However,
a further 35,000 households with mortgages shifted from employed
to unemployed status, suggesting that these households would experience particularly severe pressures around mortgage arrears. In 2009,
early on in the crisis, the very poorest 20 per cent of households
had low rates of home-ownership and mortgage arrears difficulties
were not as widespread (3.9 per cent were in arrears on rent or
mortgages). However, the next poorest 20 per cent had the highest
rate of rent or mortgage arrears at 9.9 per cent (CSO, 2012). By 2013,
the mortgage arrears problem had escalated very seriously, with
94,500 mortgages over 90 days in arrears and 23,500 over two years
behind with payments.

The inequalities in Irish society that had been in place in the late
1990s and had been papered over through the 2000s came to the fore
once more in the years of the crisis. The persistent vulnerability and
marginalisation at the bottom of the income distribution continued,
with heavy reliance on social transfers and very high rates of
unemployment. Groups with higher levels of education maintained
reasonably steady employment rates, even if there were significant
losses of income. Poverty rates, however measured, increased steadily
through the course of the crisis. The sharpest relative impact of the
crisis was felt in the lower middle classes, where many workers with
craft and related qualifications had obtained employment in the
construction and related fields and had been able to purchase private
houses through this employment. When the crisis hit, these workers

were seriously damaged by the bursting of the construction bubble, the decline in employment and their persistently high mortgage payments. The recovering sectors, dominated by professional occupations, offered them few opportunities for re-employment. The structural weaknesses that Ireland had failed to address at the end of the late 1990s came back to haunt it once more.

Legitimacy: reputational and political crises

In a crisis where economic and social well-being plummets and where the financial and fiscal systems are locked in a downward spiral, much is asked of a country's citizens. The basis of trust and legitimacy of the institutions of the society is undermined even as the need for trust and collective agreement in making the difficult decisions needed to form paths out of the crisis is greater than ever. As will be seen later on, Ireland's crisis is distinctive both for the degree to which elites have been able to implement the austerity programme with relatively little protest and the degree to which the political system and the institutions of the society have been unable to generate more creative alternative or even complementary strategies.

More specifically, however, it is clear that Ireland has undergone an external reputational crisis indicated in its inability to borrow funds to support its public debt. If the confidence of the financial markets in the Irish state was lost, so too in many respects was the confidence of its citizens. It is the interplay of the state, the citizenry and the international political and financial institutions that have come together to form Ireland's crisis of legitimacy. Between the (second) referendum on the Lisbon Treaty in 2009 and the Fiscal Treaty referendum in 2012, Ireland submitted to direct governance by the EU/IMF funders of a government bailout in 2010 and decimated Fianna Fáil in the General Election of 2011. These were historically tumultuous events, but perhaps the more striking aspect of the crisis is the steady erosion of public trust and political legitimacy, even in the absence of widespread disruptive protest.

Figure 6.7 shows the levels of distrust among citizens in particular institutions and the long-term interest rates on Irish government bonds, an indicator of the degree of trust of private financiers in the ability of the state to repay its debts (with higher rates indicating greater distrust). Trust in European institutions was much greater than in

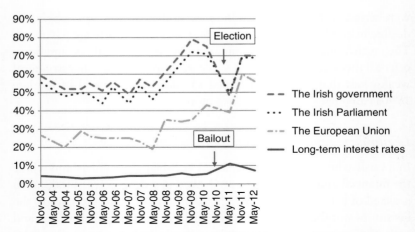

Figure 6.7 Levels of distrust among public citizens and private financiers (absolute levels)

Notes: Public attitudes: the question for the citizen responses is as follows: 'I would like to ask you a question about how much trust you have in certain institutions. For each of the following institutions, please tell me if you tend to trust it or tend not to trust it?' The figure shows the percentage of people saying they tend not to trust the institution. Long-term interest rates: the OECD defines 'long-term rates' as 'secondary market yields of long term (usually 10 year) bonds'. The OECD rates mirror almost exactly the Bloomberg estimates of nine-year government bond yields from 2008 to 2013 (available at www.bloomberg.com)

Sources:

Public attitudes: Eurobarometer, 2003–12

Long-term interest rates: OECD Monthly Monetary and Financial Statistics

domestic parliamentary and government institutions. Levels of trust and distrust were very stable until the eve of the crisis in the summer of 2008, including a reduction in distrust of the EU over this period. However, once the crisis hit, levels of distrust in public institutions increased rapidly – initially on the domestic front, but over time extending to the EU, to the point that levels of distrust in the EU were only 10 per cent less than in domestic institutions by 2011. In the period around the General Election in 2011, which swept Fianna Fáil out of power and greatly reduced its parliamentary representation, distrust in the government and parliament fell once more to pre-crisis levels. However, a short six months after the election,

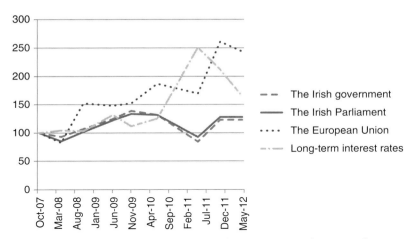

Figure 6.8 Levels of distrust among public citizens and private financiers (relative to October 2007)
Notes and sources: see Figure 6.7

distrust in political institutions in Ireland had surged once more. The figures for long-term interest rates on Irish government bonds also show a similar increase in levels of distrust over this period, with significant improvement from May 2011 onwards after Mario Draghi's commitment to defend the euro.

However, these trends are better compared in Figure 6.8, which takes the level of each index in October 2007 as equal to 100 and tracks subsequent changes. This figure shows that although overall levels of distrust in domestic institutions were higher than in international institutions and continued to grow during the period, it was the relation between Ireland and Europe that became increasingly fractious. The distrust of Irish citizens in the EU grew rapidly early on in the crisis and then spiked again in mid-2011. This is mirrored in the trends in long-term interest rates, reflecting the distrust of international financial markets in the Irish state. These spiked from mid-2010 to mid-2011 and only dropped once more after Draghi's commitment. While the state of domestic political institutions was hardly something to boast about, the reputational and political crisis in Ireland has been sharper in Ireland's external relations. This also suggests that the weakening of trust and legitimacy across borders has been a two-sided affair, with Irish citizens not only

Table 6.7 *Reasons for Fiscal Treaty votes, 2012*

	Positive – Europe	Negative – Europe	Positive – domestic political process	Negative – domestic political process	Ambiguous
Yes voters	9.0%	17.2%	6.0%	3.7%	8.2%
No voters	0.7%	21.9%	3.0%	21.4%	8.7%
All voters	9.7%	39.2%	9.0%	25.2%	17.0%

Source: Eurobarometer, 2012
Notes: percentages are given as a percentage of all answers given (total answers added up to more than 100 per cent as respondents could choose more than one reason).
Main reasons include:

Yes/positive Europe (good for Ireland, pro-EU).
Yes/negative Europe (uncertainty/instability attached to no vote; access to funding/future bailouts/no side fail to show how debt can be financed; dependent on EU; no other option).
Ambiguous (economic necessity/stability; foreign investment).
No/negative Europe (loss of political/economic sovereignty; anti-EU; bad for Ireland; austerity).
No/negative domestic (anti-government; distrust of politicians/misleading the people; lack of information/understanding).
No/ambiguous (anti-referendum; economic factors).

increasing their distrust of domestic institutions but also of the once-widely legitimated EU.

This erosion of trust in Europe is also reflected in the voting patterns around the Fiscal Treaty in 2012. Irish voters had endorsed the Lisbon Treaty by a vote of 67 per cent to 33 per cent in October 2009 (a swing from a 53 per cent no vote at the first time of asking in June 2008). In May 2012 Irish voters were given the choice in a constitutional referendum whether to allow the government to sign the European Fiscal Treaty or not and the yes vote largely held up as the Treaty was passed with 60 per cent in favour. Apparently an endorsement of the European response to the crisis, Table 6.7 shows that the reasons for voting both yes and no were dominated by negative assessments of both Europe and the domestic political process. While we might not be surprised that no voters' assessments were rooted in negative views of Europe and of the domestic political process, the pattern of responses among yes voters is more striking. Here the domestic political process was much less significant as a factor in shaping voting. What is most striking is the large number of voters who voted yes despite, or indeed because of, assessments of the European situation which were largely negative. In particular, many voters voted yes because they did not believe that Ireland would gain access to crucial European resources (especially further bailout financing) if they did not ratify the Fiscal Treaty. Of the yes voters, 15 per cent voted yes for positive reasons, while 21 per cent voted yes for primarily negative reasons, most of which were to do with Europe.

While recovery would demand political creativity and institutional legitimacy of the state, these resources appeared to be in very short supply in both national and transnational political relations during Ireland's crisis years. In late 2010 and early 2011, these came together particularly dramatically in the bailout and electoral defeat of Fianna Fáil. However, by 2013, the dominant picture appeared to be one of constant erosion of public trust combined with fatalism – even as international lenders' faith in the Irish state was increasingly being restored.

The crisis trilemma

The previous sections have outlined how the six main dimensions of the crisis are entangled along three main clusters of problems – the interdependence of private and public debt, turning financial crisis into fiscal crisis; the crises in the real economy, as high unemployment combined with limited economic growth, and then mainly in sectors that were some distance from the bulk of the unemployed; and the ways in which Ireland's external reputational crises of the state were intertwined with a collapse of the legitimacy of domestic and European political institutions among the citizenry. These three clusters of difficulties are themselves inter-related. Indeed, these can be characterised as forming a trilemma within the crisis (Figure 6.9).

The trilemma consists of the interactions between these three parts. As will be seen later on, measures taken to tackle any one or pair of the corners of this trilemma are likely to aggravate problems in the other corners. Indeed, the trilemma of the Great Recession reflects other trilemmas that have been identified in contemporary capitalist development. Iversen and Wren (1998) argue that the service economy is characterised by a trilemma in which they identify the core problem as

Figure 6.9 The crisis trilemma

the difficulty in combining fiscal stability, employment growth and economic equality. For them, each variety of capitalism is well placed to solve two, but only two, of these challenges. Their trilemma shadows the crisis trilemma presented here – both contain a fiscal crisis, their employment crisis relates strongly to the growth crisis, and questions of equality are closely tied to the issues of political legitimation and social solidarity. Equally, we can see similar underlying patterns in the earlier arguments of Habermas (1976) and Offe (1984) regarding 'legitimation crises' in contemporary capitalism. Habermas and Offe see legitimation crises as driven by the contradiction between the demands of capital accumulation (or of 'growth') and the demands of the population for the expansion of welfare and other social protections and services, which can drive a fiscal crisis of the state (O'Connor, 1973).

Iversen and Wren's trilemma of the service economy begins most fundamentally from what they see as the demands of growth in a post-industrial economy, tracing outwards from this the difficult problems of balancing strategies for equality and fiscal discipline. The analyses of Habermas and Offe start instead from the legitimation crises that they perceive in 1970s capitalism as expectations rose and were dashed in an era of stagflation. By contrast, the trilemma of the Great Recession starts most fundamentally with the fiscal crisis and traces how attempts to deal with the fiscal crisis generated further intense dilemmas in terms of growth and public legitimacy and trust. In this sense, the crisis trilemma is significantly different in terms of its internal dynamics compared to those of the service economy or of the stagflation era.

However, it is also necessary to be careful about placing too much emphasis on the 'impossibility' of resolving trilemmas. For example, while Iversen and Wren argue that the three elements of their trilemma are irreconcilable, it was shown in Chapter 4 that social democratic economies in the 2000s have managed to combine persistently high levels of equality, growth levels equalling the best performance in the OECD and strong underlying fiscal discipline. Similarly, Scharpf (1999) agrees with Offe and Habermas that there are significant tensions between capital accumulation and welfare state demands in capitalism. However, he argues that the history of capitalism is in many respects not a story of the impossibility of reconciling these competing demands, but of the constantly shifting institutional and political compromises in managing these contradictions and dilemmas (Ó Riain, 2000a). Identifying trilemmas is important in showing how already-difficult problems are intertwined with other clusters of challenges. However, it should not be taken as evidence in itself of the impossibility of resolving these trilemmas.

The primary means of tackling this trilemma in Ireland and in Europe has been through strategies of austerity and fiscal consolidation. The focus of this policy has been firmly on reducing fiscal deficits and bringing the expansion of general government debt under control across Europe, and particularly in the periphery. The main goal of this policy, especially in Ireland since the bailout of 2011, has been the restoration of creditworthiness – in other words, tackling countries' external legitimation crises in the financial markets. The dilemma here is that the fiscal contraction measures to achieve these twin goals are damaging to economic and employment growth, and undermine domestic political legitimacy. Whereas some analysts had argued that fiscal contraction would produce economic expansion by bolstering investor confidence, most Irish commentators recognised that it would in fact have contractionary effects on the economy. However, in practice, the resumption of growth is largely seen as following the restoration of stability to the public finances and external creditworthiness, and growth predictions have had to be revised downwards regularly during the course of the crisis. The motors of growth are largely seen as market liberalisation combined with improved competitiveness and the restoration of investor confidence as stability is restored to the public finances (Lane, 2011).

Given the scale of Ireland's fiscal contraction, the question of whether fiscal consolidations are up to the task of restoring creditworthiness and growth or whether they are self-defeating is a central one. It has received increasing attention in the Eurozone as the European economy has continued to stagnate a full five years after the crisis began. A number of papers have examined the question, to the extent that EU Commissioner Ollie Rehn was moved in February 2013 to write a note to the ECB describing the wave of new studies of fiscal multipliers during an economic crisis as 'unhelpful'. The IMF report on the World Economic Outlook in 2012 brought a lingering debate into public view when it argued that austerity policies were at fault for the failure of Europe's economy to match the growth rates that have been forecast for it over the course of the crisis (IMF, 2012). The point was echoed by prominent economist Olivier Blanchard (Blanchard and Leigh, 2013), whose paper was one of those that attracted the direct attention of Commissioner Rehn. Other analyses carried out more extensive assessments. Holland and Portes (2012) argued that austerity in the Eurozone was self-defeating as the effect of cuts on growth weakened revenues to such an extent that it under-mined the direct fiscal benefit of cuts in expenditure or increases in revenue. De Grauwe and Ji (2013) showed that the countries imple-menting the largest austerity packages within the Eurozone were those that saw the greatest increases in their debt to GDP ratio in 2011.

Perhaps the most comprehensive analysis is that of IMF economists Eyraud and Weber, who argue that fiscal multipliers in a crisis are much higher than in normal economic times and that the effect of fiscal consolidation under such conditions is in many cases to increase the debt to GDP ratio in the short term as 'fiscal gains are partly wiped out by the decline in output' (Eyraud and Weber, 2013: 1). They state that this effect is temporary and that debt eventually declines, although under certain scenarios, this decline is only evident after between two and five years. These effects of delayed debt reduction are higher in high-debt countries and in periods of crisis when multipliers are stronger (Eyraud and Weber, 2013; see also Irish Fiscal Advisory Council, 2012: 45). Arguably, the most accurate summary of this debate is that, compared to a scenario with no fiscal adjustment, fiscal contraction will reduce government debt, but only after initially increasing the debt to GDP ratio and damaging economic growth.

Barnes and Wren (2012) argue that the liberal economies of the UK and Ireland faced a choice in how they would emerge from the crisis. They could seek to recover the liberal model of the 2000s, a form of 'privatised Keynesianism' (Crouch, 2009), or they could seek a path towards greater reliance on export competitiveness, more or less along the lines of the European model. This suggests that Ireland now faces much the same choices as it did at the end of the 1990s, although under much more difficult circumstances. Indeed, Ireland's path out of the crisis in practice harks back to the earliest period of the Celtic Tiger era in the early 1990s, seeking to stabilise the macroeconomy with a secondary focus on developing a dynamic Irish-owned export sector. While unravelling the worst effects of privatised Keynesianism, the transition to a 'European' export economy is only pursued in a 'thin' version of competitiveness. Furthermore, given Ireland's already comparatively liberalised labour and product markets, the potential contribution of liberal market 'structural reforms' is likely to have only minimal impacts on growth, even leaving aside the debate as to whether such measures are typically growth-promoting or not.

A fuller strategy for becoming a more 'European' economy would have involved, as outlined in Chapter 4, a combination of establishing fiscal discipline with significant investments in social protections and economic growth.

Such a view balances fiscal consolidation with measures focused on social and productive investment and growth, which becomes the basis for tackling the fiscal crisis. The restoration of creditworthiness, in this view, largely follows an improvement in economic and employment growth rather than being a condition of that growth. Nonetheless, economically, it appears that a programme of fiscal consolidation that generated permanent shifts in the structure of the public finances but was combined with a counterbalancing significant programme of productive and social investments might well be an effective strategy for escaping the crisis while minimising economic and social damage. Indeed, this is in practice what many of the Continental European countries pursued as a strategy, at least in the early years of the crisis.

The comparison of fiscal consolidation with a zero consolidation scenario tells us little about the choice between fiscal consolidation and some version of fiscal stimulus, whether as an alternative or a complement to consolidation in the public finances. The primary alternative identified to this strategy focuses first on providing a stimulus for tackling growth (Taft, 2010; NERI, 2012). NERI (2013; see also O'Farrell, 2012; Social Justice Ireland, 2012) argues that a stimulus programme centred on investment would generate the same fiscal savings without damaging the economy to the same extent as the strategy of fiscal consolidation. In addition, as Central Bank of Ireland economists Kelly and McQuinn argue, fiscal multipliers may be even higher when the state is responsible for bank solvency: 'Government policies which return distressed households back into employment are likely to yield an additional benefit above and beyond that traditionally considered. Namely, by alleviating levels of mortgage distress, the solvency position of these institutions is ameliorated, thereby reducing the Irish State's future capital obligations' (Kelly and McQuinn, 2013: 16).

It is also worth noting that there were significant opportunity costs to the state taking on the costs of the financial crisis in Ireland and the contribution by the state of a large portion of the national pension reserve fund to the 2010 bailout programme. Had these funds been available, or had the Irish debt ratio not risen above the level that the IMF projected for it in the absence of a cost to the state of the banking crisis, then it would have been much easier for the state to finance an investment stimulus programme.

Both austerity and stimulus appear to be initially costly and damaging to public finances and government debt – stimulus through the cost of investment and austerity through its effects on output. Each arguably provides an (uncertain) return over the long term in terms of creditworthiness. The effects on the real economy appear to be quite different, although they are contested by analysts.

Deciding on the relative merits of the strategies is partly a technical matter, as debates rage about the extent of different multipliers under different conditions. It is also, however, a political matter, not simply of choices in the balance and composition of consolidation and stimulus, but also in terms of the political capacity to allow experimentation or the creative recombination of different elements of different strategies. There are significantly different political and social dynamics to austerity and stimulus strategies. Austerity appears to offer certainty through its application to specific identifiable groups and expenditure and revenue targets, masking a set of more complex, hidden long-term effects. Stimulus investments are often focused on uncertain future returns where the benefits and costs are often collective rather than targeted on specific groups. The political mobilisation involved around a stimulus programme, whether combined with fiscal consolidation or not, is challenging, not least in that it demands significant trust in public institutions at a time when that is being eroded.

The Irish response was distinctive and has been commended by its international funders for 'meeting its targets' in terms of deficit reductions. At the same time, it has been slow to undertake a number of projects which might have been very significant in enhancing recovery, including projects which were within the Programme for Government of Fine Gael and Labour, such as the re-organisation of training, the formation of a state investment fund or bank (Ó Riain and O'Sullivan, 2011), the promotion of credit to small businesses and so on. By 2013, these initiatives were much further advanced but would have no impact on the course of the crisis until at least six years after it began. The response to the crisis has been telling in both its resolute pursuit of deficit reduction and its slow development of alternative or complementary strategies. Why has government been strong in the management of consolidation and weak in terms of creative strategies?

Ireland's fiscal position is such that it, possibly more than any other European country, is poised on the knife-edge of debt sustainability. While there is significant controversy about the sustainability of Ireland's debt, domestic and international elites shared a view that recovery to a more sustainable position is possible for Ireland without requiring a default on any portion of its debt. Internally, while almost all incomes have declined to some extent, the 'iron triangle' of the Fine Gael/Labour government (no new taxes, public pay cuts or cuts in social transfer rates) largely allowed it to hold back widespread protests even in the face of declining living standards. As was discussed above, the sharpest declines in economic status and vulnerability have been among those households hit by unemployment and now carrying significant debts and mortgage arrears. In this respect, while details are not forthcoming, the government was significantly helped by the main banks not pursuing house repossessions due to mortgage arrears.

This fiscal political balancing act also functions as a constraint on options for recovery, of course. Most significantly, deep problems in the public finances reduce the funds available for investment. More generally, the political space, both domestically and internationally, to generate finance for recovery has been narrowed as Irish policy makers and international lenders focus almost exclusively on Ireland's creditworthiness. The Irish position between debt sustainability and default has left citizens with complex mixes of interests in both resisting specific measures and acceding to the general strategy of fiscal consolidation. This is consistent with the combination of the erosion of trust in institutions with the comfortable victory of the Fiscal Treaty referendum, which consolidates the policies that are eroding that trust.

Furthermore, the institutional resources available to chart a path out of the crisis based on a new round of export-oriented developmentalism had themselves been significantly eroded during the 2000s, as was shown in the previous chapter. Nowhere was this clearer than in the area of active labour market policy, where the urgent need for effective public action in the face of rapidly increasing unemployment was matched only by the scale of the collapse in the effectiveness and legitimacy of the training agencies in a series of scandals relating to management self-aggrandisement, political corruption and low standards in the training provided by external contractors. The broader institutions of 'creative corporatism', already weakened and hollowed out through the 2000s, played a relatively small role in shaping strategies for recovery.

Ireland walked a dangerous fiscal tightrope, drawing on an institutional structure where many of the capacities that would have been useful in rebuilding development had been eroded through the 2000s. The erosion of institutional capacities and the hollowing out of the social compact in the 2000s had a profoundly damaging effect, as the scope for public action and even a willingness to consider it as a vehicle of recovery was extremely limited. Ironically, the election of 2011 may have contributed to dampening political protests and dissatisfaction by allowing for protests against the existing government, while providing the new government with a five-year term within which it could pursue its own strategy.

The management of Ireland's response to the crisis was highly centralised as the Fine Gael/Labour government formalised the already-strong oligarchic tendencies within Irish politics in an economic management council consisting of the two party leaders and the Ministers for Finance and Public Expenditure and Reform. Even government ministers complained of their exclusion from overall policy development, but the power of the government and of the ministerial elite within government was crucial in managing the process of fiscal consolidation.

However, the great difficulty faced by the coalition government elected in 2011 in terms of pursuing creative responses to the crisis was also rooted in the deeper structures of Irish politics. The politics of coalition are unusual in Ireland – not just in terms of electoral numbers

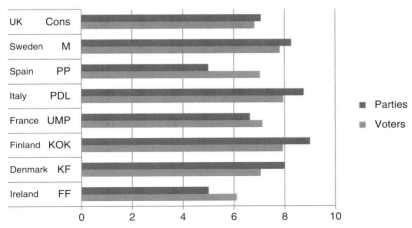

Figure 6.10 Conservative parties in Europe: left–right positioning of party voters and party members of the European Parliament, 2009
Source: Belchior, 2013

but also in terms of ideological and policy alignment. Belchior (2013) has compared the policy profile of political parties across Europe and those who vote for them, using party policy positions and interviews with European Parliament members from different parties across Europe in 2009. While the Irish Labour Party is similar to most European social democratic parties in the self-positioning of party voters and party members on a left–right scale, Fine Gael and Fianna Fáil are quite distinctive in their profile. Fianna Fáil is rightly classified as a conservative party, but its position on the left–right scale is significantly further to the centre than most other European conservative parties (see Figure 6.10). Moreover, Fine Gael is significantly further to the right of other Christian democratic parties in Europe (see Figure 6.11). This indeed places it well to the right of Fianna Fáil, particularly in terms of its parliamentarians, who are over two points further to the right on the scale than Fianna Fáil, while the party voters are relatively similar.

It is striking then that, in these admittedly simplified terms, the organisation of coalitions in Irish politics is quite complex in terms of policy coherence. Fianna Fáil and Fine Gael are closest on the right-leaning end of the political spectrum, but have been largely defined by their historical rivalry with one another. Labour and Fianna Fáil are

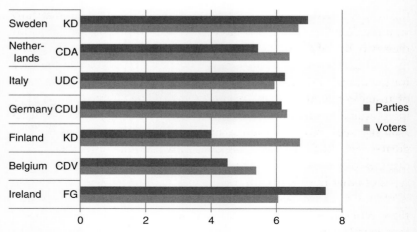

Figure 6.11 Christian democratic parties in Europe: left–right positioning of party voters and party members of the European Parliament, 2009
Source: Belchior, 2013

closest on the left-leaning end of the spectrum, but Fianna Fáil's conservatism and the perception of its dominance in a coalition has meant that Labour has only once entered into a coalition with it (1992–4). The most common coalition combination (Fine Gael and Labour) combines the two parties furthest apart on the left–right spectrum. The social liberalism that unites these parties is less relevant in an economic crisis than the economic orientations that tend to divide them.

These factors shaping Ireland's unusual response to the crisis show that the Irish crisis remains marked by the features of a liberal political economy – where the fiscal foundations of public action are fragile, the institutional capacities tend towards centralism and oligarchy rather than diversity and experimentalism, and where the legitimacy of public action and the coherence of public policy are difficult to achieve. This has reinforced a disciplinary role for government rather than a creative or developmental approach.

The European crisis

However, given Ireland's fiscal constraints, European politics was more significant than Irish politics in shaping Ireland's economic strategy during the recession. Eurozone-level strategies for managing through the crisis trilemma have also been found to be dramatically wanting. Why has it been so difficult for European countries to chart their way out of the economic crises? On the one hand, the Continental, and to a lesser extent Nordic, countries have emphasised the need for the liberal and Mediterranean countries to implement programmes of austerity that are in many respects self-defeating in the context of an international recession. On the other hand, the peripheral countries typically seek more Keynesian measures from the core as well as greater relief of the debts arising out of the financial crisis itself. These disputes often end up tapping into nationalist or xenophobic stereotypes of other European countries. The European response to the crisis is often contrasted with the response of the US and the UK. Where these economies are said to have focused on Keynesian strategies of monetary 'quantitative easing' and (to a lesser extent, and mainly in the US) public investment, Europe has pursued a policy of 'austerity'. Overall, Europe appears to be caught in a bind. The 'Keynesian' measures necessary to exit the crisis cannot be pursued because of a lack of funds in the periphery and because of a lack of trust in the core that peripheral countries will deliver on their commitments over the medium to long term.

The European response is considerably more complex than this, as we will see. However, before Europe pursued austerity, it put a different fundamental plank of its response in place – the firewalling of the financial system itself from the crisis that it had largely created. The European response therefore consisted of two key steps: first, measures to protect the financial system, including the transfer of the debts of the financial system into the public purse, the insulation of financial institutions from losses across the financial system and a set of associated policies to boost the financial sector, particularly its underlying capital and assets; and, second, the pursuit of a set of policies aimed at restoring fiscal balance in national economies across the Eurozone. All this was undertaken in the context of legal and ideological prohibitions on a European-level Keynesian monetary response.

Figure 6.12 indicates the operating profits of domestic EU banks across the EU from 2007 to 2011, showing that after a sharp dip in 2008, the operating profits of EU banks recovered to pre-crisis levels in 2009 and remained relatively stable. Similarly, ECB figures show that the assets of EU banks increased across this period (ECB, 2012). European banking, it appears, recovered and returned to business as

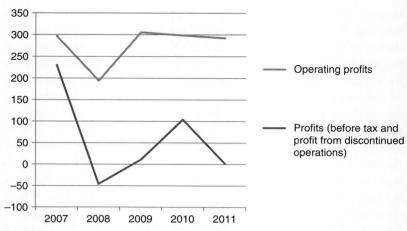

Figure 6.12 Profit rates of domestic EU banks, 2007–11
Source: ECB statistics

usual after the shock of the crisis in 2008. However, Figure 6.12 also shows the ongoing fragility of the European banking system, reflected in the much more volatile trend in 'profits before tax and not including profits from discontinued operations'. These profits show a very large gap from the baseline operating profits, which is largely accounted for by the continuing problems of impaired assets and non-performing loans. The shock to underlying profits in 2008 was much greater than to operating profits and the recovery much less. Indeed, these profits fell once again in 2011. There has been great volatility within the banking sector, a fact reflected in the significant drops in the position of most of the large banks within the Fortune Global 500 (Fortune, 2012). However, the same figures show that some banks, such as JPMorgan, have done extremely well through the crisis period, while others, such as Deutsche Bank, have returned to a very healthy profit rate after a number of exceptionally difficult years. Nonetheless, overall the banking sector remains fragile.

The banks are not the only institutions to have returned more or less to business as usual while still dealing with the overhang of the crisis. Table 6.8 shows the revenues and operating profits of two of the big three credit rating agencies, Fitch and Standard & Poor's. Standard & Poor's, the larger of the two, saw a dramatic drop in revenues and operating profit in 2008, but has largely stabilised its operations since then. While Fitch's revenues have decreased, the agency has

Table 6.8 *Financial performance of credit rating agencies, 2007–11*

	Fitch			Standard & Poor's ratings		
	Consolidated revenue	Recurring operating profit	Profit as % of revenue	Revenues	Operating profit	Profit as % of revenue
2007	744.8	159.1	21.4%	2138	1159	54.2%
2008	568.9	163.6	28.8%	1583	749	47.3%
2009	559.1	151.3	27.1%	1537	712	46.3%
2010	487.5	145	29.7%	1695	762	45.0%
2011	525.7	162.8	31.0%	1767	719	40.7%

Sources: Fimilac Annual Reports; McGraw-Hill, 2012

maintained its operating profit and has increased profit as a percentage of revenue. The problems of credit rating agencies have been well rehearsed and these figures suggest, along with the lack of serious reform in this area, that the agencies are largely operating along the same business models as before the crisis.

Public policy has been crucial to this restoration of the stability of the financial sector. As noted above, the creation of a firewall around the most damaged parts of the European financial system was the earliest European policy response and has been crucial to the recovery of the financial sector and the associated threats to the public finances – and, indeed, the euro. These efforts were not enough in themselves to shore up the financial position of European banks. The ECB has undertaken a variety of major policy initiatives at the level of the EU to recapitalise banks and prop up the value of their assets (Figure 6.13). These included the acquisition of securities by the ECB in two covered bond purchase programmes and the Securities Markets Programme of 2010, where the ECB and national central banks were able to purchase Eurozone public and private debt. The uptake by banks of these programmes was very strong, reflecting their relatively fragile position, as indicated in both European banking authority stress tests and in Figure 6.12. To put the scale of these operations by the ECB into context, the value of these operations in 2011 was just under three times larger than the €347 billion budget for the European structural funds from 2007 to 2013. Although this is hardly comparing similar kinds of financing, it provides a broad indication of the dominant form of the European

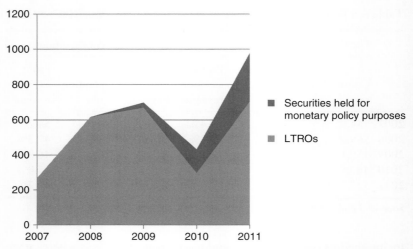

Figure 6.13 Scale of ECB Long-Term Refinancing Operations (LTROs) and purchase of securities, 2007–11
Source: ECB Annual Reports

policy response. The public banking system at the national level also played an important role in the recovery of certain economies. The German state investment bank, KfW, increased its lending substantially from 2008 to 2011 (Ó Riain and Rhatigan, 2013). This diversified state bank was central to the German stimulus programmes of 2008 to 2009, despite having a low profile in public policy discussions.

These financial operations were accompanied by a weaker programme of reform. A number of countries pursued a coordinated policy introducing a financial transaction tax (but not including Ireland and the UK), a number of efforts were made to control bankers' bonuses to weaken incentives for non-prudent lending, and some progress was made towards an EU banking union which would provide in the future for the transnational prudential regulation of banks. However, despite a great deal of early discussion on the topic, no progress was made on the development of banking resolution regimes that would enable the tackling of losses in the financial system arising out of the crisis itself. While some reforms were put in place, the overall thrust of European banking policy has been to shore up the banking system as it stands and look to the public finances of Member States to fund this programme.

The irony of the financial crisis is that the financial markets that were the primary cause of the bubble through their speculative activity, and that were significantly bailed out by public actors during the course of the crisis, have been placed once more at the centre of European policy. The future of Eurozone states is being adjudicated in large part by the same financial system which damaged their position so dramatically to begin with. This raises the question of what these financial markets 'want'. The easiest answer is to assume that financial markets seek neoliberal responses of fiscal consolidation and market reform to any change in economic fundamentals, such as increasing government debt. However, the picture is not that simple. De Grauwe and Ji (2013) argue that financial markets in the Eurozone have responded primarily to emotions of panic and fear rather than to economic fundamentals. They argue that the interest rate spreads on government borrowing in the Eurozone are best explained not by changes in government debt ratios, but by the changing commitments of the ECB to maintaining the euro. The ECB announced a programme of unlimited support of government bond markets in the middle of 2012, moving the Eurozone from a position of radical uncertainty regarding the future of the euro to one where, despite ongoing economic difficulties, the key actors had provided a credible commitment that the euro would persist. In the months after this announcement, the interest rate spreads on government bonds in the European periphery declined dramatically, despite the fact that debt to GDP ratios were not falling and indeed were almost universally getting worse. De Grauwe and Ji find that the change in interest rate spreads was explained almost entirely by the countries' initial levels of spread. Whereas the financial markets had panicked in 2011 and had driven up interest rates as a result of fear of a euro meltdown, they now rowed back on that panic based on Eurozone-level commitments – responding to the political environment rather than to economic fundamentals.

De Grauwe and Ji also argue that the financial markets responded to their panic by promoting austerity in the European periphery. Indeed, the countries with the highest interest rate spreads applied the most severe austerity measures. They conclude that for 2011, 'there can be little doubt. Financial markets exerted different degrees of pressure on countries. By raising the spreads they forced some countries to engage in severe austerity programmes. Other countries did not experience increases in spreads and as a result did not feel much urge to apply the austerity medicine' (2013: 1). Although De Grauwe and Ji assume that financial markets have an intrinsic preference for austerity measures, this is not necessarily the case. Mosley (2005) argues that financial markets have a complex relation to national governments. In advanced capitalist economies, where the markets have a degree of historically established trust in countries' self-management, financial markets exercise 'strong but narrow' control over national governments. In other words, they do not intervene significantly in micro-level policies or in supply-side decisions as long as the key macroeconomic indicators conform to their expectations. In less developed countries, by contrast, Mosley finds that financial markets exert 'strong and broad' control, extending to a broader range of interventions in policy making. Such tendencies towards broad control are most likely heightened in a financial crisis when uncertainty looms largest.

Indeed, it is the importance of uncertainty regarding government capabilities and commitments that is the common thread between De Grauwe and Ji's analysis and that of Mosley. The Eurozone then represents an unusual mix of governments with different relations to the financial markets. Some governments, such as that in Germany, have an almost unimpeachable record with international bond markets. The link between Germany and the euro was important in extending that certainty both to the euro itself and to its broader membership of countries that had weaker records in the bond markets. The European policy of 'kicking the can down the road' from 2008 to 2012 seriously threatened this formula, damaging belief in the stability of the euro and opening up a space for punitive interest rate spreads on government bonds in peripheral Eurozone members. The radical policy uncertainty regarding the euro proved to be a crucial feature in making it necessary for peripheral economies to engage in bailout programmes through 2010 and after. As De Grauwe and Ji document, this virtuous link between core economies, peripheral economies and a stable euro was significantly repaired by the ECB commitment of 2012. It is also telling that this commitment was quite open-ended and was relatively vague in terms of the specific policies that would be pursued to support the euro. In keeping with Mosley's analysis, the most important feature was the restoring of certainty about the credible commitments of governments rather than the formulation of a specific policy regime.

This suggests that there has been more room for creative public policy during the crisis than Eurozone and EU governments have been willing to pursue. The prioritising of funding through private markets over government-level initiatives, from mutualised risk to transnational public investment, has been a defining element of European policy. Even within this, we have seen that financial markets primarily reward certainty – and there may be many policy regimes that are consistent with the provision of that certainty. Where negative contagion across the Eurozone was the great fear of European policy makers during the crisis, they have largely ignored the potential of positive contagion, as indicated in the response of the bond markets to the ECB defence of the euro in 2012.

This leads us to the question of the specific character of the European policy response and how that might be rooted in the particular national models of capitalism in Europe and their interaction within the EU. In many respects the core policy goal of the Eurozone response has been to enforce new mechanisms for ensuring 'fiscal discipline' in the peripheral economies. This is in many ways the mirror image at the intergovernmental level of Mosley's relationship between financial markets and national governments, as the core governments demand new credible commitments from the peripheral political economies that they will place their public finances on a more secure footing.

However, in Chapter 4 it was shown that in practice, such fiscal discipline is broadly associated with social compacts that are only weakly developed in the peripheral and liberal economies within Europe. 'Social Europe', often seen as a pleasant 'add-on' to the European project, is shown to be a key condition for securing this fiscal discipline. The building of Social Europe would, it seems, strengthen the capacity of European public finances to maintain fiscal discipline. However, this itself raises profound difficulties. As Ferrera argues, the 'virtuous nesting' of welfare states within the EU as a whole 'entails the strengthening of an EU "social space", capable of safeguarding the closure pre-conditions for multi-level social sharing arrangements' (2009: 219). This of course is not easy. Hemerijck (2013) argues that there is a 'double bind of social Europe'. National social compacts and welfare states are undermined by the market integration associated with globalisation and also with the EU itself. However, differences in national policies make cooperation at the transnational level and the building of a strengthened European social space very difficult. Social Europe is weakened at the national level, but the national level remains strong enough to block its emergence at the European level.

Chapter 4 suggested some reasons why it might be so difficult to reconcile these national models, given not only the distinctive profile of welfare but also the links between welfare, production regimes and macroeconomic management in Europe's worlds of capitalism. It documented the quite different interlocking systems at the national level within Europe, even as these systems pursued a political programme of institutional convergence. These differences go deeper still as they relate not just to the dominant institutions but also to the field of action within the different countries in responding to the crisis of 2008.

Karl Polanyi's notion of the double movement is useful here. For Polanyi, the double movement consists, first, of a movement to establish a market society, where market relations dominate social life, and, second, of counter-movements by groups within the society to protect themselves against the corroding effects of market society. Figures 6.14 and 6.15 show that this creates different dynamics within liberal and social democratic economies. In liberal political economies, these movements are particularly volatile because of the dominance of market society. They are characterised by strong inequalities in market power and by weak credible commitments on the part of all actors to long-term goals and action, including economic security, social protection, and economic and social investment. The promotion of market society is also a feature of social democratic societies, but takes a quite

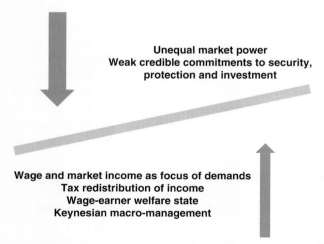

Unequal market power
Weak credible commitments to security,
protection and investment

Wage and market income as focus of demands
Tax redistribution of income
Wage-earner welfare state
Keynesian macro-management

Figure 6.14 The Polanyian double movement in liberal political economies

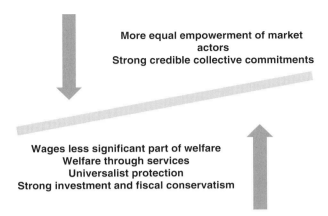

Figure 6.15 The Polanyian double movement in social democratic political economies

different form. As Pontusson (2011) has noted, most citizens are market actors with very high levels of employment and economic participation. However, they enter the market in a much more empowered position than citizens and workers in liberal political economies. Given this fact, and the strong historical development of the welfare state, most actors are in a position to make and expect strong, credible, collective long-term commitments.

More significant still, the nature of the second part of the double movement is different in the two different types of political economy. In liberal economies, the most realistic avenues of action mean that social protection is most likely to be pursued through market-centred mechanisms. These include Keynesian macroeconomic policy, the demand for welfare state expansion linked to wages and occupational earnings of benefits, the attempt to protect wage and market income as a focus of labour's demands rather than the expansion of welfare, and the redistribution of income through the taxation system. In macroeconomic policy, welfare state development, tax policy and industrial relations, the focus of movements for social protection is the securing of gains in the market, as the development of large-scale welfare or other programmes is a much more risky political prospect.

The double movement in social democratic political economies is quite different. The second part of the double movement relies much less on market-centred social protection. Instead, universalist collective systems of social protection, a strong emphasis on long-term social and economic investments, the expansion of the welfare state as a compensation for wage restraint, and the distribution and redistribution of welfare through universal services and the overall size of the welfare states rather than through progressive taxation are key features of the social democratic double movement.

Each of the contending views of how to exit the crisis draws on different strands of Keynesianism. While Keynes is often read as an advocate of counter-cyclical spending and quantitative easing, this relies purely on a reading of Keynes as macroeconomic manager. Keynes also emphasised a more general role for government, particularly in securing social protection and investment, and generally managing the economy and ensuring the appropriate level of investment and other long-term economic requirements (Block, 2012). While most commentators associate the social democratic worlds of capitalism with Keynesianism, in practice, it is this more general argument by Keynes for social investments and long-range planning and management that is most characteristic of the social democratic and Christian democratic countries. The Keynes who advocated counter-cyclical spending and macroeconomic reflation to escape from crisis is in practice more widely favoured in liberal political economies – as seen in the persistently higher deficits run in such economies.

Underlying this, each political economy relies on a different system for managing risks. In social democratic countries the risk is internalised within the society itself through high levels of taxation and spending linked to strong underlying fiscal discipline. The society insulates itself relatively effectively from the vagaries of capitalist business cycles and crises. However, in liberal political economies, risk is externalised as the society tends to follow the ups and downs of the business cycle, and indeed of boom and crisis, relying on external adjustments to escape from crisis. These external adjustments include measures such as currency devaluation and international borrowing to fund domestic counter-cyclical measures.

In addition, the two double movements relate to quite significantly different notions of the state and its role in the economy and vulnerability in an economic crisis. In liberal models, the state itself becomes an instrument of flexibility through monetary and currency policy.

Table 6.9 *The EU response to the crisis*

	Liberal capitalisms	Social market capitalisms	EU, 2008–12
Macroeconomic management	Keynesian demand management	Fiscal consolidation	Fiscal consolidation
Supporting real economy recovery	'Confidence' and private investment	State-led investment	'Confidence' and private investment

In social market economies, the focus is on defending the state from the vagaries of capitalist business cycles and crises. Fiscal discipline is not simply a matter of prudence or conservatism, but in some systems is based on – ironically – a view where the state (and, by extension, the society) needs to be protected from capitalism.

The kinds of demands made from the periphery for more Keynesian responses and similar anti-crisis measures were always likely to fall on deaf ears until some reconciliation of these different logics within European capitalism could be found. Table 6.9 provides a schematic outline of the typical response to economic crisis in liberal and social market capitalisms. Despite being highly schematic (and reproducing the binary distinction between capitalisms that I have critiqued throughout this book!), the table gives us a sense of the set of typical options available within the worlds of European capitalism. It suggests that in each world of capitalism, a contractionary response is combined with a counterbalancing expansionary response. The liberal approach relies primarily on private investment to drive recovery, restricting the expansionary contribution of the public sector, but compensates for this with flexibility in expansionary monetary, currency and sometimes fiscal policy. Despite their association with Keynesian demand management, social market capitalisms are typically more conservative in terms of fiscal consolidation, at least in recent decades. However, they are willing to use state investment to drive recovery (for example, the activities of the German state investment bank after 2008).

Both approaches combine expansionary and contractionary elements in their stylised 'policy mix'. However, the Eurozone-level response has emphasised the contractionary dimensions of both models without taking on the counterbalancing expansionary measures. This transnational response has involved fiscal consolidation and restoring confidence in public finances in order to drive future private investment (an investment that has been predictably weak, at least where it is needed most). There was been some discussion of Keynesian measures in the core, including a loosening of fiscal policy and an increase in wages to boost demand (and ideally, though not necessarily, imports from peripheral economies). However, this made limited progress and in 2013 both France and Germany were planning significant national fiscal consolidation. Less prominent in public debate were suggestions for the expansion of transnational state-led investment – and, indeed, the EU budget for 2014–20 was cut by 3.3 per cent, particularly in growth-promoting investments including R&D and structural funds for regional development. The European-level policy response has primarily combined the two contractionary elements from each national policy mix and has ignored their expansionary counterweights, providing a policy mix of the worst of both worlds of capitalism.

This is of course a somewhat rigid representation of the policy choices available. Figure 6.16 represents the same set of options not as a table, but as a set of overlapping circles, indicating that the range of options was more flexible than is recognised in the Eurozone-level response. It is telling that the Eurozone response is the most firmly located in the combination of fiscal consolidation and private investor

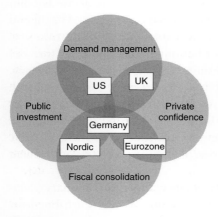

Figure 6.16 Policy mixes in the crisis

confidence, while the Nordic and German national strategies have drawn more heavily on supply-side investment, and the US and the UK have leaned towards monetary loosening (and, in the case of the US, some increases in public investment). While at the national level, most countries engaged in some version of stimulus programme between 2008 and 2010 (Cameron, 2012), the coordination of the Eurozone involved no such efforts. As De Grauwe and Ji (2013) document, this resulted in austerity programmes in the countries where they did the most damage in terms of increasing debt to GDP ratios and damaging international creditworthiness.

Armingeon and Baccaro (2012) document the variety of Eurozone-level responses that were possible and that were mooted at the European level during the crisis. One possibility was a more activist monetary policy by the ECB, loosening its dedication to maintaining low levels of inflation. The European Commission in 2011 also endorsed an alternative involving the introduction of Eurobonds to be jointly guaranteed by Eurozone members. Financial guarantees voluntarily provided by Eurozone members are another option and are the basis of the European Stability Mechanism (ESM), which was put in place in 2012. Despite the large amounts of funds available (approximately €1 trillion), these funds are dwarfed by the overall level of debt within the Eurozone. Crucially, 'all proposals discussed would mutualise, and hence reduce, the risk associated with GIIPS [Greece, Italy, Ireland, Portugal, Spain] sovereign debt' (Armingeon and Baccaro, 2012: 184).

These strategies would all face significant legal and political difficulties. Crucially, in our terms they involve a mixing of the internal logics of Europe's capitalisms. Behind the accounting and financial flows of 'mutualisation' lies a fusing of two different social logics. One emphasises the externalisation of economic risk and the flexible revaluing of state and society alike, while the other emphasises the internalisation of risk and a kind of defence of state and society even at the cost of significant losses of national and household income. The European crisis has made demands on the European economic system that go to the heart of the differing socio-political and socio-economic logics at work within the social field of the EU. Where the response required seems to demand a more creative and deeper form of integration or a complete loosening of the bonds within Europe, the response has been to fall back on the 'thin integration' of the fiscal rules at the heart of the euro. While these rules and criteria have been expanded and their legal basis and enforcement mechanisms have been strengthened in the Fiscal Treaty of 2012, the underlying relations between Europe's capitalisms remain much the same. Europe has largely continued to kick the can down the road, hoping to ride out the debt crisis without having to face up to these structural dilemmas of integration.

Conclusion

This book has made a number of arguments. Chapter 2 examined how the Celtic Tiger years were linked to the ebb and flow of different versions of success in 'the market'. In particular, an early period of stabilisation was followed in the 1990s by deepened development, but this in turn was trumped by financialisation in the 2000s. The rest of the book has explored the reasons for this victory of financialisation and its consequences. Chapter 3 examined this first through analysing the dynamics of the financial and property bubble, and tracing how they shifted over time, becoming increasingly detached from the real economy in the 2000s. Institutions of market liberalism in the Irish and European banking and property systems were crucial in 'making rational' the bubble.

Chapter 4 then followed this thread from financialisation into the broader process of European integration, showing how a European agenda of developmentalism and regional development in the 1990s was firmly sidelined by the spread of financialisation, facilitated by Anglo-American financial globalisation and by European economic and monetary union. The rules around the euro and fiscal discipline failed to act as a buffer against the effects of this financialisation, despite significant institutional convergence across Europe on these rules and their supporting institutions. The analysis found that this failure was linked in large part to the important differences between the social compacts that in practice underpin fiscal discipline in Continental Europe and those that are linked to the macroeconomic models of the Mediterranean and liberal economies. These institutional differences combined with uneven development within Europe in the 2000s to pose a very significant structural challenge to Europe's peripheral economies.

Chapter 5 showed that Ireland proved to be weak in managing these challenges. The 2000s saw the erosion of developmental capacities and coalitions that had been developed in the 1990s but were now sidelined by property and credit growth machines. This logic of financialisation also found its way into the public finances through the structure of taxation and levels of public spending. The institutional features of a liberal political economy – the fragmentation of production regimes in a system of coordinated pluralism, a pay-related or wage-earner welfare state, a dualist public administration and a highly centralised parliamentary system – facilitated a system of macro-level coordination that focused on growth and the distribution of cash benefits rather than on development and enhanced public services.

I have interpreted these features of the real world of liberalism in Ireland through two sets of connected lenses – Karl Polanyi's discussion of the relations between market and society, and the insights of political economy and economic sociology into the specific institutions of economic liberalism. I began in Chapter 2 by recognising that all market action is socially embedded, characterising different projects within the Irish political economy at different times in terms of the institutions and social relations that made this possible. The promotion of economic liberalism was an outcome of these multiple projects, each of which promoted the liberalisation of the economy, but in a different way and with different consequences. Economic liberalism is real, but is also made real in different ways at different times. Chapter 3 showed the continuing relevance of Polanyi's warning that 'finance is the enemy of production' and added to his analysis of market society by documenting the institutions of the market that enabled the commodification of land and money in the Irish property and credit bubble.

The analysis of European integration in Chapter 4 examined the interplay of economic flows and stabilising forces within the international political economy. In many respects, the fiscal rules around the euro were designed to serve a stabilising function in much the same way as Bretton Woods and the gold standard had done in earlier eras. However, these rules were unable to withstand the pressures of aggressive financialisation in Europe and beyond. In particular, Europe missed its social dimension in the 2000s, not just in terms of the benefits that it would provide to European citizens but also in the stabilising foundations that it would provide to the public finances and the development of the real economy. Chapter 5 then explored the political dimension of the relationship between the market and society in more detail. While Polanyi recognises an autonomous space for politics (Bohle and Greskovits, 2012) he has relatively little to say about its content. This chapter identified a number of key features of Ireland's polity that are linked to its often-liberal character. These included: the decay of institutional capabilities for development and stability; the triumph of finance and the power of capital markets in deciding the allocation of resources across the economy; the presence of coordination in production, but only of a corporate pluralist nature; the building upon the minimal welfare state of liberal regimes, but in a way that emphasised a wage-earner status and market income; the building of a dualist state as a poorly resourced general public sector was supplemented by targeted roles for additional public agencies; and the highly centralised form of policy making in an apparently open liberal democracy. This chapter has extended this further by analysing the course of the crisis itself and tracing the difficulties that Europe and Ireland face in escaping the crisis. These difficulties are rooted in the failure of the EU to find an effective way of combining the different social compacts in its Member States and their different macroeconomic, production and welfare regimes. In the course of the crisis, one-sided European policies have ironically made it more difficult for the peripheral economies to pursue a truly 'European' road towards recovery.

Europe in 2013 is locked into a perverse path. If the project of fiscal consolidation and saving the financial system fails, disaster looms for the European project and the place of Europe on the global stage. If it succeeds, it may be at such a cost that the public legitimacy of the European project will be deeply undermined. Ireland and other peripheral countries could have been facilitated to emerge from this crisis in a way that was consistent with the European model. The classic European model, combining fiscal discipline and productive investment as well as social protection, had been important in significant if unrecognised ways in the recovery of Continental economies (as was noted in the case of the German state investment bank and its key role in promoting recovery in 2009 and 2010). However, this project has not been promoted at the European level since the 1990s. Having been undermined by financialisation and current account imbalances in the 2000s, it is now weakened by the exclusive focus on fiscal discipline at significant cost to the real economy and society. Given their external constraints and their poor institutional capacities, peripheral countries were poorly placed to make better use of any opportunities for more creative pathways out of the crisis than appeared obvious.

Europe, if it is to succeed as Europe, must once more both rediscover and re-imagine its historical project. The prioritisation of the financial sector has been disastrous and has placed a huge burden on the public finances of the European periphery, particularly in the parts of that periphery that were linked closely to the European project (Ireland and Spain) and were most successful in its development era in the 1990s. In order to protect liberal values in the broadest sense in Europe, European economies and societies will need to rediscover their own distinctive 'non-liberal' policies, institutions and social compacts. This would be deeply challenging – and not only in the core countries that would fund most of these processes. It would also be challenging in the liberal and Mediterranean periphery, where citizens and institutions would be asked to create new, demanding social compacts. However, the recovery of this transnational project is essential if the current political exchange of fear for consent between citizens and governments is to be transcended.

Bibliography

Abdelal, R. 2007. *Capital Rules*. Princeton University Press.

AIB. Various years. *Annual Reports*.

Allen, K. 2003. 'The Celtic Tiger, Inequality and Social Partnership', *Administration*, 51(1): 119–42.

2007. *The Corporate Takeover of Ireland*. Dublin: Irish Academic Press.

Amable, B. 2004. *The Diversity of Modern Capitalism*. Oxford University Press.

Anglo Irish Bank. Various years. *Annual Reports*. Dublin: AIB.

Armingeon, K. and Baccaro, L. 2012. 'The Sorrows of Young Euro: Policy Responses to the Sovereign Debt Crisis' in N. Bermeo and J. Pontusson (eds.), *Coping with Crisis: Government Reactions to the Great Recession*. New York: Russell Sage Foundation, pp. 162–98.

Arrighi, G. and Silver, B. 2000. *Chaos and Governance in the Modern World System*. Minneapolis: University of Minnesota Press.

Avdagic, S., Rhodes, M. and Visser, J. (eds.) 2011. *Social Pacts in Europe: Emergence, Evolution, and Institutionalization*. Oxford University Press.

Bank of Ireland. Various years. *Annual Reports*. Dublin: Bank of Ireland.

Barnes, L. and Wren, A. 2012. 'The Liberal Model in the Crisis: Continuity and Change in Great Britain and Ireland' in N. Bermeo and J. Pontusson (eds.), *Coping with Crisis: Government Reactions to the Great Recession*. New York: Russell Sage Foundation, pp. 287–324.

Barry, F. 2003. 'Economic Integration and Convergence Processes in the EU Cohesion Countries', *Journal of Common Market Studies*, 41(5): 897–921.

Barry, F., Görg, H. and Strobl, E. 2005. 'Foreign Direct Investment and Wages in Domestic Firms in Ireland: Productivity Spillovers versus Labour-Market Crowding Out', *International Journal of the Economics of Business*, 12(1): 67–84.

Barry, F. and Van Egeraat, C. 2008. 'The Decline of the Computer Hardware Sector: How Ireland Adjusted', *Quarterly Economic Commentary*, 38–57.

Beckert, J. 2002. *Beyond the Market: The Social Foundations of Economic Efficiency*. Princeton University Press.

Belchior, A. M. 2013. 'Explaining Left–Right Party Congruence across European Party Systems: A Test of Micro-, Meso-, and Macro-Level Models', *Comparative Political Studies*, 46(3): 352–86.

Berman, S. 2006. *The Primacy of Politics*. New York: Cambridge University Press.

Beyer, J. and Hopner, M. 2003. 'The Disintegration of Organised Capitalism. German Corporate Governance in the 1990s' in H. Kitschelt and W. Streeck (eds.), 'Germany Beyond the Stable State?' *West European Politics*, Special Issue, 26: 179–98.

Blanchard, O. J. and Leigh, D. 2013. 'Growth Forecast Errors and Fiscal Multipliers', Working Paper No. w18779. National Bureau of Economic Research.

Block, F. 2012. 'Varieties of What? Should We Still Be Using the Concept of Capitalism?', *Political Power and Social Theory*, 23: 269–91.

Bohle, D. and Greskovits, B. 2012. *Capitalist Diversity on Europe's Periphery*. Ithaca, NY: Cornell University Press.

Boyle, G., McElligott, R. and O'Leary, J. 2004. 'Public-Private Wage Differentials in Ireland, 1994–2001', *Quarterly Economic Commentary*, Special Article. Dublin: Economic and Social Research Institute.

Bradley, J. and Whelan, K. 1997. 'The Irish Expansionary Fiscal Contraction: A Tale from One Small European Economy', *Economic Modelling*, 14(2): 175–201.

Breen, R., Hannan, D. F., Rottman, D. B. and Whelan, C. T. 1990. *Understanding Contemporary Ireland: State, Class and Development in the Republic of Ireland*. London: Macmillan.

Brenner, N. 2004. *New State Spaces*. Oxford University Press.

Brenner, N., Peck, J. and Theodore, N. 2009. 'Variegated Neoliberalization: Geographies, Modalities, Pathways', *Global Networks*, 10(2): 182–222.

Brenner, N. and Theodore, N. 2004. *Spaces of Neoliberalism*. Oxford: Blackwell.

Burawoy, M. 2001. 'Neoclassical Sociology: From the End of Communism to the End of Classes', *American Journal of Sociology*, 106(4): 1099–120.

2003. 'For a Sociological Marxism: The Complementary Convergence of Antonio Gramsci and Karl Polanyi', *Politics and Society*, 31(2): 193–261.

Byrne, E. 2012. *Political Corruption in Ireland 1922–2010: A Crooked Harp?* Manchester University Press.

Callan, T., Keane, C., Savage, M. and Walsh, J. R. 2012. 'Distributional Impact of Tax, Welfare and Public Sector Pay Policies: 2009–2012', *Quarterly Economic Commentary*, Special Article: 47–56.

Cameron, D. R. 2012. 'Fiscal Responses to the Economic Contraction of 2008–09' in N. Bermeo and J. Pontusson (eds.), *Coping with Crisis: Government Reactions to the Great Recession*. New York: Russell Sage Foundation, pp. 91–129.

Carruthers, B. G. and Stinchcombe, A. L. 1999. 'The Social Structure of Liquidity: Flexibility, Markets, and States', *Theory and Society*, 28(3): 353–82.

Castles, F. G. 1985. *The Working Class and Welfare: Reflections on the Political Development of the Welfare State in Australia and New Zealand 1890–1980*. Wellington: Allen & Unwin.

Cedefop. 2010. *Employer-Provided Vocational Training in Europe: Evaluation and Interpretation of the Third Continuing Vocational Training Survey*, Cedefop Research Paper No. 2. Luxembourg: Publications Office of the European Union.

Cerny, P. G. 1995. 'Globalization and the Changing Logic of Collective Action', *International Organization*, 49(4): 595–625.

  2000. 'Restructuring the Political Arena: Globalization and the Paradoxes of the Competition State' in R. D. Germain (ed.), *Globalization and its Critics: Perspectives from Political Economy*. London: Palgrave, pp. 117–38.

Chubb, Basil. 2006. *The Government and Politics of Ireland*. London: Longman.

Clancy, P. 1989. 'The Evolution of Policy in Third-Level Education' in D. Mulcahy and D. O'Sullivan (eds.), *Irish Educational Policy: Process and Substance*. Dublin: Institute of Public Administration, pp. 15–35.

Coffey, S. 2013. 'Debts and Deficits Decomposed', *Economic Incentives Blog*. Available at: http://economic-incentives.blogspot.ie/2013/01/debt-and-deficits-decomposed.html.

Cole, R. E. 1991. *Strategies for Learning: Small-Group Activities in American, Japanese, and Swedish Industry*. Berkeley: University of California Press.

Coleman, S. and Coulter, C. 2003. *The End of Irish History?: Critical Approaches to the Celtic Tiger*. Manchester University Press.

Collins, M. and Walsh, M. 2010. *Ireland's Tax Expenditure System: International Comparisons and a Reform Agenda*. Studies in Public Policy No. 25, TCD Policy Institute.

Connor, G., Flavin, T. and Kelly, B. 2012. 'The U.S. and Irish Credit Crises: Their Distinctive Differences and Common Features', *Journal of International Money and Finance*, 31: 60–79.

Cousins, M. 2007. 'Political Budget Cycles and Social Security Budget Increases in the Republic of Ireland, 1923–2005', MPRA Paper No. 5359. Available at: http://mpra.ub.uni-muenchen.de/5359.

Cox, L. 2011. 'There Must Be Some Kind of Way Out of Here: Social Movements and the Crisis in Ireland', *New Left Project/Crisisjam*, May Day International joint issue. Available at: www.newleftproject. org/index.php/mayday/article/6278.

Crouch, C. 2009. 'Privatised Keynesianism: An Unacknowledged Policy Regime', *British Journal of Politics & International Relations*, 11(3): 382–99.

2011. *The Strange Non-Death of Neo-Liberalism*. Cambridge: Polity Press.

CSO. 2012. *Survey on Income and Living Conditions SILC 2010*. Cork: Central Statistics Office.

2013. *Survey on Income and Living Conditions SILC 2011 & Revised 2010 Results*. Cork: Central Statistics Office.

Cullen, P. 2002. *With a Little Help from my Friends: Planning Corruption in Ireland*. Dublin: Gill & Macmillan Ltd.

Cusack, T., Iversen, T. and Soskice, D. 2007. 'Economic Interests and the Origins of Electoral Institutions', *American Political Science Review*, 101(3): 1–34.

Davis, G., 2011. *Managed by the Markets*. Oxford University Press.

De Grauwe, P. and Ji, Y. 2013. 'Panic-Driven Austerity in the Eurozone and its Implications', VoxEU Blog. Available at: www.voxeu.org/article/ panic-driven-austerity-eurozone-and-its-implications.

Deeg, R. 2007. 'Complementarity and Institutional Change in Capitalist Systems', *Journal of European Public Policy*, 14(4): 611–30.

Dellepiane, S. and Hardiman, N. 2012. 'Governing the Irish Economy: A Triple Crisis' in N. Hardiman (ed.), *Irish Governance in Crisis*. Manchester University Press, pp. 83–109.

Deutsche Bank. Various years. *Annual Reports*.

Döring, H. 2001. 'Parliamentary Agenda Control and Legislative Outcomes in Western Europe', *Legislative Studies Quarterly*, 145–65.

Ebbinghaus, B. and Manow, P. 2001. 'Introduction: Studying Varieties of Welfare Capitalism' in B. Ebbinghaus and P. Manow (eds.), *Comparing Welfare Capitalism: Social Policy and Political Economy in Europe, Japan and the USA*. London: Routledge, pp. 1–26.

ECB. 2011. *Financial Integration in Europe*. Brussels: ECB.

2012. *Annual Report of the European Central Bank*. Brussels: ECB.

Enterprise Ireland. 2007. *Venture Capital in Ireland*. Dublin: Enterprise Ireland.

Epstein, G. A. (ed.) 2005. *Financialization and the World Economy*. Cheltenham: Edward Elgar.

Erixon, L. 2008. 'The Swedish Third Way – An Assessment of the Performance and Validity of the Rehn–Meidner Model', *Cambridge Journal of Economics*, 32(3): 367–93.

Ertürk, I. and Solari, S. 2007. 'Banks as Continuous Reinvention', *New Political Economy*, 12(3): 369–88.

Esping-Andersen, G. 1990. *The Three Worlds of Welfare Capitalism*. Cambridge: Polity Press.

1999. *Social Foundations of Postindustrial Economies*. Oxford University Press.

Eurobarometer. 2012. *Fiscal Compact Post-referendum Survey, Ireland 31 May*. Brussels: Public Opinion Monitoring Unit.

Evans, P. B. 2002. 'Collective Capabilities, Culture, and Amartya Sen's Development as Freedom', *Studies in Comparative International Development*, 37(2): 54–60.

EVCA. 2010. *EVCA Yearbook*.

Eyraud, L. and Weber, A. 2013. 'The Challenge of Debt Reduction during Fiscal Consolidation', IMF Working Paper WP/13/67.

Favell, A. and Guiraudon, V. 2009. 'The Sociology of the European Union: An Agenda', *European Union Politics*, 10(4): 550–76.

Federation of Small Businesses. 2012. *Alt+ Finance: Small Firms and Access to Finance*. London: Federation of Small Businesses.

Félix, B. 2007. 'Venture Capital Investments' in *Statistics in Focus: Science and Technology*. Brussels: Eurostat.

Ferrera, M. 2009. 'National Welfare States and European Integration: In Search of a "Virtuous Nesting"', *Journal of Common Market Studies*, 47(2): 219–33.

Fimilac. Various years. *Annual Reports*.

Flaherty, E. and Ó Riain, S. 2013. 'Labour's Declining Share of National Income in Ireland and Denmark: Similar Trends, Different Dynamics', New Deals in the New Economy Working Paper 1, Department of Sociology and the National Institute for Regional and Spatial Analysis, NUI Maynooth.

Fligstein, N. 2008. *Euroclash*. Oxford University Press.

Fortune. 2012. *Fortune 500 Global*. Available at: http://money.cnn.com/magazines/fortune/fortune500/2012/full_list.

Fourcade-Gourinchas, M. and Babb, S. L. 2002. 'The Rebirth of the Liberal Creed: Paths to Neoliberalism in Four Countries', *American Journal of Sociology*, 108(3): 533–79.

Friends First. 2006. 'Are We Too Dependent on the Property Market?' Dublin: Friends First.

Garvin, T. 2004. *Preventing the Future: Why Was Ireland So Poor for So Long?* Dublin: Gill & Macmillan.

Girma, S., Gorg, S., Strobl, E. and Walsh, F. 2008. 'Creating Jobs through Public Subsidies: An Empirical Analysis', *Labour Economics*, 15(6): 1179–99.

Gkartzios, M. and Norris, M. 2011. '"If You Build it, They Will Come": Governing Property-led Rural Regeneration in Ireland', *Land Use Policy*, 28(3): 486–94.

Granovetter, M. 1985. 'Economic Action and Social Structure: The Problem of Embeddedness', *American Journal of Sociology*, 91(3), 481–510.

Gunnigle, P. and McGuire, D. 2001. 'Why Ireland? A Qualitative Review of the Factors Influencing the Location of US Multinationals in Ireland with Particular Reference to the Impact of Labour Issues', *Economic and Social Review*, 32(1): 43–68.

Haas, E. 1958. *The Uniting of Europe*. Stanford University Press.

Habermas, J. 1976. *Legitimation Crisis*. London: Heinemann.

　2012. *The Crisis of the European Union: A Response*. Cambridge: Polity Press.

Hall, P. A. and Soskice, D. W. (eds.) 2001. *Varieties of Capitalism: The Institutional Foundations of Comparative Advantage*. Oxford University Press.

Hannan, D. F. and Commins, P. 1992. 'The Significance of Small-Scale Landholders in Ireland's Socio-economic Transformation' in J. Goldthorpe and C. Whelan (eds.), *The Development of Industrial Society in Ireland*. Oxford University Press, pp. 79–104.

Hardie, I. and Howarth, D. 2010. 'What Varieties of Financial Capitalism? The Financial Crisis and the Move to "Market-Based" Banking in the UK, Germany and France', paper presented at the annual meeting of *Theory vs. Policy? Connecting Scholars and Practitioners*, New Orleans, 17–20 February.

Hardiman, N. 1988. *Pay, Politics and Economic Performance in Ireland, 1970–1987*. Oxford: Clarendon Press.

　1992. 'The State and Economic Interests: Ireland in Comparative Perspective' in J. Goldthorpe and C. Whelan (eds.), *The Development of Industrial Society in Ireland*. Oxford University Press, pp. 329–58.

　1998. 'Inequality and the Representation of Interests' in W. Crotty and D. E. Schmitt (eds.), *Ireland and the Politics of Change*. Harlow: Addison Wesley Longman, pp. 122–43.

Hardiman, N., Murphy, P. and Burke, O. 2008. 'The Politics of Economic Adjustment in a Liberal Market Economy: The Social Compensation Hypothesis Revisited', *Irish Political Studies*, 23(4): 599–626.

Hardiman, N. and Whelan, C. T. 1994. 'Values and Political Partisanship' in C. T. Whelan (ed.), *Values and Social Change in Ireland*. Dublin: Gill & Macmillan, pp. 136–86.

Hayek, F. A. 1973. *Law, Legislation and Liberty*. University of Chicago Press.

Hechter, M. 1975. *Internal Colonialism: The Celtic Fringe in British National Development*. Piscataway, NJ: Transaction Publishers.

Hemerijck, A. 2013. *Changing Welfare States*. Oxford University Press.

Hirschman, A. 1970. *Exit, Voice and Loyalty*. Cambridge, MA: Harvard University Press.

Holland, D. and Portes, J. 2012. 'Self-defeating Austerity?', *National Institute Economic Review*, 222(1): F4–F10.

Holm, J. R., Lorenz, E., Lundvall, B. Å. and Valeyre, A. 2010. 'Organizational Learning and Systems of Labor Market Regulation in Europe', *Industrial and Corporate Change*, 19(4): 1141–73.

Honohan, P. 2004. 'Book Review – "Preventing the Future: Why was Ireland so Poor for so Long?" by Tom Garvin', *Economic and Social Review*, 35(3): 351–5.

    2006. 'To What Extent Has Finance Been a Driver of Ireland's Economic Success?', *ESRI Quarterly Economic Commentary*, Winter: 59–72.

Honohan, P., Maître, B. and Conroy, C. 1998. 'Invisible Entrepôt Activity in Irish Manufacturing', *Irish Banking Review*, Summer: 22–36.

Honohan. P. and Walsh, B. 2002. 'Catching Up with the Leaders: The Irish Hare', *Brookings Papers on Economic Activity*, 1: 1–77.

Hooghe, L. and Marks, G. 2009. 'A Postfunctionalist Theory of European Integration: From Permissive Consensus to Constraining Dissensus', *British Journal of Political Science*, 39(1): 1–23.

Hopkin, J. 2006. *Clientelism and Party Politics*. London: Sage.

Huber, E. and Stephens, J. D. 2001. *Development and Crisis of the Welfare State: Parties and Policies in Global Markets*. University of Chicago Press.

Huo, J., Nelson, M. and Stephens, J. 2008. 'Decommodification and Activation in Social Democratic Policy: Resolving the Paradox', *European Journal of Social Policy*, 18: 5–20.

IMF. 2009. *Germany* IMF Country Report No. 09/15.

    2012. *World Economic Outlook WEO: Growth Resuming, Dangers Remain*. Washington DC: IMF.

Irish Banking Federation. 2006. *About Banking*, 4th edn, November.

Irish Fiscal Advisory Council. 2012. *Fiscal Assessment Report*, April. Dublin: Irish Fiscal Advisory Council.

Iversen, T. 1999. *Contested Economic Institutions*. Cambridge University Press.

    2005. *Capitalism, Democracy and Welfare*. Cambridge University Press.

Iversen, T. and Stephens, J. 2008. 'Partisan Politics, the Welfare State, and Three Worlds of Human Capital Formation', *Comparative Political Studies*, 41(4/5): 600–37.

Iversen, T. and Wren, A. 1998. 'Equality, Employment, and Budgetary Restraint: The Trilemma of the Service Economy', *World Politics*, 507–46.

Jacoby, S. 1988. *Employing Bureaucracy*. New York: Psychology Press.

    1997. *Modern Manors: Welfare Capitalism since the New Deal*. Princeton University Press.

Jessop, B. 2002. *The Future of the Capitalist State*. Cambridge: Polity Press.

    2007. 'Knowledge as a Fictitious Commodity: Insights and Limits of a Polanyian Perspective' in A. Bugra and K. Agartan (eds.), *Reading Karl Polanyi for the Twenty-First Century: Market Economy as a Political Project*. Basingstoke: Palgrave Macmillan, pp. 115–34.

Katzenstein, P. J. 1985. *Small States in World Markets: Industrial Policy in Europe*. Ithaca, NY: Cornell University Press.

Kelly, M. 2007. 'Banking on Very Shaky Foundations', *Irish Times*, 7 September.

Kelly, R. and McQuinn, K. 2013. 'On the Hook for Impaired Bank Lending: Do Sovereign-Bank Inter-linkages Affect the Fiscal Multiplier?" Central Bank of Ireland, Research Technical Paper 1/ RT/ 13. Available at: www.centralbank.ie/publications/Documents/01RT13.pdf.

Kelly, S. 2010. *Breakfast with Anglo*. London: Penguin.

Kennedy, K. 1992. 'The Context of Economic Development' in J. Goldthorpe and C. Whelan (eds.), *The Development of Industrial Society in Ireland*. Oxford University Press, pp. 5–30.

Kenworthy, L. 2012. 'Is the U.S. Tax System More Progressive Than Those of Most Other Rich Countries?', Consider the Evidence Blog. Available at: http://lanekenworthy.net/2012/02/16/is-the-u-s-tax-system-more-progressive-than-those-of-most-other-rich-countries.

Killian, S., Garvey, J. and Shaw, F. 2011. 'An Audit of Irish Debt', University of Limerick. Available at: www.debtireland.org/download/pdf/audit_of_irish_debt6.pdf.

Kingspan Group plc. Various years. *Annual Reports*.

Kinsella, S. 2012. 'Is Ireland Really the Role Model for Austerity?', *Cambridge Journal of Economics*, 36(1): 223–35.

Kirby, P. 2002. *The Celtic Tiger in Distress: Growth with Inequality in Ireland*. Basingstoke: Palgrave.

    2010. *Celtic Tiger in Collapse: Explaining the Weaknesses of the Irish Model*. Basingstoke: Palgrave Macmillan.

Kirby, P. and Murphy, M. 2011. *Towards a Second Republic: Irish Politics after the Celtic Tiger*. London: Pluto Press.

Kitchin, R., Gleeson, J., Keaveney, K. and O'Callaghan, C. 2010. 'A Haunted Landscape: Housing and Ghost Estates in Post-Celtic Tiger Ireland', NIRSA Working Paper Series. No. 59.

Kitchin, R., O'Callaghan, C., Boyle, M. and Gleeson, J. 2012. 'Placing Neoliberalism: The Rise and Fall of Ireland's Celtic Tiger', *Environment and Planning A*, 44: 1302–26.

Komito, L. 1992. 'Brokerage or Friendship? Politics and Networks in Ireland', *Economic and Social Review*, 23(2): 129–42.

Krippner, G. 2011. 'The Elusive Market: Embeddedness and the Paradigm of Economic Sociology', *Theory & Society*, 30: 775–810.

Krippner, G., Granovetter, M., Block, F., Biggart, N., Beamish, T., Hsing, Y., Hart, G., Arrighi, G., Mendell, M., Hall, J., Burawoy, M., Vogel, S. and Ó Riain, S. 2004. 'Polanyi Symposium: A Conversation on Embeddedness', *Socio-Economic Review*, 2(1): 109–35.

Kus, B. 2012. 'Financialisation and Income Inequality in OECD Nations: 1995–2007', *Economic and Social Review*, 43(4): 477–95.

Kvist, J. and Greve, B. 2011. 'Has the Nordic Welfare Model Been Transformed?', *Social Policy & Administration*, 45(2): 146–60.

Laeven, L. and Valencia, F. 2012. 'Systemic Banking Crises Database: An Update', IMF Working Paper, WP/12/163.

Lane, P. R. 2003. 'Assessing Ireland's Fiscal Strategy: Recent Experiments and Future Plans' in T. Callan, D. McCoy and A. Doris (eds.), *Budget Perspectives 2004*. Dublin: Economic and Social Research Institute, pp. 4–22.

  2011. 'The Irish Crisis', IIIS Discussion Paper No. 356, IIIS: TCD.

Larragy, J. 2006. 'Origins and Significance of the Community and Voluntary Pillar in Irish Social Partnership', *Economic and Social Review*, 37(3): 375–98.

Larragy, J., Ó Cinnéide, S. and Ó Riain, S. 2006. 'Social Foundations for an Uncertain Future', Report to Forfás, Departments of Sociology and Applied Social Studies, NUI Maynooth.

Leetmaa, P., Rennie, H. and Thiry, B. 2009. 'Household Saving Rate Higher in the EU than in the USA Despite Lower Income: Household Income, Saving and Investment, 1995–2007', *Eurostat Statistics in Focus 29/2009*. Brussels: Eurostat. Available at: http://epp.eurostat.ec.europa.eu/cache/ITY_OFFPUB/KS-SF-09-029/EN/KS-SF-09-029-EN.PDF.

Lewis, M. 2010. *The Big Short: Inside the Doomsday Machine*. New York: W. W. Norton & Company.

Lundvall, B.-Å. (ed.) 1992. *National Systems of Innovation: Towards a Theory of Innovation and Interactive Learning*. London: Pinter Publishers.

McAleese, D. 1990. 'Ireland's Economic Recovery', *Irish Banking Review*, 18–32.

McCabe, C. 2011. *Sins of the Father: Tracing the Decisions that Shaped the Irish Economy*. Dublin: History Press.

MacCárthaigh, M. 2012. 'Mapping and Understanding Organisational Change: Ireland 1922–2010', *International Journal of Public Administration*, 35(12): 795–807.

MacDonald, F. and Sheridan, K. 2009. *The Builders*. London: Penguin.

McGauran, A., Verhoest, K. and Humphreys, P. C. 2005. *The Corporate Governance of Agencies in Ireland: Non-Commercial National Agencies*. Dublin: Institute of Public Administration.

McGraw-Hill. 2012. *Investor Fact Book 2012*. New York: McGraw-Hill.

McGuinness, S., Kelly, E. and O'Connnell, P. J. 2010. 'The Impact of Wage Bargaining Regime on Firm-Level Competitiveness and Wage Inequality: The Case of Ireland', *Industrial Relations: A Journal of Economy and Society*, 49(4): 593–615.

McInerney Holdings plc. 2005. Chairman's Statement Annual General Meeting, 10 May.

2007. Press release.

McKenzie, D. 2006. *An Engine, Not a Camera*. Cambridge, MA: MIT Press.

2012. 'The Credit Crisis as a Problem in the Sociology of Knowledge', *American Journal of Sociology*, 116(6): 1778–841.

MacLaran, A. 1993. *Dublin: The Shaping of a Capital*. London: Belhaven Press.

2012. 'Dublin's Fifth Office Boom – Some Characteristics', paper given at the Conference of Irish Geographers, Trinity College Dublin.

MacLaran, A. and Murphy, L. 1997. 'The Problems of Taxation-Induced Inner City Housing Development – Dublin's Recipe for Success?', *Irish Geography*, 30(1): 31–6.

Mahoney, J. 2010. *Colonialism and Development: Spanish America in Comparative Perspective*. Cambridge University Press.

Mjøset, L. 1992. *The Irish Economy in a Comparative Institutional Perspective*. Dublin: National Economic and Social Council.

Molotch, H. 1976. 'The City as a Growth Machine', *American Journal of Sociology*, 82(2): 309–32.

Mosley, L. 2005. 'Globalisation and the State: Still Room to Move?', *New Political Economy*, 10(3): 355–62.

Mouzelis, N. 1985. *Politics in the Semi-periphery: Early Parliamentarism and Late Industrialisation in the Balkans and Latin America*. London: Palgrave.

Murphy, M., forthcoming 2013. 'Interests, Institutions and Ideas: Explaining Irish Social Security Policy', *Policy and Politics*.

NERI. 2012. 'NERI Quarterly Economic Observer', Spring.

2013. 'NERI Quarterly Economic Observer', January.

NESC. 2004. *Housing in Ireland: Performance and Policy*. NESC Report No. 112. Dublin: NESC.

2005. *The Developmental Welfare State*. Council Report No. 113. Dublin: NESC.

2009. *Ireland's Five-Part Crisis: An Integrated National Response*. Dublin: NESC.

2012. *Promoting Economic Recovery and Employment*. Dublin: NESC.

2013. *The Social Dimension of the Crisis*. Dublin: NESC.

Norris, M. and Gkartzios, M. 2011. 'Twenty Years of Property-led Urban Regeneration in Ireland: Outputs, Impacts, Implications', *Public Money & Management*, 31(4): 257–64.

O'Brennan, J. 2009. 'Ireland Says No Again: The 12 June 2008 Referendum on the Lisbon Treaty', *Parliamentary Affairs*, 62(2): 258–77.

O'Brien, A. 2011. *The Politics of Tourism Development: Booms and Busts in Ireland*. Basingstoke: Palgrave Macmillan.

O'Brien, J. 2006. 'IFSC Seen as Financial Wild West', *Irish Times*, 9 January.

O'Connell, P. J. and Byrne, D. 2012. 'The Determinants and Effects of Training at Work: Bringing the Workplace Back in', *European Sociological Review*, 28(3): 283–300.

O'Connor, J. 1973. *The Fiscal Crisis of the State*. Piscataway, NJ: Transaction Publishers.

O'Donnell, R. 2000. 'The New Ireland in the New Europe' in R. O'Donnell (ed.), *Europe: The Irish Experience*. Dublin: Institute of European Affairs, pp. 161–214.

O'Donnell, R. 2008. 'The Partnership State – Building the Ship at Sea' in M. Adshead, P. Kirby and M. Millar (eds.), *Contesting the State: Lessons from the Irish Case*. Manchester University Press, pp. 73–99.

O'Donnell, R., Cahill, N. and Thomas, D. 2010. 'Ireland: The Evolution of Social Pacts in the EMU Era' in P. Pochet, M. Keune and D. Natali (eds.), *After the Euro and Enlargement: Social Pacts in the EU*. Brussels: Observatoire Social Européen/ETUI, pp. 191–221

O'Donnell, R. and Moss, B. 2005. 'Ireland: The Very Idea of an Open Method of Coordination' in J. Zeitlin, P. Pochet and L. Magnusson (eds.), *The Open Method of Coordination in Action: The European Employment and Social Inclusion Strategies*. Brussels: PIE-Peter Lang, pp. 311–51.

OECD 1966. *Investment in Education: Ireland*. Paris. OECD.

2008. *Review of the Irish Public Service*. Paris: OECD.

2010. *Tax Expenditures in OECD Countries*. Paris: OECD.

2011. *Economic Outlook 2011*. Paris: OECD.

2012. *Competition and Credit Rating Agencies*. Paris: OECD.

O'Farrell, R. 2012. 'An Examination of the Effects of an Investment Stimulus', NERI Working Paper No 4. Dublin: NERI.

Offe, C. 1984. *Contradictions of the Welfare State*. London: Hutchinson.

Ó Gráda, C. and O'Rourke, K. 2000. 'Living Standards and Growth' in J. W. O'Hagan (ed.), *The Economy of Ireland*. Dublin: Gill & Macmillan, pp. 178–204.

O'Hearn, D. 2001. *The Atlantic Economy: Britain, the US and Ireland*. Manchester University Press.

O'Leary, J. 2010. 'External Surveillance of Irish Fiscal Policy during the Boom', Working Paper Series N210-10, Department of Economics, Finance and Accounting, NUI Maynooth.

O'Malley, E., Kennedy, K. A. and O'Donnell, R. 1992. *Report to the Industrial Policy Review Group on the Impact of the Industrial Development Agencies*. Dublin: The Stationery Office.

Ó Riain, S. 2000. 'The Flexible Developmental State: Globalization, Information Technology and the "Celtic Tiger"', *Politics and Society*, 28(2): 157–93.

  2000a. 'States and Markets in an Era of Globalization', *Annual Review of Sociology*, 26: 187–213.

  2004. *The Politics of High-Tech Growth: Developmental Network States in the Global Economy*. Cambridge University Press.

  2006. 'Time Space Intensification: Karl Polanyi, the Double Movement and Global Informational Capitalism', *Theory and Society*, 35(5/6): 507–28.

  2009. 'Addicted to Growth: Developmental Statism and Neo-Liberalism in the Celtic Tiger' in M. Bøss (ed.), *The Nation-State in Transformation: The Governance, Growth and Cohesion of Small States under Globalisation*. Aarhus University Press, pp. 163–90.

  2010. 'The Developmental Network State under Threat: Markets and Managerialism in the Irish Innovation System' in F. Block and M. R. Keller (eds.), *State of Innovation: Perspectives on U.S. Innovation Policy 1969–2009*. Boulder, CO: Paradigm.

  2011. 'Human Capital Formation Regimes: States, Markets and Human Capital in an Era of Globalisation' in A. Burton Jones and J. C. Spender (eds.), *Handbook of Human Capital*. Oxford University Press, pp. 588–617.

Ó Riain, S. and O'Connell, P. 2000. 'The Role of the State in Growth and Welfare' in B. Nolan, P. O'Connell and C. Whelan (eds.), *Bust to Boom? The Irish Experience of Growth and Inequality*. Dublin: Economic and Social Research Institute/Institute for Public Administration, pp. 310–39.

Ó Riain, S. and O'Sullivan, M. 2011. 'State Investment Bank Can Shift Focus from Property', *Irish Times*, 31 October.

Ó Riain, S. and Rhatigan, F. 2013. 'State Investment Banks as Agents of Recovery and Transformation', paper presented at the Alternatives for Transformation Conference, NUI Maynooth, March.

Ornston, D. 2012. *When Small States Make Big Leaps: Institutional Innovation and High-tech Competition in Western Europe*. Ithaca, NY: Cornell University Press.

O'Toole, F. 1994. *Black Hole, Green Card: The Disappearance of Ireland*. Dublin: New Island Books.

2009. *Ship of Fools: How Stupidity and Corruption Sank the Celtic Tiger*. London: Faber & Faber.

Papaioannou, E., Kalemli-Ozcan, S. and Peydró, J. 2009. 'What is it Good for? Absolutely for Financial Integration', Vox.eu column, 20 June. Available at: www.voxeu.org/article/euro-s-financial-integration-europe.

Parsons, C. 2010. 'How – and How Much – are Sociological Approaches to the EU Distinctive?', *Comparative European Politics*, 8: 143–59.

Paus, E. 2012. 'The Rise and Fall of the Celtic Tiger: When Deal-Making Trumps Developmentalism', *Studies in Comparative International Development*, 47: 161–84.

Peillon, M. 1982. *Contemporary Irish Society: An Introduction*. Dublin: Gill & Macmillan.

1994. 'Placing Ireland in a Comparative Perspective', *Economic and Social Review*, 25(2): 179–95.

Perez, C. 2002. *Technological Revolutions and Financial Capital: The Dynamics of Bubbles and Golden Ages*. Cheltenham: Edward Elgar.

Peterson, J. and Sharp, M. 1998. *Technology Policy in the European Union*. Basingstoke: Macmillan.

Piattoni, S. (ed.) 2001. *Clientelism, Interests, and Democratic Representation: The European Experience in Historical and Comparative Perspective*. Cambridge University Press.

Polanyi, K. 1957 [1944]. *The Great Transformation*. Boston: Free Press.

Polillo, S. and Guillén, M. F. 2005. 'Globalization Pressures and the State: The Worldwide Spread of Central Bank Independence', *American Journal of Sociology*, 110(6): 1764–802.

Pontusson, J. 2005. *Inequality and Prosperity: Social Europe vs. Liberal America*. Ithaca, NY: Cornell University Press.

2011. 'Once Again a Model: Nordic Social Democracy in a Globalized World' in J. Cronin, G. Ross and J. Shoch (eds.), *What's Left of the Left: Democrats and Social Democrats in Challenging Times*. Durham, NC: Duke University Press, pp. 89–115.

Prasad, M. 2006. *The Politics of Free Markets: The Rise of Neoliberal Economic Policies in Britain, France, Germany, and the United States*. University of Chicago Press.

Regan, A. 2011. 'The Political Economy of Institutional Change in European Varieties of Capitalism: The Rise and Fall of Irish Social Partnership', PhD thesis, University College Dublin.

2012. 'The Political Economy of Social Pacts in the EMU: Irish Liberal Market Corporatism in Crisis', *New Political Economy*, 17(4): 465–91.

Regling, K. and Watson, M. 2010. *A Preliminary Report on the Sources of Ireland's Banking Crisis*. Dublin: Government Publications Office.

Reinhart, C. M. and Rogoff, K. S. 2009. *This Time it's Different: Eight Centuries of Financial Folly*. Princeton University Press.

Roche, W. K. 1998. 'Between Regime Fragmentation and Realignment: Irish Industrial Relations in the 1990s', *Industrial Relations Journal*, 29(2): 112–25.

2007. 'Social Partnership in Ireland and New Social Pacts', *Industrial Relations: A Journal of Economy and Society*, 46(3): 395–425.

Rodrik, D. 2012. *The Globalization Paradox*. New York: W. W. Norton.

Rokkan, S. 1970. *Citizens, Elections, Parties: Approaches to the Comparative Study of the Processes of Development*. Oslo: Universitetsforlaget.

Ruane, J. 2010. 'Ireland's Multiple Interface-Periphery Development Model: Achievements and Limits' in M. Bøss (ed.), *The Nation-State in Transformation: The Governance, Growth and Cohesion of Small States under Globalisation*. Aarhus University Press, pp. 213–32.

Russell, H., Smyth, E. and O'Connell, P. J. 2005. *Degrees of Equality: Gender Pay Differentials among Recent Graduates*. Redlands, CA: Esri.

Sabel, C. 1996. *Ireland: Local Partnerships and Social Innovation*. Paris: OECD.

Sassen, S. 2006. *Territory, Authority, Rights: From Medieval to Global Assemblages*. Princeton University Press.

Scharpf, F. 1991. *Crisis and Choice in European Social Democracy*. Ithaca, NY: Cornell University Press.

1999. *Governing in Europe*. Oxford University Press.

Schmitter, P. C. 2003. 'Neo-Neo-Functionalism' in A. Wiener and T. Diez (eds.), *European Integration Theory*. Oxford University Press, pp. 45–74.

Seers, D. 1979. *Underdeveloped Europe*. London: Branch Line.

Sen, A. K. 1999. *Development as Freedom*. Oxford University Press.

Senghaas, D. 1985. *The European Experience: A Historical Critique of Development Theory*. Dover, NH: Berg.

Shelbourne Development Group. Various years. *Annual Reports*.

Silver, B. and Arrighi, G. 2003. 'Polanyi's "Double Movement": The Belle Époques of British and U.S. Hegemony Compared', *Politics and Society*, 31(2): 325–55.

Simon, H. 1957. *Models of Man, Social and Rational: Mathematical Essays on Rational Human Behavior in a Social Setting*. New York: Wiley.

Social Justice Ireland. 2012. *Shaping Ireland's Future*. Dublin: Social Justice Ireland.

Solinger, D. J. 2009. *States' Gains, Labor's Losses: China, France, and Mexico Choose Global Liaisons, 1980–2000*. Ithaca, NY: Cornell University Press.

Somers, M. R. and Block, F. 2005. 'From Poverty to Perversity: Ideas, Markets, and Institutions over 200 Years of Welfare Debate', *American Sociological Review*, 70(2): 260–87.

Stinchcombe, A. L. 1995. *Sugar Island Slavery in the Age of Enlightenment: The Political Economy of the Caribbean World*. Princeton University Press.

1997. 'On the Virtues of the Old Institutionalism', *Annual Review of Sociology*, 23(1): 1–18.

2000. 'Liberalism and Collective Investments in Repertoires', *Journal of Political Philosophy*, 8(1): 1–26.

Streeck, W. 1997. 'Beneficial Constraints: On the Economic Limits of Rational Voluntarism' in J. R. Hollingsworth and R. Boyer (eds.), *Contemporary Capitalism: The Embeddedness of Institutions*. Cambridge University Press, pp. 197–219.

2009. *Re-forming Capitalism: Institutional Change in the German Political Economy*. Oxford University Press.

2011. 'Taking Capitalism Seriously: Towards an Institutionalist Approach to Contemporary Political Economy', *Socio-Economic Review*, 9(1): 137–67.

Taft, M. 2010. 'The Urgent Priorities', Progressive Economy Blog. Available at: www.progressive-economy.ie/2010/06/urgent-priorities.html.

TASC. 2010. *Mapping the Golden Circle*. Dublin: TASC.

Teague, P. and Donaghey, J. 2009. 'Why Has Irish Social Partnership Survived?', *British Journal of Industrial Relations*, 47(1): 55–78.

Treasury Holdings. 2007. Press release, 24 January.

2008. Press release, 17 November.

Various years. *Annual Reports*.

Van der Pijl, K., Holman, O. and Raviv, O. 2011. 'The Resurgence of German Capital in Europe: EU Integration and the Restructuring of Atlantic Networks of Interlocking Directorates after 1991', *Review of International Political Economy*, 18(3): 384–408.

Varley, T. and Curtin, C. 2002. 'Community Empowerment via Partnership?' in G. Taylor (ed.), *Issues in Irish Public Policy*. Dublin: Academic Press, pp. 127–50.

Vartiainen, J. 2011. 'The Finnish Model of Economic and Social Policy: From Cold War Primitive Accumulation to Generational Conflicts?', *Comparative Social Research*, 28: 53–87.

Visser, J. 2012. *ICTWSS: Database on Institutional Characteristics of Trade Unions, Wage Setting, State Intervention and Social Pacts in*

34 Countries between 1960 and 2010. Amsterdam Institute for Advanced Labour Studies AIAS, University of Amsterdam.

Vogel, S. K. 1996. *Freer Markets, More Rules: Regulatory Reform in Advanced Industrial Countries*. Ithaca, NY: Cornell University Press.

Whelan, C. T., Nolan, B. and Maître, B. 2012. *Work and Poverty in Ireland*. Dublin: ESRI.

Whelan, K. 2010. 'Policy Lessons from Ireland's Latest Depression', *Economic and Social Review*, 41: 225–54.

White, R. 2010. *Years of High Income Largely Wasted*. Dublin: Davy Stockbrokers.

Woods, M. 2007. 'A Financial Stability Analysis of the Irish Commercial Property Market', Part Two in *Annual Financial Stability Report 2007*. Dublin: Central Bank of Ireland.

Young, S. and Hood, N. 1983. *Multinational Investment Strategies in the British Isles: A Study of MNEs in the Assisted Areas and in the Republic of Ireland*. London: HMSO.

Index